The Art of Retreat

TRANSITS

LITERATURE, THOUGHT & CULTURE, 1650–1850

A landmark series in long-eighteenth-century studies, *Transits* publishes monographs and edited volumes that are timely, transformative in their approach, and global in their engagement with arts, literature, culture, and history. Books in the series have engaged with visual arts, environment, politics, material culture, travel, theater and performance, embodiment, connections between the natural sciences and medical humanities, writing and book history, sexuality, gender, disability, race, and colonialism from Britain and Europe to the Americas, the Far East, the Middle/Near East, Africa, and Oceania. Works that make provocative connections across time, space, geography, or intellectual history, or that develop new modes of critical imagining are particularly welcome.

Recent titles in the series:

The Art of Retreat: Domestic Romanticisms in the Early United States
Laurel V. Hankins

Charles Johnson's "General History of the Pyrates" and Global Commerce
Noel Chevalier

Revisiting Richardson
Rebecca Anne Barr and Bonnie Latimer, eds.

British Romanticism and Prison Reform
Jonas Cope

Prolific Ground: Landscape and British Women's Writing, 1690–1790
Nicolle Jordan

Consuming Anxieties: Alcohol, Tobacco, and Trade in British Satire, 1660–1751
Dayne C. Riley

The Part and the Whole in Early American Literature, Print Culture, and Art
Matthew Pethers and Daniel Diez Couch, eds.

Teaching the Eighteenth Century Now: Pedagogy as Ethical Engagement
Kate Parker and Miriam L. Wallace, eds.

Women and Music in the Age of Austen
Linda Zionkowski with Miriam F. Hart, eds.

For more information about the series, please visit bucknelluniversitypress.org.

The Art of Retreat

DOMESTIC ROMANTICISMS IN THE EARLY UNITED STATES

LAUREL V. HANKINS

BUCKNELL UNIVERSITY PRESS
LEWISBURG, PENNSYLVANIA

Library of Congress Cataloging-in-Publication Data

Names: Hankins, Laurel V., author.
Title: The art of retreat : domestic romanticisms in the early United States / Laurel V. Hankins.
Description: Lewisburg, Pennsylvania : Bucknell University Press, 2025. | Series: Transits: literature, thought & culture, 1650-1850 | Includes bibliographical references and index.
Identifiers: LCCN 2024041382 | ISBN 9781684485628 (paperback) | ISBN 9781684485635 (hardcover) | ISBN 9781684485642 (epub)
Subjects: LCSH: American literature—19th century—History and criticism. | Home in literature. | Romanticism—United States. | Domestic fiction, American—History and criticism. | LCGFT: Literary criticism.
Classification: LCC PS217.H64 H36 2025 | DDC 813/.309355—dc23/eng/20250101
LC record available at https://lccn.loc.gov/2024041382

A British Cataloging-in-Publication record for this book is available from the British Library.

∞ The paper used in this publication meets the requirements of the American National Standard for Information Sciences—Permanence of Paper for Printed Library Materials, ANSI Z39.48-1992.

bucknelluniversitypress.org

Distributed worldwide by Rutgers University Press

For my parents, Joseph Hankins and
Virginia Shipley Hankins

CONTENTS

Introduction: Inventing Domestic Retreat 1

1 Charles Brockden Brown's Domestic Scenes 18

2 *Salmagundi*'s Elbow-Chair Domesticity 39

3 The Voice of Nature: *Hope Leslie* and Early American Romanticism 56

4 Epicene Genius in Theodore Winthrop's *Cecil Dreeme* 76

5 Tracking Harriet E. Wilson's Spiritualist Visions 101

Coda: #WFH 122

Acknowledgments 125

Notes 129

Bibliography 159

Index 171

The Art of Retreat

INTRODUCTION

Inventing Domestic Retreat

THE SHORT SKETCH "A Literary Wife," published in *The Literary Magazine and American Register* in March 1805 and most likely written by Charles Brockden Brown, opens by asserting that "Nothing is so terrible, to most men, as a literary wife."[1] The problem for this narrator is not an intellectual woman per se, but that the demands of domestic labor make it impossible for most women to continue their intellectual pursuits after marriage:

> Whatever a woman is, as to literature, science, or the arts, before marriage, she generally lays aside all her learning with her maiden state. Other avocations then engross her attention, and either her mind is not sufficiently capacious, or her taste sufficiently versatile, to enable her to divide her time between her old pursuits and her new. One of them must be neglected for the other, and the happiness of life is probably promoted by the preference usually given, in this dilemma, to the occupations of a nurse and housekeeper. (195)

Although the narrator assumes that it is the woman who will sacrifice her intellectual and creative pursuits to domestic labor, it is also clear that this sacrifice is necessitated by the arbitrary constraints of the sexual contract rather than any essential difference between genders. Lamenting as a "rarity" the "circumstances as enable a married couple both of them to devote themselves to learning and study, without material detriment to their happiness or comfort in other respects," the narrator concludes "*Intolerabilius nihil est quam fœmina* studiosa" [There is nothing more intolerable than a studious woman].[2] Maintaining the material circumstances that allow for the domestic scene to be a space of "learning and study" and "happiness or comfort" is women's work, and it is precisely this condition that renders the position of the studious woman so intolerable. "A Literary Wife" represents an early moment in a political, economic, and cultural transition that began to conceive of the home as a space of retreat, and we can understand this essay's ambivalence toward this ideal as marking its contrived incoherence. Even as the home is imagined as a space of aesthetic and intellectual potential, a gendered distinction is drawn within the home between this potential and the material obligations that support it. The narrator celebrates the home as a space of "learning and study" but laments the ways that "material detriment" interferes with these intellectual prospects. Rather than pastoralizing the labor that supports an emerging notion of domestic retreat, the essay insists on its inconvenient persistence. The essay can't seem to reconcile the liberatory promise of autonomous private retreat with the coercive social conditions that render this promise unevenly attainable. *The Art of Retreat* focuses on the aesthetic possibilities of domestic retreat imagined in the fiction of the early United States in the early stages of its development as a trenchant fantasy. While a diverse range of authors imagine the intellectual and aesthetic potential of the domestic scene, these authors are also acutely aware of how access to this potential is limited by gender, race, and class. Capturing the uncertain movement toward a familiar conception of domestic retreat that solidifies throughout the nineteenth century, *The Art of Retreat* aims to return the labor behind its development to our literary histories.

A new idealization of the home as retreat created the conditions of the two major literary movements of the nineteenth century, domestic fiction and Romanticism. Both movements imagine an inviolate private sphere free from political and economic interests as the realm of aesthetic production, but in our gendered critical narratives domestic retreat takes on different valences depending on the literary movement an author is associated with. For the performatively beleaguered male author, alienation from consumer culture becomes an important marker of dissenting literary genius but risks charges of political quietism. For the ideologically programmed woman, isolation within the domestic sphere grants great cultural power but leaves her restricted by narrow standards of feminine virtue. In general our critical narratives assume that domestic retreat for women is capitulation—they are granted moral authority over the private sphere as a tradeoff for their political disempowerment—while for men domestic retreat is a sign of dissent, as they temporarily reject the benefits and obligations of public life.[3] Tracing a moment of transition when private retreat was being imagined in all sorts of ways, including those that don't align with our contemporary methods for approaching and defining domestic fiction and American Romanticism, *The Art of Retreat* repositions these two literary movements as sharing an origin that is itself a contested transition. I contend that a diverse range of authors wished to stake a claim to the aesthetic potential of domestic retreat and, in doing so, exploited the interpretive vulnerability of the political fictions that rely on the idealization of a transcendent private sphere. The concept of the home as a retreat from the coercive pressures of the world undergirds a liberal narrative that invents the right to an autonomous private life as a signifier of consensual citizenship. Emerging out of a literary culture in transition, the early national periodicals, sketches, and novels I examine imagine the home as a space of self-interested pleasure, coerced labor, creole social reproduction, homosocial intimacy, bachelor whimsy, petty tyranny, racial abuse, and transgender capacity. In turn, the varied prospects for social arrangements and self-determination generated by domestic retreat exert pressure on a mode of political affiliation that fetishizes privacy as the grounds for consensual citizenship. The ambivalent responses to the freedom and constraints of domestic retreat this study traces suggest that the gendered public-private divide imagined by the liberal narrative is itself a generative fiction, subject to diverse reimaginings.

THE MUSIC OF A LOFTIER SPHERE

The connections between the ideal of the home as a retreat from the coercive pressures of the world and the major economic and political developments of the late eighteenth century are well established. In her history of middle-class women's experiences of labor in New England during the market revolution of the late eighteenth and early nineteenth century, Nancy F. Cott determines that by the early nineteenth century, "'home' became synonymous with 'retirement' or 'retreat' from the world at large."[4] The shift to market-oriented production changed the household from a space of shared labor, where men and women labored together to directly support the needs of their household, to a space that was defined against wage labor and the manufacturing industry. This distinction required the pastoralization of the labor, particularly childcare, that continued to take place within the home. Idealizing the home as a space free of coercion also served to delineate the conditions of freedom and enslavement. As Amy Dru Stanley has established, following the Civil War, "the promise of a home unscathed by the market distinguished the rewards of free contract and chattel slavery."[5] Whereas domestic labor was distinguished from wage labor, wage labor came to be distinguished from slave labor through the ability to support domestic dependents within a private home untouched by the market. A man's right to an inviolate private sphere was held up as the precise condition the institution of slavery violated. The marriage contract supports the distinction between freedom and slavery by establishing that a woman entered a state of submission freely in exchange for the protection of her husband. The free household is contrasted to one marked by slavery through this notion of submission chosen freely: unlike the private household of voluntary dependents that establishes the independence of its patriarchal head, the enslaved person's household, subject to intrusion at any time and undifferentiated by gendered divisions of labor, establishes only the subjection of its members.[6] Following Emancipation, reformers went to work encouraging the formerly enslaved to establish their suitedness for the rights and duties of freedom by establishing their own private households that enacted the sexual division of the marriage contract. Additionally, as Anne McClintock has established, as household labor was pastoralized to support the notion of a domestic sphere defined by its freedom from the market, the labor needed to support that ideal became increasingly racialized. The symbolically trenchant notion of the woman at home as a woman of leisure became an anxiety-ridden fantasy precisely because so few households could support it through the hiring of domestic servants. Domestic servants enabled the fantasy of invisible domestic labor but also corrupted the notion of a domestic sphere defined against the specter of wage labor. In this way, domestic servitude became increasingly associated with Black workers over the course of the nineteenth century.[7]

Even as the ideology of domesticity became firmly established by the mid-nineteenth century, these historical accounts also remind us that it remained a contested ideal: women in New England found freedom in factory work, formerly enslaved women resisted being rendered domestic dependents to establish their husbands' freedom, and, as I argue in this book, men looked covetously upon the freedom and intimacy promised by domestic retreat and questioned its gradual association with an essentialized femininity.[8] As scholars of domesticity have established, the notion of the home as a retreat from the world is not simply a condition that is produced by historical contexts like the market revolution or the age of contract. Instead, domestic retreat is an ideologically powerful fantasy that is necessary for the emergence of the liberal subject.[9] Cott carefully notes that the rhetoric of domestic retreat was "an intriguing development in language usage."[10] This insight points to the centrally generative role that literature played in imagining this new fantasy, not only through the marriage plots that are so easily read as allegories of consensual citizenship but also through portrayals of the domestic scene as the site of literary production.

The pastoralization of domestic labor developed in tandem with romantic theories of genius that associated artistry with the feminine.[11] We can see this connection between the ideology of domesticity and theories of romantic genius in Rufus Wilmot Griswold's preface to his 1848 anthology *The Female Poets of America*, where he proposes "feminine genius" as the answer to charges that Americans are "too much devoted to business and politics" to produce a national literature.[12] In the expanded preface to the second edition published four years later, Griswold goes on to argue that "youthful female voices" "soften and enrich the tumult of enterprise, and action, by the interblended music of a calmer and loftier sphere."[13] In the same way that women's domestic labor became increasingly idealized as a moral calling rather than an economic contribution, feminine genius came to be understood as natural impulse rather than artful craft. This belabored development can be understood as a defensive reaction to the sneaking suspicion that feminine isolation from the masculine world of "business and politics" might also give women greater access to genius. Even as Griswold's comments attempt to establish gender as a fundamental category for organizing literary collections, they also remind us that theories of romantic genius were informed by nineteenth-century understandings of gender difference as performative and polar rather than essential and oppositional.[14] This confusion is encapsulated in Griswold's claim that "it does not follow, because the most essential genius in men is marked by qualities which we may call feminine, that such qualities when found in female writers have any certain or just relation to mental superiority."[15] As Eliza Richards has demonstrated, this comment "neutralizes" feminine genius and sets the stage for masculine genius being defined through the performance of the feminine.[16] Even as the masculine literary establishment defensively characterized feminine genius as artless instinct rather than artful creation, Griswold's preface is also representative of the instability held in check by these codes, as the increasing association of the apolitical with the feminine is covetously seen as allowing more direct access to romantic notions of genius.

By the middle of the nineteenth century, gatekeepers like Griswold can confidently attribute the source of feminine genius to women's circulation within a "calmer and loftier sphere." The fantasy of domestic retreat on which this understanding of feminine genius relies is not yet securely available to early national authors like Charles Brockden Brown and Washington Irving. In the early national essay that opens this introduction, "A Literary Wife," the narrator distinguishes between "literature, science, or the arts" and "the occupations of a nurse and housekeeper." For this narrator, the disciplinary distinctions between the sciences, visual and musical arts, and literature that have traditionally been applied to define the aesthetic are secondary to a more fundamental contrast between intellectual-aesthetic production and supporting material conditions.[17] This distinction, between material and immaterial labor, comes to be elided by the aesthetic of nineteenth-century sentimental domestic ideology that imagines household labor as spiritual impulse.[18] The resulting tension plagues representations of feminine genius that grant access to the aesthetic through the very material conditions that are understood to corrupt the aesthetic ideal. At the same time, supplemented with artistic whimsy, romantic retreat comes to exploit the freedom of the private sphere established through domestic ideology to claim a position of literary autonomy that has traditionally been unavailable to the domestic author because of her material burdens and financial dependence. If domestic ideology conflates the material and the spiritual, while romantic retreat reinforces a divide within the private sphere between material and intellectual labor, there is a third position that sees these labors as distinct but not antithetical. This third position reconciles the confusion between the spiritual and the material that plagues romantic notions of feminine genius not by sentimentalizing domestic labor as spiritual impulse, thus participating in a mode of authorship that would erase the coercive conditions of the sexual contract, but by insisting on the material and embodied dimensions of literary production. This third position is most forthrightly claimed by the subject of my final chapter, Harriet E. Wilson, in her experimental novel-narrative *Our Nig; or, Sketches from the Life of a Free Black* (1859). Along the way to this concluding intervention, we will see authors experiment with the possibilities and constraints of an aesthetic theory that locates the source of genius within a domestic scene increasingly being imagined as feminine.

Alienation from the restrictions of domesticity has become closely associated with a narrow sense of the romantic author in U.S. fiction. This label continues to stubbornly adhere to a small group of authors associated with mid-century Transcendentalism.[19] Although the critical history surrounding American Romanticism is relatively self-conscious about problems of generic coherence, the critical history surrounding domestic fiction seems to be more certain of its object—a result, I assert, of the conflation of women writers with domestic fiction. My aim is less to return any kind of formal or generic stability to American Romanticism than to open up our definitions of domestic fiction. What would it mean to imagine domestic fiction as distinct from realism? From sentiment? From femininity? When domestic retreat is untethered from the disciplinary function of the realist novel, it becomes an imaginatively generative space of play, adornment, and sensuality that resists narrative consolidation. Unsettling domesticity as the opposing term that stabilizes our understanding of romanticism, this book realigns studies of domestic fiction and aesthetic retreat in three ways. First, telling the prehistory of American Romanticism and domestic fiction, when the gendered associations of each were still in the process of being institutionalized by the literary public sphere, my account of the early national period finds that the aesthetic possibilities of domestic and natural retreat were not defined by gender in the ways we might imagine. In the chapters that follow, I show that Charles Brockden Brown, Washington Irving, and Theodore Winthrop are drawn to the aesthetic possibilities of domestic fiction, while Catharine Maria Sedgwick and Harriet E. Wilson reject the constraints of domestic fiction and experiment with romantic historiography and embodied feminine genius. Second, examining fiction that insists on the visibility of the material labor that supports an ideal of domestic retreat, this study moves past a gendered critical binary that sees private retreat as either privileged escapism or ideological capitulation. Third, by considering the aesthetic potential of the domestic scene, this study considers domestic fiction within a critical turn toward the formal properties of early American literature. This critical shift threatens once again to leave behind genres like domestic fiction that are frequently read for their cultural work rather than their imaginative aesthetics. In general, we might say that romanticism has been associated with formal experimentation, while genre-bound domestic fiction has mostly been attended to through a cultural-studies approach that has sought to establish it as a vehicle for social and political commentary. A recent aesthetic turn in American literary studies has been particularly attentive to romanticism, presenting the conjectural reading experience the romance encourages as an imaginative corrective to the historicist methods that have privileged the cultural work of realist domestic fiction. I aim to establish domestic retreat as a crucial component of this conjectural, speculative tradition, rather than its realist other.

DOMESTIC FICTION AND THE AESTHETIC TURN

Domestic fiction has traditionally been interpreted as using sentimental reading practices to seduce readers into socially reproductive behavior.[20] Studies of the early American novel have emphasized the fraught possibilities of that strategy, noting a thematic obsession with desires gone astray like seduction and incest. This literary preoccupation with illicit desires reflects an ambivalence toward the unpredictable trajectories of the private sentiments that were appealed to in political rhetoric attempting to establish a government founded on the laws of nature and the wills of the people.[21] In these critical histories, as Marion Rust has shown, *sentimental* and *domestic* become "interchangeable terms."[22] Conventions such as the affectionate marriage plot and portrayals of the home as a space governed by moral impulse serve to naturalize political belonging or, in some cases, critique its artificial constraints. The chapters that follow are informed by but ultimately diverge from a body of scholarship that primarily sees domestic fiction as a means of programming obedient subjects. I argue that because the rhetoric of consent requires the availability of pliable private desires to naturalize its authority, domestic fiction is uniquely equipped to stage confrontations with the social conventions that are presented as individual choices, a necessary performance for preserving the notion of dissent in an increasingly ascriptive state.[23] Affirming consent required the right of disaffiliation to be at least imaginatively available. Although, as Elizabeth Barnes has argued, "sentimental fiction effectively bridges the gap between internal and external authority," this strategy does not only internalize external authority, producing self-regulating modern subjects.[24] It also places political rhetoric that appeals to the "wills of the people" in an uneasily appropriative and adaptive relationship to individual private desires, where dissent can just as easily highlight the unnaturalness of social convention as it can demarcate idiosyncratic unfitness.

Domestic retreat becomes an opportunity to imaginatively reenact the fictional moment of consent enshrined by the social contract. Carrie Hyde has recently argued that our critical narratives of the early national period overemphasize the Lockean legacy of consent, noting that the right to disaffiliate was regularly contested during the early national period and only belatedly enshrined following the Civil War. Debates about the meaning of citizenship weighed the duties of citizenship alongside the rights it promised in return.[25] We can see the tension between these two facets of citizenship if we turn again to the essay "A Literary Wife." Although the marriage plots of domestic fiction are frequently read as literary analogues to consensual citizenship, where a subject consents to certain obligations in exchange for certain protections, in "A Literary Wife," the obligations of this arrangement are given much more attention than any protections the literary wife might be granted. Recognizing the extent to which the idea of consensual citizenship is being invented during this period also reminds us of the fundamentally imaginative nature of the fantasies it relies upon. Portrayals of domestic retreat that are not supplemented with sentiment hold open a gap between nature and culture that allows consensual citizenship to be imagined as a process punctuated by moments of dissent and revisionary reinscription.[26] My archive provides potentially disorienting examples of fiction that is invested in the notion of domestic retreat but is not organized by sentimental conventions like affectionate marriage, virtuous labor, and spontaneous reform. If the plots of the novels, periodical fragments, and experimental autobiographies I examine seem haphazard or unfulfilling, it is because they refuse to make formal or emotional sense of the arbitrary hierarchies that emerge from historical contexts such as the market revolution or the age of contract that are traditionally understood to structure and explain domestic plots.

Early national authors openly debated the relationship between history and fiction, and they placed debates surrounding reading practices and professional criticism in relation to questions about national identity and individual subjectivity. Brown's frequently cited essay "The Difference Between History and Romance," which I take up in the first chapter, argues that history writing that presumes itself to be merely descriptive of facts does not fulfill a naturally speculative human curiosity. By the time of Sedgwick's *Hope Leslie*, the subject of my third chapter, history writing was valued for its explicitly subjective and ideological bent, as its primary objective was to tell history in a way that supported the author's individual vision of national character. Early national authors provide useful precedent for historicizing our own contemporary debates about critical method, particularly a discontentment with historicist critique and a turn to methods that are more attentive to literary form. For most scholars, a return to aesthetics does not require a strict departure from the cultural studies of the past decades. As Christopher Looby and Cindy Weinstein write in their introduction to the collection *American Literature's Aesthetic Dimensions*, rather than returning to a New Critical attempt to establish timeless aesthetic standards or to study literary form removed from historical context, the goal is "to demonstrate the ways in which aesthetics and politics are dialectically engaged."[27] This dialectical engagement is frequently cited in recent scholarship on aesthetic writing in the early United States, as early national intellectuals used a shared vocabulary to discuss politics and aesthetics, particularly the paradoxical relationship between consent and submission experienced by the liberal subject that is similarly allegorized in the marriage plots of domestic fiction.[28] The early national authors in this study are self-conscious of the ways that political ideology relies on aesthetic modes and is therefore susceptible to imaginative revision.

The aesthetic turn in early American studies is part of a much broader shift in literary studies that has seen numerous critics proposing methodological corrections to the symptomatic reading practices of historicist criticism that understand critique to be the work of excavating a text's hidden ideological programming. One of the most generative of these polemics continues to be Eve Kosofsky Sedgwick's essay charting the different possibilities of paranoid and reparative reading.[29] I have found most useful for this project approaches to these debates from scholars who think of paranoid and reparative reading less as choices to be fully occupied by critics than as reactive positions subjects constantly move between.[30] We can see this movement reflected historically in the narrative experimentation of the early national period. One example of this movement appears in the sophisticated narrative theory of Charles Brockden Brown. Brown is frequently cited as an inaugurator of the romance tradition that positions him as a precursor to canonical practitioners like Nathaniel Hawthorne and Henry James, in part because his precisely developed theory of the romance is a rare moment of generic stability in the history of the notoriously unwieldy form. Brown's emphasis on the conjectural nature of romance aligns his narrative theory with a recent critical interest in the political efficacy of speculative, as opposed to realist, fiction.[31] As I argue in my first chapter, however, Brown's fiction is often characterized by an exhaustion with a conjectural mode that encourages the very paranoid reading practices the post-critical turn has grown disenchanted with.[32] Out of the thwarted courtship plots, same-sex utopias, and creole domestic spaces my first chapter examines, it is a housewife, strictly preoccupied by the mundane daily tasks of household labor, who stands out as the most imaginatively powerful advocate for new social relations emerging out of the revolutionary Atlantic world of Haiti, France, and the United States. Brown's Woldwinite understanding of romance as a mode that fulfills a natural curiosity to speculate about unconscious motives and unintended consequences potentially aligns the romance with what Sedgwick describes as the anticipatory mode of paranoid reading practices.[33] Brown theorizes that because romance is preoccupied with conjecturing an always uncertain relation between cause and effect, the province of romance is generatively but also overwhelmingly infinite. The romance's anticipatory mode generates narrative, but it is also vulnerable to requisition by xenophobic nationalist scripts, heteronormative marriage plots, and paralyzing determinism. Brown experiments with episodic domestic scenes to pause this drive toward resolution, allowing readers to linger in sensual and aesthetic pleasures that remain temporarily unencumbered by the consolidating force of nationalist and heteronormative plots. Brown theorizes that writing in the anticipatory mode of the romance forecloses certain possibilities precisely because it is so difficult to resist social impositions like gender hierarchy that pose as natural inevitabilities. But crucially, Brown also understands conjecture to be fundamental to the act of creating a satisfying narrative.

Domestic fiction of course explicitly invites considerations of interiority: the domestic space is within the home, rhetorically defined through its very isolation from the exterior public, and the conventional marriage plots of domestic fiction establish character through affective inner states rather than the superficial markings of lineage and nobility. It is thus particularly conducive to a kind of criticism that, in Sedgwick's words, "places its faith in exposure," as critics work to excavate the ideological programming beneath domestic fiction's understanding of the private as a space of authenticity.[34] In the moment of transition that opens this book, however, when the literary public sphere is actively constructing fictions of an inviolate private sphere as incubator for self-determined individuals, there is also a clear self-consciousness about the fact that, in the words of a wise mentor in Theodore Winthrop's novel *Cecil Dreeme* (1861), "publicity makes privacy."[35] Rather than a repressed source of anxiety, these texts forthrightly experiment with the possibilities that follow from recognizing that the very private desires the law relies on to present itself as consensual are products of social invention. As I argue in my fourth chapter, *Cecil Dreeme* borrows from the Gothic genre a "social and relational" understanding of identity but eschews the paranoia that is traditionally understood to accompany this understanding.[36] The central character's determination to resist suspicion and cynicism leads to forms of intimacy and caretaking that allow for privacy without shame.[37] In this sense, the novel resists what Christopher Castiglia has called the disposition of critique and proposes an alternative to the modes of detection and quietism that have emerged as caricatures out of our debates about critical method.[38] As a prototrans novel, *Cecil Dreeme* understands gender ideology as surpassing the materiality of the body, but it remains committed to a connection between external markings of racial otherness and internal depravity. As we will see in my final chapter, Wilson's *Our Nig* is equally preoccupied with questions of surface and depth, but Wilson's novel harnesses sentimental antislavery fiction's incoherent romantic racialism to claim exceptional embodiment as the source of her creative genius. Even as *Cecil Dreeme* and *Our Nig* ask readers to interrogate their own investment in exposure and detection, they are not naive about the fact that popular nineteenth-century aesthetic modes and pseudoscientific discourses like the Gothic romance, portraiture, sentimental antislavery fiction, physiognomy, and spiritualism that work to fix readable surfaces as signifiers of innate depths create the surfaces they claim to describe. Winthrop and Wilson do not only denaturalize discourses of gender or racial essentialism that authorize themselves through supposedly neutral descriptions of bodily surface; they also recognize that what is a fundamentally and inevitably creative act does not always need to work in the service of heteronormativity or white supremacy.[39]

A study of the debates surrounding the aesthetic and political value of domestic retreat as it is being invented at the turn into the nineteenth century finds early national authors confronting many of the same questions that inform our own debates about critical method, including the interdependence of political ideals and fictional conventions, the indeterminate primacy of surface and depth, and the consequences of acts of exposure and disregard. As I now propose, although this book does not offer much in the way of methodological prescription, in its investigation of how domestic retreat is imagined as a space of critique in the early United States, it does offer some insight into how our contemporary debates about critical method can be historicized.

LITERARY HISTORIES: DOMESTIC FICTION AND AMERICAN ROMANTICISM

If we compare some of the most established accounts of domestic fiction and romanticism, a pattern emerges that suggests our critical practices consistently use gender to organize our own shifting relationship as literary scholars to the possibilities of critique. Historically situated as responses to the market revolution, both domestic fiction and American Romanticism have been associated with a performative discomfort with the commodification of literature and the public demands of professional authorship. In his important study *American Romanticism and the Marketplace*, Michael Gilmore countered a well-established understanding of romanticism and domestic fiction as having opposing relationships to the marketplace: "ambivalence toward the exchange process also links the romantics to more popular authors, such as the literary women, who are ordinarily perceived as their opposites."[40] Despite this inclusive gesture, the reasons for this shared discomfort are located in tellingly different registers. For Gilmore discomfort with the market emerges, for domestic authors, from a contrast between the private life celebrated by domesticity and the publicity of authorship, and for romantic authors, from a desire to resist the commodification of their art. In this narrative, the domestic author's discomfort with publicity is attributed to the acceptance of ideology, while the romantic author's discomfort is a sign of dissent. Even as both movements imagine an inviolate private sphere free from social and economic constraints as the realm of aesthetic production, retreat takes on different valences depending on the literary movement an author is associated with—for romantic authors, retreat is considered to be an antisocial statement of aesthetic independence, while for domestic authors, retreat is understood as providing access to moral truths that can then be communicated to the sentimental reader. Both of these positions can be understood, in the words of Lora Romero, as "textual productions."[41] Decades of criticism have established the performative nature of these positions of feminine retreat and masculine alienation, primarily through arguments that "see through" the counterculture status both romanticism and domesticity claim. In addition to sharing a historical origin, domestic fiction and romanticism share a critical narrative that is preoccupied with the relationship between aesthetics and critique. The critical histories of domestic fiction and romanticism consistently return to the question of each movement's effectiveness as a vehicle of critique. Rising and falling with our own critical shifts between the poles of aesthetics and cultural studies, each movement comes to depend on the other for generic coherence.

Once characterized as aesthetically deficient and politically irrelevant, domestic fiction was restored to the canon through attention to what Jane Tompkins famously called its "cultural work." Tompkins made this argument by continuing to position domestic fiction in relation to the canonical romantic authors it had been unfavorably compared to: domestic fiction potentially "offers a critique of American society far more devastating than any delivered by better-known critics such as Hawthorne and Melville."[42] Complicating this celebratory approach, a next generation of New Historicist scholars then investigated how this cultural work perpetuated the ideologies of its time.[43] As Shirley Samuels wrote in her introduction to the important collection *The Culture of Sentiment*, in recognizing the fraught nature of the cultural power domestic ideology granted white middle-class women, the question became "whether the sentimental gaze acts to conservative ends . . . or seeks to produce radical reform."[44] Noting a tendency in New Historicist scholarship to uncritically reproduce a nineteenth-century narrative of a culture dominated by women, scholars worked to historicize this gendered divide, pushing the conversation past debates that presented domestic fiction as either subversive or hegemonic.[45] More recently, critics have noted that approaches primarily informed by cultural studies have sidestepped the charges of aesthetic inferiority once leveled against the women's writing of the nineteenth-century, but these reassessments have primarily privileged the category of sentimental rather than domestic, terms that are frequently conflated but that, as I argue, are worth prying apart.[46]

The category of American Romanticism was first established by F. O. Matthiessen's claims of aesthetic excellence: rather than considering Emerson, Hawthorne, Melville, Thoreau, and Whitman in relation to literary history or as products of economic or social developments, Matthiessen claimed to be solely interested in "*what* these books were as works of art."[47] Claiming unpopularity as a sign of aesthetic merit, by the fourth page of his introduction Matthiessen turns to Warner, Cummins, and Southworth as apparently obvious counterpoints to his, quoting Pound, interest in "masterwork" rather than "failures or mediocrity."[48] In their critiques of an approach that assumed the timeless universality of aesthetic criteria, feminist scholars like Tompkins and Nina Baym noted that the judgment that great American literature should be divorced from context-specific social conditions is more reflective of the priorities of the critic making that argument than the literature used as representative evidence in support of that claim.[49] The characterization of the romantic canon as divorced from the historical upheavals directly addressed by the women's protest novel tradition was next countered by approaches that linked the alienation claimed by the romantic author to a challenging and experimental literary form. While some critics characterized a romantic aesthetic of inaccessibility as dissent rather than escapism, others unfavorably contrasted canonical Romanticists' impotent "aesthetic dissent" to texts written within the antislavery and women's rights movement that directly link "cultural work" to "specific political practices."[50] Most recently, scholars have returned to the fiction writers associated with American Romanticism to reconsider the political possibilities of the antirealist tendencies of romance.[51] As Paul Gilmore notes, this renewed interest has occurred "by almost always avoiding the term" romanticism, "in part because it still carries a charge of formal, aesthetic universalism or cultural nationalism."[52] Thus although the category of American Romanticism has been deemphasized because of its origin as a canon of exclusion (even as the gravitational pull of its authors continues to hold sway in our teaching practices), a renewed interest in the romance genre marks a shift from the historicist preoccupation with realism's explicitly mimetic critique of society to an aesthetic interest in romance's imaginative antirealism.[53] As I argue throughout this project, this move to excise "romance" from romanticism leaves behind the early national poets who have been dismissed as derivative "stepchildren of British and European Romanticism," a move that also surrenders expansive and fluid conceptions of gender and genius to American Romanticism's narrow history.[54]

When we place these familiar critical narratives of American Romanticism and domestic fiction side by side, we see how clearly our conceptions of domestic fiction and romanticism depend on one another for generic stability: romanticism's aesthetic transcendence is first defined against domestic fiction's conventionality; domestic fiction's cultural work is then defined against romanticism's disengagement; romanticism's imaginative possibilities are then defined against domestic fiction's realist foreclosures. This is not to say that these categories are meaningless but that they have gained coherence through a firmly entrenched sense of retroactively established author networks rather than predictable formal attributes. Our understanding of a text as domestic or romantic predetermines our readings in ways that force an alignment between generic conventions and content that don't always do justice to the messy possibilities texts might imagine. The problem is twofold. First, the fictional category of "romance" that has become a preferred circuit back to the canonical novelists associated with American Romanticism is not itself a stable genre. As defined by early theorists of the American romance tradition like Charles Brockden Brown, the romance is more accurately accounted for as a speculative mode that appears across genres and is just as likely to influence marriage plots and descriptions of household arrangements as tales of spontaneous combustion and mysterious ventriloquists.[55] Additionally, the notion of private retreat that is foundational for both a tradition of domestic fiction and romanticism is itself a supporting fantasy for the political invention of liberal citizenship. Just as there is value in separating the terms sentimental and domestic, we might also pry apart realist and domestic. Although the domestic novel has been nearly inseparable from realism in our critical histories, the fundamentally imaginative nature of the notion of domestic retreat is aligned with rather than oppositional to the speculative mode of the romance. In the chapters that follow, this realignment of terms affords new ways of thinking about the trope of domestic retreat, particularly its function in registering dissent through the withholding of naturalizing emotional supplement and the mutually adaptive relationship it enjoys with the encroachment of social sanction.

THE CHAPTERS

This study traces a moment of transition when the literary public sphere is actively constructing fictions of an inviolate private sphere. This transition is a moment when private retreat was being imagined in all sorts of ways, including those that don't align with our contemporary methods for approaching and defining domestic fiction and romanticism. I begin with the domestic fiction of Charles Brockden Brown. Acutely aware of how gender and class determine access to the possibilities of domestic retreat, Brown's fiction associates the domestic space with aesthetic and intellectual pleasures while resisting the consolidating narrative pressures of the marriage plot and the conflation of labor and virtue that will eventually characterize domestic ideology in the nineteenth century. The fiction of a transcendent private sphere both inspires and frustrates Brown, as he attempts to imagine domestic scenes that are not limited by the sentimentalizing of a gendered labor divide. Brown's domestic fiction does not sentimentalize the household as a space free from material labor, nor is it emotionally invested in naturalizing the categories of sexual difference that undergird the liberal fiction of a public-private divide. This first chapter considers the genre glitches that evacuate the traditional conventions of domestic fiction of their emotional force. Excised from the consolidating futurity of the marriage plot, for example, domestic scenes become largely episodic and thus temporarily unconstrained by the expectations of genre and the pressures of resolution. Circulating within periodicals that aim for conversation rather than resolution, Brown's domestic fragments imagine homosocial and cosmopolitan possibilities for domestic spaces, temporarily unburdened by the obligations of duty and dependence that threaten to corrupt both the republican ideal of companionate marriage and the romantic ideal of domestic retreat. Emphasizing the term *domestic* rather than *sentimental,* I use Brown as an opening example of how reconfiguring domestic retreat as a right rather than an obligation yields possibilities for dissent not only in romance's fantastic world making but also in the mundane daily practices that are denaturalized through the refusal of emotional supplement.

Although a new privileging of gender difference accompanied the transition from republican periodical culture to liberal novel culture, a diverse range of authors responded ambivalently to this very transition. This shift from republican to liberal print culture is often described in gendered terms that exclude American women writers from a Romantic canon characterized by critique and individualism, as the perceived rise of a feminized reading public either marks a shift from republican collaboration to liberal privatization or signals a conservative investment in republican collaboration out of step with the innovative individualism cultivated by the period's Romantic authors.[56] My second and third chapters address the contradictions of this critical narrative. Chapter 2, on James Kirke Paulding and William and Washington Irving's literary periodical *Salmagundi; or, the Whim-Whams and Opinions of Launcelot Langstaff, Esq. and Others* (1807), considers the new policing of gender conventions that accompanied the transition from republican periodical culture to the liberal literary marketplace. Through the self-conscious assumption of aristocratic bachelor personas, the magazine editors' aggressively masculine domestic retreat can be read as a reaction to the insufficiently reductive categories of a literary culture increasingly organized by gender difference. Rather than retreating from the restrictive codes of domesticity, *Salmagundi* works to reinvest the reformative promises of domesticity with the bachelor's imaginative whimsy. This strategy, however, depends on the careful construction of a division within the domestic space that distinguishes the bachelor-author's imaginative output from the termagant's domestic labor.

After resituating Irving as a producer of domestic fiction, chapter 3 offers a similar repositioning as I approach Catharine Maria Sedgwick's frontier romance *Hope Leslie; or, Early Times in the Massachusetts* (1827) as an early romantic experiment rather than as a straightforward precursor to mid-nineteenth-century domestic novels. Drawing a correspondence between the domestic and the frontier, early romantic historiography called upon feminine genius to naturalize fantasies of progressive national history. Although Sedgwick's experimental romanticism protests the artificial confines of domesticity, it can do so only by replacing the disenfranchised white woman of domestic fiction with the forsaken Indian woman of romantic historiography as the figure who must remain the unassimilated source of the natural values that the United States claims for itself. As my reading of Magawisca's revolutionary dissent in *Hope Leslie* suggests, because we tend to read women's fiction as always making an argument on behalf of a liberal model of citizenship that argues for inclusion based on universal rights, it is easy to overlook moments when the assimilationist pressure of this citizenship is presented as a threat to be resisted. Rather than seeking a correspondence between private identity and public recognition, the early national fiction I examine desperately attempts to preserve divergence. Withholding emotional investment from socially sanctioned forms of attachment, this fiction's imaginative force lies less in revealing individual choice as a ruse of all-encompassing power than in flushing out the assimilative pressures of liberal inclusion from the naturalizing rhetoric of sentiment.

Chapter 4 moves us from early national settler-colonist fantasies of the New England frontier to the decidedly queer New York City of Theodore Winthrop's midcentury urban novel *Cecil Dreeme* (1861). Perhaps less familiar to readers than Charles Brockden Brown, Washington Irving, and Catharine Maria Sedgwick, Theodore Winthrop initially had a posthumous revival of popularity after becoming one of the first Union officers to be killed in a Civil War battle. Winthrop's writing has more recently received renewed critical attention as a rich repository of early national representations of same-sex desires and transgender capacities before the imposition of sexology's classifying schemes at the end of the nineteenth century. The story of a virtuous young American who finds himself drawn to a magnetic and unscrupulous blackmailer, *Cecil Dreeme* would appear to be especially well suited for readings in the queer Gothic tradition. But *Cecil Dreeme* also highlights the distinct affordances of transgender studies for domestic fiction and romantic genius. At the center of *Cecil Dreeme* is a reclusive artist who is granted the status of genius through the "epicene character" of his work (206). Nineteenth-century theories of genius organized around the appropriative availability of femininity help us to see that *Cecil Dreeme* is not structured by a cross-dressing plot that represses and displaces queer desire but instead is structured around a straightforward recognition and acceptance of transmasculinity. One of the many single-gender domestic spaces of this book's archive, the primary setting for *Cecil Dreeme* is a boardinghouse for unmarried men that becomes a middle ground of public privacy where a shared vulnerability to influence can be experienced as generative rather than a weakness to be exploited. While previous chapters have considered the diverse possibilities of domestic retreat as it is being invented in the early decades of the nineteenth century, this chapter considers the transportability of domestic ideology across unexpected social arrangements once its conventions come to be increasingly fixed over the course of the nineteenth century. The partnership that develops between two men in *Cecil Dreeme* survives the ending of the novel in part because their relationship seamlessly conforms to the gendered roles of husband and wife, suggesting that as domestic ideology solidifies over the course of the nineteenth century, its protections become more accessible to those willing to inhabit its increasingly recognizable conventions. In these last two chapters we also see that the ideas of gender performance that inform nineteenth-century theories of genius are increasingly restricted by race. As Kyla Schuller and Jules Gill-Peterson write, "unevenly distributed plasticity, rather than biological determinism, characterizes nineteenth-century ideas of racial and sexual difference."[57] Even as domestic virtue and respectability are extended to the queer partnership of *Cecil Dreeme*, the novel's understanding of gender as a mutable and social potential takes shape only in contrast to its insistence that race is an immutable and expressive trait.

Emerging out of critical accounts of privacy in the early nineteenth century is the question of how private individuals can critique the structures that gain power through the desire of those very individuals for social recognition and political inclusion.[58] I argue in my final chapter that Harriet E. Wilson's radically experimental novel-narrative *Our Nig; or, Sketches from the Life of a Free Black* (1859) provides one possibility, as Wilson deploys her protagonist's exceptional embodiment to highlight the anemic freedom granted to those who accept the abstracting terms of liberal recognition. Wilson rejects the conventions of domestic and romantic fiction that require a performative discomfort with the financial implications of publishing and with the material circumstances that have generated and hindered her own literary production. Refusing to participate in the fiction of a transcendent domestic sphere that we see some authors in this book attempt to revise and make their own, Wilson's novel is an unsparing portrait of violently coerced domestic labor that condemns domestic retreat as a supporting structure for consensual citizenship. Additionally, recognizing that sentimental domestic fiction's generic turn to interior character traits constructs the racialized surfaces it claims to disregard, Wilson reimagines the mutability of surface as a source of creative freedom. Mobilizing the incoherent fantasies of romantic racialism for her own creative purposes, Wilson claims the position of a spiritual medium that allows her to speak for her white domestic tormentors in public. Untethered from supporting fantasies of domestic retreat, Wilson redirects readers' attention away from her protagonist's interiority to their own investment in confession and exposure. In turn, the novel asks what new modes of protest and persuasion can be imagined that don't hinge on scenes of suffering or require us to continue looking below and within to confirm what we already know. Denied the protections of white womanhood, Wilson showcases the labor behind sentimental conventions that maintain a readerly conceit of innocent unknowingness and advertises the literary contrivance behind conventions consumed as spontaneous impulse or artless testimony. Wilson's novel provides a powerful conclusion to a book that begins with Charles Brockden Brown's speculative uncertainty about how to reconcile the aesthetic freedom promised by domestic retreat with its supporting material conditions. Telling a story of coerced domestic labor in a narrative that foregrounds the literary labor behind the seductive conventions of domestic fiction, Wilson connects domestic and literary labor precisely by refusing the sentiment that pastoralizes both as effortless.

1
CHARLES BROCKDEN BROWN'S DOMESTIC SCENES

THE PRECEDING INTRODUCTION characterized the position of domestic retreat as a contested invention of the early national period. Additionally, I argued that the two major literary movements of the nineteenth century, domestic fiction and Romanticism, share a foundational investment in this ideal of domestic retreat. These movements have gained categorical coherence through relational contrasts that can obscure the portability of the speculative mode of the romance and of the literary trope of domestic retreat across genres. Writing in the final decades of the eighteenth century, when the fantasy of domestic retreat begins to emerge, Charles Brockden Brown is an ideal author to begin establishing this argument. Brown is a deliberative theorist of fiction, particularly the romance. He also writes across genres and print mediums, from long-form novels to fragments collected in early national periodicals. Additionally, although Brown is most often characterized as an author of Gothic romances, he brings his experimental Woldwinite interest in class and gender politics to bear on the marriage plots and domestic arrangements that populate his fiction. As we will see in this chapter, Brown's fiction serves as a potent opening example of the expansive and surprising possibilities of domestic retreat emerging out of the early national period.

In his frequently cited essay "The Difference Between History and Romance" (1800), Brown writes that the difference between the historian and the romancer is the difference between a writer who "faithfully enumerates the appearances which occur" and a writer who "adorns these appearances with cause and effect."[1] The historian observes and describes "facts in their disconnected and natural order," while the romancer "adorns" "natural appearances" with "speculations on the past or future." For Brown, the primary distinguishing feature of romance is its conjectural and speculative nature, particularly when it comes to forging connections—past motives and future consequences—between seemingly disparate events. Rather than maintaining a clear generic distinction between romance and history, Brown claims "the same man is frequently both historian and romancer in the same compass of the same work" (252). Because human curiosity is not content with factual description, but is naturally conjectural, a writer who does not blend history and romance "is essentially defective" (253). Brown's essay, with its dual emphases on the generative relationship between history and romance and its understanding of romance as a response to a fundamental human impulse, conceives of romance less as a formally coherent genre than as a mode that can be found across genres. In this chapter I consider how Brown experiments with romance's conjectural mode within episodic fantasies of domestic retreat to counteract the deterministic impulses of romantic conjecture that plague the characters of his long-form Gothic plots.

Brown's essay has become an important touchstone for understanding his fiction more generally, as critics claim the conjectural nature of romance to be crucial to his Woldwinite project of political critique and his narrative method.[2] We can also see that, in practice, his novels are characterized by an exhaustion with the relentlessly speculative logic of causality and by a frustration with the long-form imposition of resolution, which can only ever offer a superficial freezing of the endless speculation about motive and consequence that has generated it. A brief detour through *Edgar Huntly; Or, Memoirs of a Sleepwalker* (1799), one of Brown's more canonical long-form romances, demonstrates this frustration with a conjectural mode of reading. Characters in the novel struggle with the utilitarian theory Brown develops in "The Difference between History and Romance": although an involuntary action differs in motive from a voluntary action, it is still the cause of potentially damaging consequences (252). The central question of *Edgar Huntly* becomes "shall we impute guilt where there is no design?"[3] The novel's antagonist, Clithero, succumbs to a contagious paranoia that the involuntary murder he commits in self-defense "could not happen without a series of anterior events paving the way for it . . . it must be the theme of design. It must spring from laborious circumvention and deep-laid stratagems" (70). An undisguised paraphrase of William Godwin's principle of necessary causality, this sense of life as plot coalesces when both Sarsefield, usually considered the novel's mature moral voice, and Clithero, the villain, agree that Huntly should take responsibility for the violent chain of events his own impulsive "rashness" eventually sets into motion (280, 284).[4] The novel ends with Huntly disenfranchised as an author, as Sarsefield takes over the final two letters. Huntly has become an unruly remainder of his own tale, his socially unproductive impulses unsatisfactorily reduced to the directive "be more circumspect and more obsequious for the future" (284). Huntly's silence following this final directive registers as a protest against the causal logic of Sarsefield's narrative coup and leaves readers with their own lingering uncertainty about what motives to attribute to his sympathetic impulses. Even as Brown theorizes that romance generates narrative by imposing motives and forging connections between seemingly unrelated events, in practice this conjectural mode can lead to a kind of narrative paralysis, as characters are no longer able to determine the intentions behind their own actions or foresee the future consequences of their choices.

This chapter considers Brown's interest in the position of domestic retreat in relation to the political affordances of overtly imaginative traditions like the romance, but it also remains mindful of Brown's claim that authors must shift between conjectural romance and descriptive history within the same text. Brown's investment in the conjectural possibilities of the romance can be found not only where we most expect it—in the sensational plots of his long-form Gothic romances—but also in the belabored marriage plots of his domestic fiction and the descriptions of household arrangements of his periodical fiction. Brown is an important precedent for nineteenth-century romance writers like Nathaniel Hawthorne and Henry James who, as Carrie Hyde puts it, were preoccupied with defining the romance as a "a *theory* of fiction that seeks to isolate its distinguishing feature: its departure from the descriptive regime of the indicative."[5] A renewed interest in what Hyde has called "the formative political power of aesthetics" has reinvigorated attention to the political affordances of the romance's conjectural mode, particularly as an imaginative corrective to historicist methods that have privileged the realist novel.[6] Domestic fiction is associated with a tradition of realism that is traditionally defined in opposition to romance. But when we think of romance as Brown does, as a conjectural mode, we can see that its portability allows for multiple affordances across genres, including domestic fiction. Brown's own understanding of the difficulty in separating historical description from romantic conjecture makes his fiction and narrative theory fertile ground for revisiting an approach to the romance that "flattens history and literature alike by figuring each as phenomenologically discrete realms."[7] Brown's fiction is situated on the cusp of the market revolution that gives rise to the figuring of the domestic sphere as a space of retreat. Writing during the decades when the literary public sphere is actively constructing fictions of an inviolate private sphere, Brown's interest in the possibilities of domestic retreat align it with the romantic conceit of "literary autonomy" as it functioned to contest and reaffirm notions of consensual citizenship.[8]

In Brown's domestic scenes, the conjectural mode operates to denaturalize the most mundane and therefore most trenchant conventions of private life. It is my contention that in Brown's fiction, scenes of domestic retreat provide relief from romance's relentlessly retrospective and anticipatory mode, where the present can only be interpreted through questions about past motives and future consequences. Excised from the consolidating futurity of the marriage plot, domestic scenes become largely episodic and thus temporarily unconstrained by the expectations of genre and the pressures of resolution. Although even the infamously digressive nature of Brown's writing cannot overcome the "power" of "generic performance" that Lauren Berlant has described as flourishing in "moments of potential collapse," the abruptly concluded and fragmentary nature of the fiction I examine in this chapter forces a confrontation with the arbitrary nature of generic conventions that highjack critical and readerly expectations.[9] In this sense, my argument is informed by recent work that aims to "un-novel" Brown by attending to his periodical fiction and to the formal experimentation within his long-form fiction.[10]

The material details of household arrangements are undoubtedly a central concern of Brown's fiction, from the prolonged and only tenuously resolved courtship plots of his early Gothic romances and his final two epistolary novels to the short portraits, fragments, and essays of his magazine writing. Even *Edgar Huntly*, a classic in the frontier Gothic genre, uses a courtship plot for its narrative framing.[11] Brown is consistently preoccupied with how gender, capital, and labor determine the intellectual and aesthetic possibilities of the domestic space. Brown's novels frequently consider relationships between men and women of unequal class, asking and unable to satisfactorily resolve the questions of how women might maintain their personal autonomy under a marriage contract that renders them dependents and how men might remain free from imputations of self-interest given that marriage acquires them property. Outside of the generic pressures of the marriage plot, Brown finds promise in the potential sensual and aesthetic freedoms of domestic retreat and imagines the domestic scene as a testing ground for alternative forms of individual autonomy.

Because Brown's preoccupation with the domestic is fundamentally Woldwinite, his fiction furnishes radically revisionary ways of thinking about domestic fiction in the early nineteenth century. Imagining versions of domestic retreat where aesthetic possibilities are not delimited by a gendered labor divide, this archive provides an avenue for challenging the stubborn divide between domestic fiction and romanticism that continues to influence the field of antebellum literary culture. Brown is an ideal figure for this challenge, as the twentieth century retroactively imposed its own critical narrative onto Brown's career. Critics once argued that Brown abandoned the experimental radicalism of his Gothic romances and succumbed to the pressures of a feminized literary marketplace at the end of his career, first returning to the already outmoded sentimental epistolary form and finally abandoning long-form fiction entirely for literary magazines.[12] Within this narrative, Brown's Gothic romances serve as important predecessors for the performatively beleaguered male writers associated with nineteenth-century romanticism. This critical narrative has been countered by mining Brown's later work for evidence that it continues the work of his political romances rather than signaling a surrender to market forces.[13] This chapter suggests a different emphasis, arguing not only that his late writing continues Brown's political experiments but also that the domestic plot has always been central to his formal and social experimentalism.[14]

This chapter will first consider how Brown's final novel, *Jane Talbot* (1801), is organized around a tension between the marriage plot and the romantic ideal of domestic retreat. Resisting the conflation of labor and virtue that will eventually characterize domestic ideology in the nineteenth century, *Jane Talbot* tentatively imagines forms of domestic autonomy uncompromised by the inevitable support of domestic labor. This fantasy, however, is consistently frustrated by characters who cannot reconcile the quality of feminine self-dependence with the generic constraints of the marriage plot and the sexual contract. The second half of this chapter connects two under-examined threads of Charles Brockden Brown's career, magazine writing and domestic fiction. A late-career turn to magazine fiction allows Brown to experiment with temporary moments of domestic retreat that can be withheld from the generic constraints that frustrate the potential for domestic autonomy tentatively imagined in *Jane Talbot*. Excised from both the consolidating logic of domestic fiction's marriage plot and the conjectural logic of the romance, the fragments and extracts unique to the world of the early national magazine imagine domestic arrangements that experiment with forms of homosocial intimacy and creole cultural capital.

THE POWER OF COMPLIANCE

In Charles Brockden Brown's final novel, *Jane Talbot*, Henry Colden warns his beloved Jane, "I cannot labour for bread; I cannot work to live. In that respect I have no parallel. The world does not contain my likeness. My very nature unfits me for any profitable business."[15] Although Henry claims his nature is exceptional, in the Brownian universe, he is only one member in a long line of morally ambiguous, marriage-averse slackers. Unsettling the categories of masculine disinterest and feminine dependence, *Jane Talbot*'s endless repetition of marital deferrals between a woman who claims she will be a "self-dependent wife" and a man who claims his "dependence must ever be on others or on fortune" suggests an ambivalence towards the new privileging of gender difference that undergirds early national celebrations of affectionate marriage (66, 57).[16] *Jane Talbot* is domestic fiction in the sense that its plot is solely focused on the courtship of Jane and Henry, but it does not follow the conventions of sentimental domestic fiction. It does not sentimentalize the household as a space free from material labor, nor is it emotionally invested in naturalizing the categories of sexual difference that undergird the liberal fiction of a public-private divide. Suggesting but not confirming Jane and Henry's marriage, the novel's abrupt ending draws attention to the structuring generic expectations of the marriage plot but does not present them as ineluctable. This chapter hitches its wagon to the work of critics who have used Brown to consider the insufficiency of the gendered categories that determine our discussions of nineteenth-century fiction. Bruce Burgett draws attention to the paradox of male sentimentalism in Brown's penultimate novel, *Clara Howard*, a text often dismissed in the same critical breath as *Jane Talbot*, noting that "U.S. literary history continues to be written as if the author of *Edgar Huntly* either never wrote *Clara Howard*, or did so only reluctantly."[17] Marion Rust has convincingly explained "why sentimental doesn't equal domestic in early American fiction." Rust argues that conflating sentimentalism and domesticity "can lead us to overlook the ways in which domesticity did not, in fact, contain either female life events or subjectivity."[18] Leonard Tennenhouse revises a flawed but pervasive critical narrative of the so-called feminization of American literary culture by demonstrating that this narrative's supposed origin, the early national seduction plot, functions to establish masculinity. Succinctly put, "domestication does not necessarily entail feminization."[19] Following these category-troubling interventions, this chapter considers *Jane Talbot* to be domestic but not sentimental fiction.[20] Excluded from the traditions of both (feminine) domestic fiction and (masculine) romanticism, Brown's vision of domestic retreat opens up new ways of thinking about the domestic as a space of aesthetic play and possibility rather than one that is inevitably reducible to discipline and consensus.[21]

After Mrs. Fielder, Jane's guardian, threatens to disinherit Jane if she marries the recovering Godwinian Henry Colden, a position that becomes only more entrenched after a forged letter suggests they have already spent a night together, most of the novel is spent trying to resolve the dilemma of whether domestic bliss is possible for two people who require domestic security but are unsuited for domestic labor. Henry explicitly links his unsuitability for "profitable business" to his intellectual pursuits: "I have no relish, indeed, for sensual indulgences. It is the intellectual taste that calls for such banquets as imagination and science can furnish" (57). Like Henry, Jane has always had a propensity for questioning the blindly conventional pursuit of duty, and she prefers the "contemplative, bookish, and romantic" Henry Colden to the husband Mrs. Fielder and her father chose for her who was "addicted to industry" and "had read no books" (37–38). If Jane and Henry share a preference for intellect over industry, they differ on how this preference will determine their future domestic scene. Although Jane claims she "looks forward to poverty without dismay," wondering if it will "strengthen [her] mind," Henry forces her to consider the material realities of poverty: "You must go into a family of strangers," "bear the humours and accommodate yourself to the habits of your inmates," and be content with "a humble dwelling . . . a low roof, a narrow chamber"; when Henry manages to visit, he will only bring "a soul harassed by unwelcome toil, eyes dim with straining at tiresome or painful objects" (54, 59). Rather than attempting, as Henry does, the hopeless project of denying the material dimension of the ideal domestic space, Jane's vision maintains a distinction between intellectual retreat and the work she might do to support that retreat and suggests that labor need not interfere with the aesthetic and autonomous possibilities of domestic retreat.

Jane responds to Henry's letter by cheekily mocking his gloomy vision: "Must I huddle, with a dozen squalling children and their notably-noisy or sluttishly-indolent dam, round a dirty hearth and meagre winter's fire? Must sooty rafters, a sorry truckle-bed, and a mud-encumbered alley, be my nuptial lot?" (62) Jane instead dreams of using what is left of her funds to rent a "little chamber, set out with perfect neatness . . . her privacy unapproachable but at her own pleasure; her quiet undisturbed by a prater, a scolder, a bustler, or a whiner; no dirty children to offend the eye, or squalling ones to wound the ear" (65). In this vision "happily she is exempt from the humiliating necessity of working to live . . . the sweet quiet of her chamber . . . or the cheerful blaze of her hearth, will invite her to mental exercise," to indulge "a taste for books" or "commune with bounteous nature" (65). Jane's vision is decidedly self-interested: as a "self-dependent wife," she will be "useful to herself" and "find delight in her own wants." From this fantasy of contemplative domestic retreat, Jane turns to wondering how "the mental powers of the artist" might relieve her husband's financial stress; teaching young women drawing and singing, she might "make a business of her sports" (66). Jane quickly moves from this utilitarian assessment of "arts" originally acquired "with no view but her own amusement" to motherhood, "a calling that may divert her from the thoughts of mere lucre." Now seeming to be in the full throes of sentimental domestic fantasy, Jane asks, "what is there but pure and sacred in the anticipated transports of a mother?"

Imagining that Henry will pay her "in caresses" rather than "money," one reading of these competing visions is that Jane is fully indoctrinated in the ideology of sentimental domesticity, where labor is rendered invisible by the bonds of love. Henry, then, might be seen as working to disabuse Jane of this illusion of pastoralized domestic labor as he "shudders at the prospect" of reducing her to "a seamstress" (77). Henry's skepticism is shared by Jane's profligate brother, Frank, who characterizes her as "one accustomed to *feed on thoughts* instead of pudding" and confronts her with his own vision of her future should she marry Henry: "you may perhaps set the good man up in a village shop,—may purchase an assortment of tapers, porringers, and twelve-to-the-pound candles. The gleanings of the year may find you in skimmed milk and hasty pudding three times a day, and you may enjoy between whiles the delectable amusements of mending your husband's stockings at one time, and serving a neighbour with a pennyworth of snuff at another" (68, 72). Unwilling or unable to recognize the pleasures of Jane's vision—an "unapproachable privacy" devoted to "mental exercise"—her suitor and her brother reduce her future to one of constant labor—the "mending of [her] husband's stockings" or working as a "seamstress." The skeptical reactions of Jane's patriarchal guardians towards her visions suggests that she is simply naive about the material underpinnings of domestic retreat. Alternatively, Jane's confident insistence on the autonomous possibilities of an approach to domestic retreat that sees material labor, "mental exercise," and communion with "bounteous nature" as necessarily coexistent instead of hopelessly oppositional eventually suggests that Henry and Frank are the ones who need to be disabused of fantasy. Precisely because labor is indeed an inevitable element of the domestic, Henry and Frank turn out to be the ones enchanted by a transcendent domestic ideal.

Jane's claims to feminine self-dependence breach the limits of Henry's radical unconventionality, and the debates between them render the structuring conventions of the marriage plot problems of the imagination rather than social inevitabilities. Disrupting essentialist arguments that coded women's domestic labor as natural impulse, Jane imagines that her labor will always be secondary, only to be pursued if her intellectual pursuits don't "suffice to fill up her time" (65). Henry warns Jane that if she should rely on his labor, "deplorable and complete would be your disappointment . . . Quickly, and by some fatal deed, should I abandon you, my children and the world" (57). But in Jane's fantasy, Henry's romantic nature makes him dependent on her labor: Jane claims the position of "self-dependent wife," happy in the knowledge that "her love adds nothing to his fatigues and cares" (65). Henry, the former Godwinian who is reputed to have once "denied that any thing but mere habit and positive law stood in the way of marriage, nay, of intercourse without marriage, between brother and sister, parent and child!" is unable to imagine a marriage between a dependent husband, unsuited for "profitable business," and a "self-dependent wife," who would happily work to support her "indolent" husband's "relish for expensive pleasure" (39, 57, 66, 98). Both Jane's lover and her villainous brother share this lack of imagination when it comes to imagining a domestic scene that centers around a solitary and "self-dependent wife" who "is not obliged to demand a share of the earnings of her husband," and, because she owes nothing to her husband, is ultimately qualified to stake a claim to republican disinterest (65–66).[22]

The endless marital deferrals that structure *Jane Talbot* point to the disruption to the marriage plot that occurs when "dependence" and "disinterest" don't properly reinforce sexual difference. The suggestive possibilities Jane imagines for a household characterized by consensual rather than coerced labor that supports rather than hinders intellectual and aesthetic activity collide with the generic constraints that have traditionally been associated with the marriage contract. Explicitly claiming that his nature means his "dependence must ever be on others or on fortune," Henry recognizes that his marriage to Jane will never be disinterested: "I am poor, indolent, devoted, not to sensual, but to visionary and to costly, luxuries, How shall such a man escape the imputation of sordid and selfish motives . . . I can never truly aver that my motives are disinterested . . . Can I place my hand upon my heart, and affirm that her fortune has *no part* in the zeal with which I have cultivated Jane's affections?" (98) Henry is confronting the logic that precluded women from being considered fit for republican citizenship: as someone who will always be dependent on others, he will never be disinterested.[23] Although Jane's claims of self-dependence pose a clear solution to the very obstacle Henry presents as standing in the way of their marriage—his inability to support her—her self-dependence would also leave him without the economically dependent wife who would establish his independence. Condemning Jane's vision of domestic autonomy as sentimental fantasy, Henry's reaction forces the visibility of domestic labor, a move that only further undermines the fantasy of masculine disinterest.

Henry's stereotypically feminine devotion to "luxuries" can be read in the context of the shift in conceptions of the home from a space of production to one of consumption, where consumption is feminized with the civilizing effects of surplus aesthetic adornment. As Lori Merish argues in her study of sentimental materialism, in the early nineteenth century, "luxury goods were endowed with *emotional* import, and were being (re)constructed as signs of a specifically *feminine* civil subjectivity."[24] Promoting a desire for luxury goods as a sign of individual choice and taste, this discourse surrounding luxury goods was interpreted as "the capacity for discriminating among objects of affection" and accompanied the trope of affectionate marriage in its functions of naturalizing heterosexual desire and portraying the domestic sphere as a space of consensual attachments and moral refinement.[25] In *Jane Talbot*, however, Henry's confessed attachment to luxury does not operate to invest "political hierarchy" with sentiment. The association of women with the civilizing force of luxury goods stemmed from the sexual contract's definition of women as property. By having Henry, rather than Jane, confess an attachment to the luxury goods accumulated within a domestic sphere associated with aesthetic adornment that exceeds material or physical need, this attraction to luxury loses its didactic orientation and political use value. More than simply reversing gender roles, *Jane Talbot* works to withhold emotional investment from socially sanctioned forms of attachment, thus refusing to offer "a sense of spontaneous, heartfelt assent to power."[26] *Jane Talbot*'s imaginative force lies less in revealing individual choice as a ruse of all-encompassing power than in frustrating the assimilative pressures of liberal inclusion.

At the beginning of this chapter I suggested that, in practice, Brown's narrative theory of conjectural romance can lead to a kind of paralysis, as characters see no way out of the ever-proliferating possibilities of motives and consequences. Henry's preoccupation with the appearance of "sordid and selfish motives" implicates him in the mode of reading for "motives" that "cannot be certainly known" Brown associates with romance (*Jane Talbot*, 98; "Difference between History and Romance," 252). Henry's policing of Jane's fantasies and his own obsessive introspection point to the difficulty of distinguishing between consent and coercion for subjects of the social contract.[27] Henry hopelessly attempts to determine "whence this incurable folly?—this rooted incapacity of acting as every motive, generous and selfish, combine to recommend? Constitution; habit; insanity; the dominion of some evil spirit, who insinuates his baneful power between the *will* and the *act*" (111). Uncertain about the cause of his "indolent habits," Henry is certain that this character flaw is "incurable," "rooted" within. Although Henry's logic of individual constitution might suggest a conservative agenda at odds with Brown's investment in Woldwinite theories of environmental and social influences on identity, it also has the potential to disrupt the process by which social convention can become determinism. Henry's dreary descriptions of a future dominated by domestic labor presents Jane's labor as financial necessity rather than natural impulse; this distinction allows Jane to spin free of the essentializing rhetoric of feminine virtue. While Henry has difficulty distinguishing between social convention and individual constitution, Jane understands that because character is formed externally, it can be refashioned. This understanding of character liberates Jane from the constraints of conventional femininity that the rhetoric of domesticity essentialized.[28] Jane proclaims that she "entertains no reverence for such a bubble" as surrounds most women, "those to whom habit or childish fear or parental authority has given their faith; who never doubted or inquired or reasoned for themselves." Claiming she was "once such a pretty fool in this respect as the rest of my sex," Jane's conversations with the religious doubter Henry have led her to question "the religion of the timorous and uninquisitive" and "to scrutinize the foundation of [her] own principles." As a result of their conversations her "belief is stronger than it ever was," her "piety has become more rational," and "a new spring has been imparted to [her] languishing curiosity" (74–76). Where Henry sees the impossibility of distinguishing between consent and coercion as hopelessly corrupting the ideal of self-determination, Jane sees influence as an inevitable and necessary factor in individual identity.

On the one hand, Jane's refashioning potentially aligns her with the rhetoric of self-improvement that has traditionally implicated domestic fiction in modern forms of self-regulating discipline. Additionally, Henry's sense of his "indolence" as a deep-seated character flaw seems to be a clear example of the ways that the early national seduction novels portray unjust social conditions as individual character flaws.[29] Alternatively, Jane's understanding of character as socially constructed becomes an opportunity to exploit the mutability of convention. While the novel presents Jane's conventional femininity as an educational misstep that can be reformed, it never suggests that Henry's constitutional indolence or devotion to luxury need to be reformed. Throughout the novel Jane does not fear being seduced by the libertine Henry Colden, but by convention.[30] In what could serve as the novel's thesis statement, Jane tells Henry that they must marry at once, because "by depriving me of the power of compliance, only can I be safe" (101). In the same letter, Jane fantasizes about the exotic and sensual domestic space she will share with Henry after they are married, when she will "become thy—." The dashes here supposedly stand in for wife, but also suggest something illicit about that possibility. Jane goes on to spin a dream for Henry of their future: "the world of thy fancy is circumscribed by four white walls, a Turkey-carpeted floor, and a stuccoed ceiling." Bidding Henry only to enter this room "in dreams," Jane conflates sex and sentiment, teasing him with a vision of a "woman's shape in negligent attire," his "hand already in hers," his cheek "already wet with her tears." The novel preserves its emotional excesses for a domestic scene that is granted an erotic charge from its freedom from the "reproaches" of guardians who might "intrude."

Articulating the link Barnes has drawn between seduction and republican discipline, Jane presents compliance as a temptation to be resisted. Once a marriage to Henry has been socially sanctioned, it loses its erotic and narrative charge. Jane and Henry continue to defer their marriage until Mrs. Fielding repents her parental tyranny on her deathbed, sanctioning the marriage with both her blessing and her fortune. In one reading, *Jane Talbot* seems to enact the reformative force of the domestic plot to its fullest, as Jane and Henry claim that through independent reflection, they have voluntarily adopted the values of pious virtue. But like so many of Brown's novels, the promised marriage will only uncertainly happen off page: the novel ends with Jane writing to inform Henry of Mrs. Fielder's change of heart, an update that resolves the problem of domestic security but not the problems of feminine self-dependence and masculine dependence. Given that the plot has been structured by Jane making commitments to Henry only to break them, the reader can only trust in the finality of this marriage proposal because the novel ends. Even in her final letter, Jane suggests that her primary turn-on has been Henry's religious doubts: "Marriage, indeed, instead of losing its attractions in consequence of your errors, drew whence only new recommendations, since with a zeal, a tenderness, and a faith like mine, my efforts to restore such a heart and such a reason as yours could not fail of success; but *till* that restoration were accomplished, never, I repeat, should I have tasted repose even in *your* arms" (131). Now that Henry claims "reflection has, at length, raised [him] to the tranquil and steadfast height of simple and true piety," Jane has traded passion for repose (129).

The abrupt conclusion to an epistolary exchange organized by deferral rather than progress refuses to make sense of the arbitrary gendered hierarchy enshrined by the marriage contract.[31] While affectionate marriages are traditionally read in early national fiction as allegorical representations of consensual government, the novel's lack of interest in a marriage that has finally been socially sanctioned withholds desire from the liberal narrative's appropriating appetite. Aligning literary convention and political form, the allegorical mode interprets private desire as public symbol. The flip side of this equation is that the rhetoric of consent requires the pliable private desires of individual citizens to naturalize its authority: as the dead women who litter the pages of early national seduction novels might attest, consent implies not only obedience but willingness. Hyde argues that our accounts of early national citizenship overlook the "deeply contested" nature of "the right of individuals to voluntarily refuse allegiance."[32] The rights and protections of citizenship also brought expectations of obligation and compliance.[33] These expectations are most visible in moments when the conditions of liberal inclusion are refused rather than sought after. If Mrs. Fielding's change of heart is a gracious act of enlightened adaptation, it is also the most conventional gesture of all in the genre of domestic fiction that works to reimagine authority as benevolent.

Henry's silence at the end of *Jane Talbot* registers as a particularly noisy form of dissent because the legal conventions of coverture ultimately render his concerns about the appearance of dependence distinctly *im*material. Additionally, Jane's resounding consent throughout the novel is difficult to read as such because the marriage contract renders women domestic dependents and thus precludes their ability to consent. Holding open possibilities that are not fully explained by a mode of reading that assumes the legal conventions of contract to be more stable than those of fiction, *Jane Talbot* also suggests that romance's relentless inquiry into "motives" which "cannot be certainly known" gives rise to a kind of paranoia that allows generic conventions to overtake any gestures of self-determination. In Brown's long-form fiction, attempts to imagine gender equality are frustrated by the property relations codified by the marriage contract, resulting in plots that are driven by the repeated and cyclical deferral of consensual and disinterested marriage. In the next section I turn to Brown's magazine fiction to argue that what Jared Gardner describes as the "anonymous, fragmentary, and willfully obscure" nature of early national periodical culture allows readers to rethink the inevitability of the larger generic narratives that condition their interpretive practices.[34] Relieved of both the conjectural pressures of romance and the heteronormative discipline of the marriage plot, the domestic scenes of Brown's magazine writing allow for more fully developed visions of the aesthetic and cosmopolitan promises of domestic retreat.

DOMESTIC FRAGMENTS AND EXTRACTS IN BROWN'S MAGAZINE FICTION

In this section I examine two pieces likely published by Brown in *The Monthly Magazine and the American Review*. "The Household: A Fragment" (August 1800) and "Portrait of an Emigrant. Extracted from a Letter" (June 1799) self-consciously frame themselves as parts of larger wholes. Their circulation in literary magazines means they are parts of publications that Jared Gardner has shown to be organized by the editorial "arrangement of fragments."[35] Smaller pieces of both fictional letters and periodical issues, the texts are doubly fragmented. The fragments of early national magazines can be understood in the spirit of what Elizabeth Harries has called planned fragments, as opposed to incomplete failures.[36] As Harries observes, "we are conditioned to see the fragment as a mere part, as what remains of a larger and more perfect whole." Harries's interest in "the possibility of a fragment that, while it appears to be broken off or partial, is not necessarily opposed to some existing or imagined whole" is helpful for thinking about the fragment in the early national magazine.[37] These fragments do more than reflect a "postmodern valorization" of "the fragment as revealing the essential discontinuity and chaos of the world."[38] Instead, the editorial mode Gardner identifies accounts for the ways that, in Matthew Garrett's words, "the whole is always the organization of its parts and that the episode's distinctive force springs from its mutable but incontrovertible relation to the whole."[39] For both Gardner and Garrett this question of the relation between part and whole is a formal analogue to the project of nation building and the competing forces of national unity and individual interests.[40] This mutually constitutive relation between part and whole does not conceive of the part only in relation to the whole but also recognizes that the whole must constantly adapt to incorporate its unruly parts. To escape the pull of generic convention, Brown's magazine fragments must be read as stand-alone fragments; at the same time, their revisionary potential is grasped in relation to the generic wholes they revise.

Daniel Diez Couch identifies the fragment as a familiar and ubiquitous form in early American print culture and eighteenth-century transatlantic romanticism more broadly. Couch argues that early Americans were uniquely invested in this form's suitability for considering the position alienated individuals would play in the nation's experimental democracy. Whereas Garrett focuses on the episodic poetics of early national literary culture, Couch carefully distinguishes between the fragment and the episode. According to Couch, while the episode "enforces a movement toward unity at the expense of minority individuals," the fragment, defined by a narrative structure that "avoids closure" and offers readers "a large degree of imaginative power" over the whole, "worked in a contrasting direction that was at odds with the amalgamating power of the episode."[41] Couch's characterization of the American fragment as particularly adept at "thinking through ways of bettering the circumstances of marginalized individuals" informs my analysis in this section of Brown's portrayals of matriarchal and immigrant households.[42] Excised from both the organizing logic of domestic fiction's marriage plot and the conjectural logic of the romance, the domestic scenes of Brown's fragments imagine alternative forms of social and familial arrangements that do not neatly accord with the consolidating logics of liberal individualism and nationalist empire.

"The Household: A Fragment," confidently but not indisputably attributed to Brown by the creators of the Charles Brockden Brown Electronic Archive, imagines the utopia of a household of "all females" characterized by a sensual freedom from the "custom and general opinion" that only occasionally interferes.[43] In addition to the narrator and her daughter, the household includes a housekeeper and two additional servants who have been rescued by the narrator from financial insecurity caused by yellow fever and a governess who has been rescued from the devious scheming of morally corrupt parents. The head of the household, Mrs. Elgar, "takes great pleasure" in her work and, in addition to overseeing the household, "thinks herself obliged" to serve as the narrator's seamstress (82). The narrator adjusts her wages accordingly, and although Mrs. Elgar expects only lodging and board, the narrator puts away three hundred dollars a year for her. Claiming "there is no inequality between us," the narrator paints a picture of equality and voluntary labor but also refuses to sentimentalize Mrs. Elgar's labor with the language of emotional obligation by carefully documenting the wages she puts aside for her.

A large part of the letter is spent describing the narrator's relationship with her daughter's governess, Lucy Franks. The narrator seems to struggle with how to characterize her relationship with Lucy to an outsider. First emphasizing that Lucy's "birth and poverty" meant she was not received as the narrator's "equal" or "friend" but as a "personal or favourite attendant," and that any "familiarity" "was to be regarded as a condescention," by the end of the letter the narrator describes an intimacy that is both maternal and sensual (85). The narrator explains, "I talk with no other as I talk with her. There is a set of objects and ideas limited to us alone. It is not narrative or reasoning. It is pure talk; the uttering all that comes, be it coherent or vague, doubtful or true. It answers more perfectly than any thing else I ever met with, to what may be called thinking aloud" (86). This "pure talk," unconstrained by the demands of "narrative or reasoning," demonstrates the extraordinary intimacy of the relationship the narrator shares with Lucy and directs the reader to let go of their own expectations for narrative logic. Describing Lucy as serving as her "amanuensis" while they "talk and sew," the narrator emphasizes Lucy's skills as a musician and a reader: "She is my only and my favourite musician . . . When I want poetry, I find it in her voice or her memory . . . I can image to myself no gratification of the senses or fancy greater than what her music and her recitations afford me" (85–86). The domestic scene imagined by "The Household: A Fragment" resembles Jane Talbot's fantasy of intellectual and aesthetic retreat, where song and poetry adorn domestic labor but do not erase it.

Unlike *Jane Talbot*, "The Household" is relieved of the knotty questions of consent and disinterest that endlessly defer marriage between men and women of unequal class in Brown's long-form fiction. A fragment that might be an interlude in a seduction novel, the narrative pretense of this fragment is a response to a male correspondent's request for a description of the narrator's unusual household. As the subtitle "A Fragment" implies, this arrangement might be temporary, given the threat of the marriage plot the correspondent potentially poses. The narrator tentatively looks ahead to "but one event which can separate us, and that is [Lucy's] marriage; but her perfect artlessness, her shyness and timidity to all persons of your sex, seems an insuperable bar to the forming of that kind of connection" (86). The daughter of a French father and an Italian mother, Lucy had been trained "in dancing, music, and the theatrical art" to secure a male companion who would reimburse her parents, regardless of "whether marriage sanctioned the intercourse" (84). "Determined to save her from the ruin that threatened her," the narrator pays the mother to allow Lucy to live with her. Written in the language of a seduction novel, the narrator explains she "had previously won the heart of the pliant and simple girl, and made her a warm advocate of my scheme. I immediately carried her away with me . . ." (85). Positioning herself as a virtuous guardian who has seduced Lucy into a life of feminine domestic retreat, the narrator revises the traditional seduction plot—Lucy's virtue is saved, and she is rescued from tyrannical parents by a substitute mother rather than a potential partner in a companionate marriage.

Rather than being exchanged between two men, and thus serving as a figure who establishes the masculinity of father and suitor, Lucy's future is negotiated by two women. Tennenhouse has demonstrated that the seduction plots of eighteenth-century fiction were "always about relations among men" and that in the early national context specifically the libertine figure is revised to imagine expansive forms of kinship ties more suitable to the early United States than the strict class hierarchies established by British rank.[44] The domestic in this context is the grounds for new forms of contract relations and property exchange between men of different classes. This exogamous orientation is frequently betrayed by stories of unwitting incest, where, as Julia Stern puts it, "an ostensibly exogamous relation is revealed to be one of endogamy: otherness becomes identity."[45] In contrast to these exogamous pretenses, "The Household" is explicitly inwardly oriented. Lucy's "timorous reserves" "concenter, as it were, her thoughts and affections" to the narrator and her child (86). This concentrating and bringing together of affections makes the positions of governess, mother, and child fluid and interchangeable: Lucy thinks of the narrator as her mother, the narrator's child "knows no difference between its mother and its nurse," and Lucy thinks of the narrator's child as her own (86). The slippage in this text between maternal and erotic intimacy shifts the traditional function of the incest plot. Most often read as an allegory of patriarchal authority gone astray, there is usually only room for dead mothers in these plots of illegitimate desire between fathers and daughters and brothers and sisters.[46] If the incest plot anxiously signals the consequences of a political model that naturalizes its authority through the use of familial metaphor, "The Household" is profoundly uninterested in the biological kinship ties that doom the affectionate marriages early national novels endlessly attempt to reimagine. Building on Tennenhouse and Armstrong, Dillon notes that the reformed libertine of early U.S. fiction serves to naturalize heterosexual desire as gender difference comes to replace class difference as the founding categorical distinction of liberalism.[47] "The Household" imagines a domestic space where the fantasy of private retreat is potentially untethered from the function of conferring social recognition via publicly sanctioned and scripted norms of heteronormativity.

The questions surrounding uncertain motives and unintended consequences that preoccupy Brown's Gothic novels hover peripherally around this fragment and originate from the narrator's relationship to Lucy rather than from a potential suitor. As Couch argues in his analysis of the collection of fragments and extracts that make up *Edgar Huntly*'s publication history, Brown published versions of moments from his longer novels as fragments and extracts to showcase the labor that went into being a professional author, and his early American critics recognized that effort in their reactions to his published fragments and novels.[48] "The Household: A Fragment" resembles one of the many episodic subplots that might be excised from the convoluted plots that characterize Brown's long-form fiction. Specifically, it resembles an episode from the life of the international revolutionary soldier Martinette in *Ormond; or, The Secret Witness*, a novel that is organized around the lifelong "master passion" between two women. One thread from Martinette's complicated history involves her relationship with Lady D'Arcy, a widow who rescues Martinette from a "loathsome" life in a convent where she is plagued by the unwelcome attentions of a priest.[49] Lady D'Arcy "speedily contracted for [Martinette] the affections of a mother" and eventually "devout affections seemed to have filled her heart, to the exclusion of any object besides [Martinette]" (150–152). Martinette does not share the intensity of Lady D'Arcy's affections and is attached merely through "gratitude and veneration" that lead her to feign a "conformity of sentiments." Lady D'Arcy eventually remarries, and while her affection is "in some degree, transferred to a new object," Martinette receives her blessing to leave. Eventually they meet again—the former Lady D'Arcy has a new husband, but her affection for Martinette has not lessened. Martinette refuses to stay with her, claiming, "I foresaw restraints and inconveniences from the violence and caprice of her passions, and intended henceforth to keep my liberty inviolate by any species of engagement, either of friendship or marriage" (155). In *Ormond*, a novel that imagines several versions of same-sex arrangements, a household organized by women is not guaranteed to be a space of freedom, and relationships like friendship that operate outside of the bounds of contractual obligation do not escape the "degrading insincerity" "institutionally enforced" by the marriage contract.[50]

If we read "The Household: A Fragment" in the context of this episode from *Ormond*, it is difficult to resist questioning the motives of the narrator who speaks on behalf of the silent and objectified Lucy, asserts her control through benevolence and obligation, and seeks to maintain Lucy's "spotless and untarnished purity" and "almost infantile innocence" (86). The narrator of "The Household: A Fragment" concludes her letter by teasingly withholding the full pleasures of the arrangement from her reader: "You may well believe that I am happy in the midst of such a family, and I am so, but far more than *you* can imagine. You can only have a glimpse of that delightful spectacle of which *I* have a full view" (86). Playfully allowing "a glimpse" of the "delightful spectacle" she has created for the letter's addressee, the narrator revels in the power her single-sex household allows her: "Such is my family. All females you perceive. I want no man about me. In that respect, I would have my house to be a convent, and I to be the mistress of it. Here I can reign without scruple; but to govern men was never my province." This reference to a convent would imply both the threat and the promise of a social structure organized by women and potentially revises Martinette's rescue from a lascivious monk into acquisition by a lascivious nun. The same-sex household gives the narrator a power that she can wield "without scruple," as she imagines that gender sameness equalizes the power imbalances of class and age difference.

Although this suspicious reading is exacerbated when the context of *Ormond* is supplied, as an anonymous fragment in a magazine, we are also relieved from this conjectural mode of reading to simply enjoy a "glimpse" of a "delightful spectacle." The veil has been established as an important symbol for how publicity constructs privacy in nineteenth-century Gothic fiction. In her invocation of the convent—where a young convert like Lucy would "take the veil"—the narrator turns her correspondent's desire for knowledge about her unconventional household into his own projection of illicit activity.[51] Within the sentimental reading practices of early U.S. literature, the spectacle the narrator creates for her correspondent would imply a distancing failure of sympathy. The public clamor of early national magazines potentially withholds this spectacle from sympathy's voracious appetite for converting difference to sameness, allowing the possibilities of a household organized along a continuum of female friendship, guardianship, and eroticism to linger, rather than serving as a digressive episode to be subsumed by the conventions of a courtship plot.[52]

While "The Household: A Fragment" celebrates the "concentering" of affections inward, my final text, "Portrait of an Emigrant. Extracted from a Letter," suggests that a distinctively cosmopolitan creole domestic space poses an alternative to the domestic narrative's traditional functions of consolidating property and policing family arrangements. Rejecting an ethos of domestic industry and republican reform, the sketch uses the stereotype of the sterility of creole culture to imagine a household free of the gendered labor expectations that consistently inhibit the domestic sphere's potential for freedom. Although the epistolary frame positions the extract as a temporary moment within a larger conversation, the text playfully leads readers to question the larger context they might instinctively apply to interpret the details of the portrait. As Couch notes, the genre of the extract differs from the fragment in its implication of authorial choice. While the fragment's "existence depends on contingencies" and posits only a "theoretically incidental" relationship between part and whole, the extract implies that the author has made a deliberate choice with the goal of accurately representing the larger whole.[53] In this sense, the label of "extract" invites readers to see the text as more than a foreclosed or temporary possibility, but as a viable and settled perspective. The certainty and choice implied by the subtitle "Extracted from a Letter" reinforces this final text's argument that the wide-angle conjectural mode of romance can prime readers to draw conclusions that are not supported by attentive and open-minded observations.

The portrait in the extract is a description Mrs. K has provided the narrator of her new neighbors, the de Lisle family. Mrs. K explains to the narrator that her new neighbors are a French couple who have recently fled the violence in Santo Domingo. Because the man is "of fair complexion" and the woman is "half negro," Mrs. K can only "suppose" that they are married.[54] The woman works as an actress and the man works in a compting-house, a job that "allows him to spend a great deal of his time at home" (162). The couple stays in bed until ten o'clock, when the man rises and smokes cigars at the back window and breakfasts on bread and wine. He leaves the house at noon and returns later in the day; while he is gone the woman "employs herself in washing every part of her body," dresses in a "perfectly brilliant and clean" dress, and sings or plays her guitar. "No attention is paid to house or furniture"; after ordering dinner to be delivered every evening, they play music and sing together until going out with visitors for the evening. The couple's only child is an orphan they have adopted after finding her wandering the streets of Philadelphia. This child is fed by the neighbors, who find her to be "harmless" and "modest," though "half-starved" (163).

As Gardner notes, this portrait evokes a number of issues we might expect to trigger a xenophobic reaction from readers in 1799 Philadelphia: the couple is a racially mixed pair of French refugees from Santo Domingo. Countering this expectation, Mrs. K concludes from her observations that "the French are the only people that know how to live." Praising their life of "the highest as well as purest sensual enjoyments," she explains that although they are impoverished exiles, they are "at ease," free from "household cares," "directing servants," cooking, laundry, "manual employment" of any kind. Sharing Mrs. K's admiration of the couple's ability to retain, despite their "extreme poverty," "their propensity to talk, laugh and sing—their flute and their guitar," the narrator encourages the reader to "grow wise by the contemplation of their example" (163–164).

Just as the portrait of the family primes and then quickly undermines xenophobic expectations, the narrator's introductory description of Mrs. K also challenges those who might assume the uneducated housewife's perspective is provided for comic relief. Although the portrait disavows any link between virtue and labor, it is a traditional domestic housewife who praises the "sensual enjoyments" of a household that is free of domestic labor. The narrator describes Mrs. K as strictly preoccupied by "domestic and every-day incidents," "the state of her own family, and her servants and children" (161). Lacking the education that would lead her to "look abroad, to investigate the character and actions of beings of a distant age and country," Mrs. K is grouped with those who are "generally attentive to what is passing under their own eye." The extract emphasizes that it is Mrs. K's narrowly domestic perspective that makes her such an astute observer of the value of her neighbors' unconventional household. "Unacquainted with what happened before she was born," and "equally a stranger to the events that are passing in distant nations, and to those which ingross the attention and shake the passions of statesmen and politicians," Mrs. K's "mind, nevertheless, is far from being torpid or inactive. She speculates curiously and even justly on the objects that occur within her narrow sphere."

Mrs. K's domestic observations operate differently than the future-oriented uncertainty that critics have identified as driving the early national romance. As Sizemore summarizes, the early national romance "registers uncertainty on a thematic level through its concerns with the cataclysmic social and political transformations set into motion by imperial conquest, colonization and settlement, and democratic revolution."[55] Woertendyke argues that exploiting "anxieties about the future of the United States," the romance's use of "geographic breadth" to compensate for "the nation's shallow historical past" results in conflicting imperialist and xenophobic impulses.[56] Mrs. K., who is uninterested in "distant nations" and unconcerned with "what happened before she was born" rejects the historical and geographic anxieties that give rise to the romance's conjectural mode. It is precisely because Mrs. K is not attuned to the "geographical breadth" that Woertendyke describes as characterizing early national romance that her observations of the emigrant family remain unprejudiced. Her open-minded observations point to the ways that romance's conjectural history is not only conducive to imagining alternative possibilities, but also vulnerable to co-option by nationalist scripts. Rather than being a suspicious reader of her cosmopolitan neighbors, Mrs. K., who is uninformed by the geopolitical uncertainty that concerns "statesmen and politicians," comes to admire their alternative domestic arrangements.

Attributing Mrs. K's astute observations and open-mindedness to her limited and focused domestic perspective, "Portrait of an Emigrant" deploys the fiction of an isolated private sphere to indict romance's conjectural mode.[57] The narrator who concludes the extract begins a classically Brownian speculation about the "ambiguous" "motives that stimulate men to action," only to turn away from those speculations as ultimately unimportant: refusing to criticize or even diagnose the carefree couple's "absence of reflection and foresight," the narrator is uninterested in the details that have established the couple and preceded their relocation (163–164). Uninvested in romance's conjectural mode, the extract instead focuses on describing a domestic space where new forms of social reproduction can be imagined that are not oriented toward the accumulation of capital, heteronormative reproduction, or civilizing reform.

In particular, the portrait revises an understanding of the geopolitics of domestic fiction. Amy Kaplan's groundbreaking analysis of domesticity's role in the work of empire demonstrated that "when we oppose the domestic to the foreign, men and women become national allies against the alien, and the determining division is not gender but racial demarcations of otherness."[58] This narrative of domesticity that is primarily framed by the Western frontier is complicated by an Atlantic world frame that positions Euro-American settler-colonists as culturally barren. Where the civilizing mission of manifest destiny works "to conquer and domesticate the foreign," inhabitants of the early United States labored to counter a colonial logic that presented the colony as an inappropriate space for social reproduction.[59] We can better understand Brown's portrait of the emigrant family in the context of creole social reproduction Elizabeth Maddock Dillon has identified as a crucial component of the early U.S. domestic novel; for Dillon, the "problems of social reproduction" that preoccupy early national novels might be viewed as "the cultural explorations of creole writers inhabiting a colonial modernity that proscribed creole social reproduction."[60] As Dillon explains, creole is a category complicated by geography: "the creole is the white or black non-native who is born (biologically reproduced) in the colony, but whose social reproduction is thus understood to be inadequate or illegitimate precisely because reproduction occurred at the site of capitalist production (the colony) rather than at the site of consumption (the metropole)."[61] Using Leonora Sansay's novel *Secret History* as her representative example, Dillon argues that early national novels potentially imagine new forms of social reproduction that "are located in the mobile, internal resources of individuals rather than in their ability to possess other human beings and property."[62] "Portrait of an Emigrant" revises the logic that rejects the possibility of creole social reproduction. The extract's portrayal of creole domesticity celebrates an impoverished but resourceful emigrant couple who make a home rooted in cultural capital rather than extraction.

The creole domestic space "Portrait of an Emigrant" imagines is celebrated for its sensuous pleasures, open sociability, and aesthetic pursuits. Mrs. K praises the musical "playing and singing" that emanates from the household, and the narrator tells us that although Madame de Lisle's profession as an actor is "not respectable according to our notions," it "is easy and amusing" (163–164).[63] Madame de Lisle fulfills all of the stereotypes of a creole mixed-race woman (including, problematically, an exotic sexuality that does not result in biological reproduction), but rather than disapproving of her amusing lifestyle as marking her as unfit for domestic virtue, the extract praises "the gratifications of sense, of conjugal union, and of social intercourse" that characterizes the de Lisle family as "among the highest in the scale" (164). Rather than attempting to redirect the cosmopolitan household's "sensual enjoyments" toward domestic industry, the sketch sentimentalizes the creole couple's carefree and sensuous impulses to establish the potential for a creole culture that the logic of colonialism denied.

Circulating within periodicals that aim for conversation rather than resolution, Brown's domestic fragments imagine homosocial and cosmopolitan possibilities for domestic spaces, temporarily unburdened by the obligations of duty and dependence that threaten to corrupt both the republican ideal of companionate marriage and the romantic ideal of domestic retreat. For Brown, periodical forms like the episode, the fragment, and the extract preserve narrative possibilities that are too easily subsumed by the long form plots of the novel. Remaining in the world of the early national magazine, the next chapter continues to consider how our conceptions of domestic fiction might expand beyond traditions like the sentimental and the novel by turning to one of the most well-known practitioners of the short-form sketch, Washington Irving. Fragmentary forms like the sketch have been recognized as central to a romantic tradition seeking to showcase the labor of professional authorship.[64] This narrative registers differently when considered alongside of a parallel movement working to link pastoralized domestic labor to an instinctual feminine genius. The critical narrative that once adopted Charles Brockden Brown as a predecessor of the beleaguered male author also once imposed itself onto Irving, who came to be known as one of the nineteenth century's most notorious critics of domestic ideology. Whereas Brown has been characterized as regressing from a writer of novels to an editor of magazines, Irving was once characterized as progressing from an editor of magazines to an author of protoromantic sketches that aim to move beyond the utilitarian didacticism of the early national seduction novel. Just as more recent scholarship on Brown has challenged a novel-centric narrative of literary regression, Irving has recently been firmly positioned as an initiator rather than a detractor of domestic fiction. The next chapter intervenes in an early defining moment in this critical narrative, a literary magazine that Irving wrote anonymously with his brother William Irving and friend James Kirke Paulding. Considering the new policing of gender conventions that accompanied the transition from republican periodical culture to the liberal literary marketplace, this next chapter recharacterizes Irving as an artful practitioner of domestic retreat.

2
SALMAGUNDI'S ELBOW-CHAIR DOMESTICITY

USING CHARLES BROCKDEN BROWN as an opening example, the previous chapter considered the expansive possibilities of domestic retreat imagined in the early national period. While Brown is fascinated by the possibilities of feminine self-dependence, homosocial kinship, and creole cultural capital that emerge out of newly developing ideas of domestic retreat, the pseudonymous collaborators behind the early national magazine *Salmagundi; or, the Whim-Whams and Opinions of Launcelot Langstaff, Esq. and Others* defensively labor to restrict access to the aesthetic possibilities of domestic retreat to the eccentric bachelor-author. In *Salmagundi* we see domestic retreat claimed forthrightly as a position of literary autonomy and reformative morality, and we also see an attempt to delimit access to the aesthetic possibilities of that position. Rather than pastoralizing domestic labor, the editors relentlessly portray feminine household labor as a hypervisible irritant to their literary pastimes. Through comically jarring editorial interjections, the editors showcase the artful labor behind their literary performance, but in doing so they enforce a sharply gendered distinction within the domestic space between material and literary labor and between authorship and source material.

In his 1819 review of James Kirke Paulding and William and Washington Irving's 1807 periodical *Salmagundi; or, the Whim-Whams and Opinions of Launcelot Langstaff, Esq. and Others*, Richard H. Dana Sr. recalls that the anonymous authors' "cavalier air, together with the mystery, and the bold declaration, 'we care not what the public think of us,' put the public upon guessing and thinking about them and nothing else."[1] Dana's retrospective review perfectly captures the paradoxically generative relationship between the belligerent editors and their receptive readers. Despite the editors' declaration in the first issue that "we *care* not what the public think of us," *Salmagundi* would become wildly popular.[2] Because of this editorial pretense of hostility towards its readers, *Salmagundi* is frequently mined for signs of Irving's protoromanticism, particularly in critical narratives that define romanticism through a perceived opposition between the aesthetic retreat of the alienated artist and the consensus-driven consumerism of a feminized reading public. A particularly vivid example of precisely this construction occurs in one of the letters written in *Salmagundi* by Mustapha Rub-a-Dub Keli Khan, a persona created in the tradition of Oliver Goldsmith's *Citizen of the World*.[3] Witnessing an election, Mustapha describes the "*mother mob*" as "the most pestilent, cross, crabbed, scolding, thieving, scratching, toping, wrongheaded, rebellious, and abominable termagant that ever was let loose in the world" (194). It is not difficult to see how Mustapha's termagant anticipates the more infamous termagant Dame Van Winkle, nor is it difficult to see Mustapha's "mother mob" as anticipating Nathaniel Hawthorne's "damned mob of scribbling women." Just as the romantic author struggles against the conventions of mother mob mass culture, his subject struggles against the tyranny of the domestic termagant.

Dana's review and *Salmagundi*'s popularity both point to the productively disingenuous nature of the editors' peevish performance. Mustapha figures the conflict between the mother mob and "the honest gentlemen bashaws" who are dependent on her favor as "a most *delectable courtship* or intrigue." Although the mother mob would occasionally "condescend to toy with them in her rough way," "woe be to the bashaw who attempted to be familiar with her." Distinguishing themselves from the politicians Mustapha describes, the editors carefully construct a position of disinterest in relation to market pressures: "thank heaven we are not like the unhappy rulers of this enlightened land, accountable to the mob for our actions, or dependent on their smiles for support" (305). But the editors' description of a coquettish mother mob, promiscuous yet capricious in her attentions, also resembles their own literary method, as any move to punish readers "who attempt to be familiar" only inflames the desire for collaboration. Additionally, the editors' frequent dramatizing of their literary output's stymied reception using figures of sexually and reproductively deviant femininity reinforces the normative codes of domesticity the Romantic author is traditionally understood to resist. This chapter first argues that rather than retreating from the restrictive codes of domesticity, *Salmagundi* works to reinvest the reformative promises of domesticity with the bachelor's imaginative whimsy. This strategy, however, depends on the careful construction of a division within the domestic space that distinguishes the bachelor-author's imaginative output from the termagant's domestic labor. The chapter concludes by arguing that because the editors' reformative project depends on readers recognizing the alienated bachelor as a humorous literary type, the hostile relationship to its readers that has earned *Salmagundi* a place in narratives of Irving's protoromanticism actually signals a collaborative relationship with readers who are repeatedly forced to acknowledge the editors' authorial design. Our contemporary critical narratives tend to naturalize gendered literary traditions that associate feminine domesticity with collaboration and consensus and masculine romanticism with individualism and critique. Reformative yet whimsical, fashionable yet eccentric, conservative yet innovative, *Salmagundi*'s contradictions signal a defensive reaction to a literary culture increasingly defined by gender difference and unsettle the gendered oppositions we have inherited from antebellum literary culture.

Concurring with my characterization of Irving as an author of domestic fiction, Claudia Stokes has recently argued that in his sketches, Irving provides surface descriptions of domestic plenitude and comfort while rendering the feminine labor required to attain that domestic ideal invisible; in his plot-driven tales, however, the women who perform domestic labor become visible but ghostly terrors.[4] For Stokes, these two portrayals of feminine domestic labor—invisibility and terror—align in a shared acceptance of "the disembodiment widely recognized as a signature trait of nineteenth-century American femininity."[5] Although Irving's later sketchbooks and collections of tales adopted this nineteenth-century ideal of "domestic labor as effortless and even bodiless," in the early national magazine *Salmagundi*, this ideal of the domestic scene as a retreat from material labor is not yet so fully available.[6] Intriguingly, Irving's own well-documented nostalgia for the preindustrial household is also a nostalgia for a time when labor and leisure were seen as distinct but not incompatible parts of a life spent within the home. The understanding of home as retreat defined by a distinction between paid labor outside of the home and labors of love within the home was in its early stages in the first decade of the nineteenth-century, even as it was quickly congealing into the ideology of domesticity that would be firmly entrenched by midcentury.[7] Rather than rendering feminine domestic labor invisible, the editors contrast household labor to their own aesthetic production, as old maids and house maids are fodder for literary sketches that only serve to demonstrate their unsuitedness for literary production. In *Salmagundi*, the bachelor-editors do not yet see themselves as outsiders to the domestic realm who appreciate from a distance. Instead, they work to establish themselves as ideally suited for appreciating the generative aesthetic potential of domestic retreat. We saw in the previous chapter Charles Brockden Brown attempting to preserve the aesthetic autonomy of private retreat from the gendered hierarchy of the sexual contract by imagining how domestic labor might support rather than impede women's self-dependence. Like Brown, the *Salmagundi* editors refuse to conflate labor with virtue, but unlike Brown, they are uninterested in imagining how women might negotiate the competing demands of household labor and aesthetic production. Reacting to an increasing but still developing association of domestic retreat with the feminine, *Salmagundi* territorially insists on the unsuitability of women for professional authorship.

LITERARY CULTURE IN TRANSITION

The history of Washington Irving criticism closely follows developments in the field of American Romanticism: once only selectively reclaimed as a primitive initiator of a movement valued for its individualism, aesthetic retreat, and national exceptionalism, Irving has more recently served as an example of a collaborative and transnational early national literary culture.[8] As Stokes has argued in her study of "the nineteenth-century aesthetic of unoriginality," Irving can be seen as representative of a literary culture marked by "a widespread preference for the traditional and the familiar."[9] For most of the twentieth century, Irving was adopted as a transitional figure not only thematically, as his sketches were read as signaling a new rejection of eighteenth-century didacticism, but also generically, as he was seen as adapting and revising British forms for the early American scene.[10] Although in *The Spirit of the Age* William Hazlitt gives a famously dour review of Irving's sketches as "taken at the rebound" and "want[ing] both freshness and probability," critics have established that *Salmagundi* parodies rather than imitates British periodicals.[11] *Salmagundi*'s fictitious contributors include Launcelot Langstaff, who writes reflective essays from his "elbow-chair," and his companions Anthony Evergreen, who serves as "a kind of patriarch in the fashionable world," and William Wizard, who presides "in the territory of criticism" (71). These contributors are "true and independent bachelors" well versed in the style and tradition of their English predecessors in *The Spectator* and *The Tatler* (229). The element of the eighteenth-century periodical essay that is most frequently parodied in *Salmagundi* is the concept that print can be used to establish any sort of broad, rational public consensus.[12] Circulating in bitterly partisan New York City a century after *The Spectator* circulated in London, *Salmagundi* seems well aware of the fiction behind Mr. Spectator's pretense of representative consensus. But what has been less acknowledged is the way that *Salmagundi*'s parody cuts backward and forward. Although the *Salmagundi* editors parody the promises of Enlightenment print culture, they are also skeptical of the very movement Irving is credited with initiating, particularly the newly developing cult of the Romantic artist and the separation it anxiously cultivated between the celebrity author and the reading public.

As the opening example of the mother mob demonstrates, the opposition between aesthetic retreat and the reading public is less a historical truth than a laborious construction of nineteenth-century literary culture. Defining romanticism "as a species of reaction-formation," Lucy Newlyn argues in her study of authorial anxiety and British Romanticism that "the defensive nature of Romanticism's sacralization of the author . . . may be seen as arising reactively, out of a resistance to the consumerism and anonymity which characterized the publishing world."[13] Reading romanticism as a defensive reaction to historical conditions including the growth of the reading public and the rise of professional criticism,

Newlyn argues that the relationship between romantic writers and readers is more dialectical than its oppositional rhetoric would suggest. Although American Romanticism is traditionally defined by a break with the British influence that characterizes early American literature, the critical narrative also emphasizes authorial anxiety toward reading consumers.[14] Even as the traditional critical narrative of American Romanticism seeks a distinctive American style, it also continues to claim overwrought expressions of authorial alienation as markers of romanticism.

Irving studies have benefitted more recently from revisionary histories that complicate this author-centric view of nineteenth-century literary culture. Jared Gardner has persuasively argued in *The Rise and Fall of American Periodical Culture* that "the privileging of individual genius and exceptional 'Americanness' has perpetuated the neglect and systematic misreading" of the early American periodical.[15] For Gardner, the *Salmagundi* editors' hostility toward their readers marks a shift away from a periodical culture organized by collaborative editors and political debate to a more familiar literary culture that valued individual authors, circulated as a retreat from politics, and was directed to readers who identified as consumers. Although Gardner attentively reinvests American literary history with the collaborative forms that disrupt our understanding of this history as "the rise and triumph of the novel," his project is also characteristic of American literary history's investment in a shift from a collaborative-republican to an individualist-liberal model of authorship.[16] This shift from republican to liberal print culture is often described in gendered terms that exclude American women writers from a Romantic canon characterized by critique and individualism. In Michael Warner's influential account of eighteenth-century American print culture, the "privatizing discourse of sentiment marks a break with the republican paradigm of diffused literature" and corresponds to a shift from a model of citizenship that required "civic action" to one achieved symbolically through the "imaginary participation" of previously excluded groups, particularly women. For Warner, this newly feminized reading public and the sentimental novels it supported corresponds to the development of a public sphere regulated by "career experts and mediating institutions" rather than the critical voices of active citizens.[17] Alternatively, accounts focused on the nineteenth century's "democratic model" of authorship argue that domestic novels written by women are characterized by lingering communal republican values that operate in opposition to American Romanticism's "incipient individualism."[18] Although a consistent picture emerges from these examples of a literary culture divided by gender, where women writers are aligned with conformity and consensus, these examples also suggest uneasy contradictions, as the perceived rise of a feminized reading public either marks a shift from republican collaboration to liberal privatization or signals a conservative investment in republican collaboration out of step with the innovative individualism cultivated by the period's Romantic authors.

The contradictions of this critical narrative demonstrate that although a new privileging of gender difference accompanied the transition from republican periodical culture to liberal novel culture, a diverse range of authors responded ambivalently to this very transition.[19] The two divergently defined movements of antebellum literary culture, domestic fiction and romanticism, emerge from a shared origin that is itself a transition. Contextualized accordingly, *Salmagundi*'s pretense of alienation from the reading public can be seen as a form of collaboration with its enamored readers. Jarring editorial disruptions, insulting descriptions of readers, and overtly comic pseudonyms never let readers escape a heavy-handed authorial presence, but these antics also characterize the authors as whimsical eccentrics who are granted the authority to produce imaginatively original and pleasantly reformative literature because of their outsider status. The *Salmagundi* editors locate the source of their imaginative whimsy within the domestic sphere's supposed transcendence of social artifice and market pressures, but they also claim authorship by distinguishing themselves from the unimaginative housewives and servants who inspire their sketches but seem indifferent to the domestic sphere's aesthetic potential. Through the self-conscious assumption of aristocratic bachelor personas, the editors' aggressively masculine domestic retreat can be read as a reaction to the insufficiently reductive categories of a literary culture increasingly organized by gender difference.

BACHELOR REFORM

Although the *Salmagundi* editors dramatically reject collaborative reading practices, they play out this drama between reader and author in a genre defined by collaborative reading conventions. Meredith McGill has demonstrated in her study of nineteenth-century reprint culture that emerging antebellum novelists called upon the periodical reading conventions that defined their early careers to performatively and comparatively establish their narrative authority.[20] If *Salmagundi* is an early moment in the construction of a divide between the alienated author and the reading public, it is also a moment that shows readers recognizing and enjoying that construction as authorial design. The very position of authorial retreat that has traditionally defined romanticism is produced through a cooperative suspension of readerly disbelief. As an early national periodical rather than a sketchbook, *Salmagundi* is an apt opportunity to consider the self-conscious performativity behind the early national bachelor-author persona that links the *Salmagundi* authors to their American Renaissance successors, particularly the ways that this performance is bolstered by a productive preoccupation with the termagants and spinsters the bachelor-author defines himself against.[21] Additionally, *Salmagundi*'s systematic use of humor to naturalize moral reform links it closely to the strategies employed by the eighteenth-century sentimental seduction novel, a genre that circulated alongside and within early national periodicals and is considered the nineteenth-century domestic novel's generic predecessor.[22] Periodical and sentimental conventions not only share an early national interest in literature's potential to naturalize virtue but also rely on an intimate relationship between reader and author. At stake in the recognition of the performativity behind the alienated bachelor-author persona is not *Salmagundi*'s status as a potentially proto-Romantic text but how our ways of claiming it as such reinforce false cultural divides between masculine and feminine literary traditions.[23]

In defining itself as operating in opposition to the consumerism of the reading public, the rhetoric of romanticism on both sides of the Atlantic gendered the reading public as feminine, through both "the association between women's reading-habits and a species of guilty, excessive consumption" and "a widespread and explicit association of excessive writing with women whose reproductive capacities were seen to be out of control."[24] Responding to an entrenched critical narrative that accepts at face value American Romanticism's rhetoric of the embattled male artist, Lora Romero has demonstrated that "the reign of women is a cultural artifact produced by the antebellum period."[25] Irving occupies a particularly trenchant place in the critical narrative that Romero interrogates. Following Leslie Fiedler's claim that "the figure of Rip Van Winkle presides over the birth of the American imagination. . . . Ever since, the typical male protagonist of our fiction has been a man on the run, harried into the forest and out to sea, down the river or into combat—anywhere to avoid 'civilization,' which is to say, the confrontation of a man and woman which leads to the fall to sex, marriage, and responsibility," Irving has served as something of an origin point for a literary canon founded in the rejection of feminine influence.[26]

Even a more recent turn in Irving studies that contextualizes him in his own time rather than in relation to midcentury American Romanticism continues this tradition of linking masculine alienation to aesthetic expression. For example, in a careful revision of Fiedler's argument, both Michael Warner and Bryce Traister note that, for Irving, authorship is less an escape from the dominant reproductive narratives of antebellum culture than a way of resolving the bachelor's sense of alienation from these reproductive narratives. But both Warner and Traister value bachelor literature as potentially innovative because of this very alienation: for Warner, Irving's patriarchal nostalgia critiques the "the normative character of modernity," and for Traister, Irving's social detachment "helps to forward a narrative of national independence and differentiation from England."[27] Irving's bachelorhood has become a recent iteration of a persistent critical narrative that finds the masculine author's marginalization from domesticity's commercially inflected reproductive narrative structures generative of potentially subversive and exceptional American literature.[28] In her study of the bachelor narrator in late nineteenth-century and early twentieth-century literature, Katherine Snyder finds that "bachelors often served in cultural and literary discourse more generally as threshold figures who marked the permeable boundaries that separate domesticity, normative manhood, and high-cultural status, from what was defined as extrinsic to these realms."[29] *Salmagundi* circulates during an early moment in the self-conscious construction of these interrelated categories, and in its pages we can see a fluid and generative rather than rigid and restrictive relationship between the potentially Romantic bachelor-author and domestic ideology. One of Irving's legacies might not be the henpecked artist's retreat from domesticity so much as working to carefully establish who is capable of using the domestic space's potential freedoms to facilitate creative genius.

Out of *Salmagundi*'s eccentric mix of spinsters and bachelors emerges a gender division within the domestic space that positions the bachelors as sentimental moralists who are able to enjoy domestic retreat without being constrained by domestic obligations. Even as Launcelot Langstaff retreats to his elbow-chair to give "free scope to his whimsical imagination," "he had rather see one of the weird sisters flourish through his key-hole on a broomstick, than one of the servant maids enter the door with a besom." While separate sphere ideology positioned the domestic woman as the moral center of the nation, *Salmagundi* positions the bachelor as the figure best suited for moral commentary because of his freedom from domestic obligations. Langstaff claims "like true and independent bachelors, having no domestic cares to interfere with our general benevolence, we consider it incumbent upon us to watch over the welfare of society" (229).[30] Although Evergreen claims that Langstaff abhors nothing more "than what is usually termed a *notable house-wife*, a pestilent being who he protests is the bane of good fellowship, and has a heavy charge to answer for the many offences committed against the ease, comfort and social enjoyments of sovereign man," the bachelors repeatedly figure their home base, the household of Langstaff's aptly named cousin Christopher Cockloft, as a space of retreat (156). Exhausted by the rage for French fashions, occasional contributor Pindar Cockloft "made a kind of growling retreat to Cockloft-Hall" during an especially bad spell of weather, Langstaff "retreated in high dudgeon to his elbow-chair," and during gatherings at the Cockloft home, Langstaff tends to "retreat to [his] elbow-chair, like a bee to his hive" (84, 153, 201). Rather than retreating from the home to clubs or the frontier, the bachelors are happy to stay "seated snugly in the old-fashioned parlour of an old-fashioned dutch house" writing their observations of New York City society (307).[31]

Distinguishing the domestic space from domestic labor, this cozy homosocial group celebrates the potential for domestic retreat to generate whimsical humor writing because of its freedom from social conventions and market pressures. But this whimsical humor is aimed toward "the welfare of society." The editors claim originality and independence in order to reform the very print culture that presents those values as assets to be commodified. Even as *Salmagundi* critiques domesticity's artificial restrictions, it does so to reestablish the possibility of making moral reform feel in tune with natural impulses. The bachelors find the source of their good humor in the domestic retreat that allows them to develop the eccentricities—"whims, and oddities, and whalebone habits"—that also signify if a man "has any genius" (135). Langstaff, for example, only gives "free scope to his whimsical imagination" when in the society of "a chosen few" (156). Elizabeth Maddock Dillon has established that the rhetoric of nineteenth-century sentimentality links the reformative function of domesticity with the play of aesthetic retreat: "the domestic setting is thus transformed from a space of constraint to one of freedom, from the location of work to the location of aesthetic experience and moral truth."[32] The rhetoric of domesticity allows the editors to negotiate the fraught relationship in Romantic discourse between what Newlyn describes as a longing for originality and the anxiety that originality was also an "asset" that furthered "the commodification of reading and writing."[33] Presenting their originality as a symptom of domestic retreat allows the editors to claim membership in a "stock of originals" while avoiding the commodification of that originality by the marketplace (202). *Salmagundi* can be understood within both a transatlantic Romantic movement that countered materialism by defining originality using standards of moral influence and within an early republican periodical culture that established the collaborative relationship between author and reader that enables the very performance of originality.[34]

Most of the moral invective in *Salmagundi* is aimed at parodying periodical culture rather than correcting the behavior of its readers, but this doesn't mean that the production refrains from proposing a new set of normative values to replace the materialist factionalism it criticizes. The larger goal of the production seems to be replacing "the sneer of illiberality with the unfeigned smile of good-humour" (229). The editors of *Salmagundi* argue that the pleasures of reading are an important strategy in projects of improvement:

> But the people of Gotham, wise souls! Are so much accustomed to see morality approach them clothed in formidable wigs and sable garbs, "with leaden eye that loves the ground," that they can never recognize her when, drest in gay attire, she comes tripping towards them with smiles and sunshine in her countenance.—Well, let the rogues remain in happy ignorance, for "ignorance is bliss," as the poet says;—and I put as implicit faith in poetry as I do in the almanack or the newspaper—we *will* improve them, without their being the wiser for it, and they shall become better in spite of their teeth, and without their having the least suspicion of the reformation working within them. (227–228)

No longer a termagant mother mob, in this moment the feminine is returned to its traditional role of embodying morality, but the editors claim to temper this morality with their whimsical humor. While the rhetoric of domesticity confused women's natural proclivity for virtue with a causal narrative that linked that proclivity to women's separation from the commercial enterprises of the public sphere, the *Salmagundi* bachelors appropriate this access to virtue provided by domestic retreat but argue that only the whimsical humor generated by a strictly masculine "single blessedness" will make this reform feel natural rather than punitive (135, 154). Positioning the bachelor-author as the figure who will reform New York City of its splenetic ill humor, *Salmagundi* works to recuperate a domestic space informed by imaginative humor and whimsy by defining it against a domestic space constrained by unimaginative conformity. Although the bachelor is figured, like the housewife, as being naturally inclined to virtue because of his domestic retreat, only the bachelor's separation from the private sphere's material obligations allows him to develop the eccentric whim-whams that lead to the laughter that eases reform.

The editors put their creative principle—"it is one of our indisputable facts, that it is easier to laugh ten follies out of countenance than to coax, reason, or flog a man out of one"—into practice in "The Little Man in Black," a sketch that has been cited as an example of Irving's proto-Romantic defiance of reform-oriented literature (227).[35] The story describes "a gloomy misanthrope" who suddenly and mysteriously arrives in Gotham. The little man in black reads and meditates all day and is ostracized by his superstitious neighbors "because he followed no trade, nor even seemed ambitious of earning a farthing" (278). Eventually he dies of neglect and starvation. Throughout the story domestic housewives allow superstition to impede sympathy as they lead the charge in suspecting the man of being a witch. Noting that his grandmother "was at that time nursing my mother" and "never left the room, without wisely putting the large family bible in the cradle—a sure talisman, in her opinion, against witchcraft and necromancy," Langstaff carefully links this superstition to domestic obligations. The little man's final moments are spent with Langstaff's grandfather, who enters the man's apartment after hearing his cries of suffering. As the starving man's death helps the grandfather overcome his "uncharitable suspicion" and recognize him as a fellow "christian," he is "amply rewarded by the approbation of his own heart" (281–282). This sentimental moment is disrupted when readers learn that the little man in black is "the last descendant of the renowned Linkum Fidelius," the scholar who provides the absurd epigraphs for many of *Salmagundi*'s essays. Linkum Fidelius, "that unheard of writer of folios" who Langstaff introduces in the first issue, is yet another of *Salmagundi*'s jokes. His "learned quotations" include "A, was an archer and shot at a frog,/But missing his aim shot into a bog," "Style, is _________ style," and "The work's all aback" (95, 157, 312). Within the periodical's larger context of whimsical bachelors who value obsolete and out-of-print books, it is easy to read "The Little Man in Black" as an allegory of the alienated romantic artist, but if we turn again to Dana's review we see that the joke doesn't completely erase the story's instructive principle. Dana recalls that the revelation that the little man in black is the descendant of *Salmagundi*'s sham philosopher serves to "ease a little the aching of the heart, and leave one in a 'most humorous sadness'" (23). From his elbow-chair, the bachelor-author crafts a tale in which his whimsical humor relieves the didacticism of a purely instructive tale about a mistreated neighbor, even as the reader's laughter signals an acceptance of the story's good-humored agenda. Rather than signaling the editors' eccentric rejection of utilitarianism, the Linkum Fidelius connection is the humorous mechanism by which the reader is seduced into accepting the story's critique of the "uncharitable suspicion" that characterizes New York City—a quality that seems to be especially prevalent in old women, children, and housewives.

The editors offer a counter piece to "The Little Man in Black" in Langstaff's description of his spinster Aunt Charity. When a French boarding house opens next to Aunt Charity's house, "it threw her into that alarming disorder denominated the *fidgets*: she did nothing but watch at the window day after day" (167). Unfamiliar with the domestic arrangements of a boarding house, Aunt Charity is horrified by the "monstrous large family" that appears to be "all men" and "wondered why there was always such a scraping of fiddles in the parlour, and such a smell of onions from neighbor Pension's kitchen." Unlike the housewife in Brown's "Portrait of an Emigrant" whose narrow domestic vision counterintuitively allows for open-minded descriptions of the music, meals, and relationships she observes in her creole neighbors' unconventional household, Aunt Charity's penchant for gossip is frustrated by her inability to gain any understanding of the boarding house and its residents, and she serves as a "warning" to the editors' "fair countrywomen" who "pry into other people's affairs and neglect those of your own household" (168). Unlike Langstaff's grandfather, who provides sympathetic care to the little man in black, Aunt Charity musters only an obsessive and monitorial curiosity for a little man "dressed in white" who arrives at the boarding house: "a little meagre, weasel-faced Frenchman, of the most forlorn, diminutive, and pitiful proportions . . . he seemed to shake in the wind, and every blast that went over him whistled through his bones and threatened instant annihilation" (167–168). Unable to reconcile "this embodied spirit of famine" with the numerous pets and trunks of clothes the refugee brings to the boarding house, Aunt Charity takes to her bed and dies a month later. Even as the sketch mocks the virulent anti-French sentiments of the Federalist political party in 1807 New York, it is Aunt Charity who becomes the face of the Cockloft family's "absurd antipathy to the French" and the sketch concludes warning "ladies" against the "evil spirit of curiosity."[36] Brown's open-minded housewife has been replaced by an impotently nosy spinster, and the cosmopolitan connections formed across a creole social imaginary have been replaced with a firmly nationalist orientation that finds sentimental accord with a ghostly

Puritan remnant (the little man in black wears a "high sugar-loaf hat") rather than a French refugee.

Claiming the domestic as a homosocial space allows the bachelor-author to produce pleasantly reformative literature, but the rhetoric of domesticity doesn't function in *Salmagundi* in quite the same way as it functioned for women writers. As Eliza Richards has argued, the rhetoric surrounding the woman writer in antebellum America demonstrates not only the fluidity of gender definitions in antebellum literary culture but also an anxiety about feminine genius that led the male literary establishment "defensively to redefine ideas of creative process."[37] Although feminine genius was considered a quality that the best male poets could also access, because it emphasized the woman writer's natural proclivity for virtue and beauty, it was valued as artless instinct rather than artful creation.[38] The bachelors' critique of feminine domesticity does not suggest that women should pay less attention to household labor and become humorists themselves. Even as the text mocks the performative virtue of feminine domesticity to usurp its position for the bachelor, it nevertheless immobilizes women by failing to imagine this performance signifying in any way other than the dull routine of household labor or the sexual frustration of spinsterhood. The editors of *Salmagundi* locate their imaginative whimsy within the domestic sphere's transcendence of artificial social convention, but they also aggressively advertise their authorial artfulness. These increasingly confident claims of authorship depend not only on the reader's complicity in recognizing the performativity of bachelor alienation but also on increasingly codified distinctions between art and instinct.

Although the relationship between author and reader in *Salmagundi* is more collaborative than might first appear, the bachelors' dismissal of the feminine literary imagination suggests that their status as authors is conferred through an exclusive logic that differentiates creative genius from the source material creative genius puts to work. In the essay "Sketches from Nature," Evergreen visits the Cockloft country estate to find his friend Langstaff "relapsed into one of his eccentrick fits of the spleen" (246). The friends stroll the grounds of Langstaff's childhood home and encounter the family servant Old Caesar. Langstaff remembers Caesar as always considering "himself on an equality with the best of us" and wonders "why a body may not like a negro, as well as a white man!" (248–249). Given both the essay's title and Caesar's role as "an oracle to resolve any question about the weather, fishing, shooting, farming and horse doctoring," it seems clear that readers are to recognize Caesar as part of the recuperative natural scenery, but the sketch ultimately emphasizes Caesar's role as a domestic emissary. Caesar served as "the chosen confidant and special agent of Pindar in all his love affairs" and Langstaff, his cousin Pindar, and Caesar are characterized as youthful allies in a myriad of failed courtships (249). Evergreen and Langstaff linger in the stable while Caesar tends to the horses and regales them with stories from Langstaff's childhood. Caesar's stories draw Langstaff out of his melancholy mood, and after "slipping a piece of money into old Caesar's hand to buy himself a new tobacco box," he returns to the house "in the best possible humor." Although this payment corrupts both the pleasure of the editors' rural retreat and the memories themselves, as Caesar's status as rural fixture and childhood sidekick is tainted with financial coercion, his status is also sentimentalized by his "affection" for the Cockloft family and Langstaff's memories of his "bosom friend and chosen playmate" (248). The story values the family servant—quite possibly a former slave—for his storytelling while his domestic labor is pastoralized as a willing choice made out of "an affection for every beast in the stable" (249).[39] Apparently tied to the Cockloft household only by bonds of affection, Caesar performs the function usually reserved for women in sentimental domestic fiction, as his primary domestic obligation appears to be generating virtuous emotion.[40] Caesar's function as a rural fixture naturalizes the multiple lessons in the restorative qualities of aristocratic nostalgia and benevolent paternalism the bachelors' encounter with him inspires.[41] Although the *Salmagundi* bachelors eliminate women as carriers of the domestic sphere's moral truths, their investment in the domestic sphere's natural moral sovereignty requires that their own reformative values be sanctioned by sentiment, even as their status as publicly circulating authors requires that they maintain an artful distance from the instinctive impulses that characterize the insights of those figures who circulate within the domestic sphere. "Sketches from Nature" naturalizes democratic exchange as Caesar is remembered as a "playmate" rather than a servant, but his value as a source of recuperative good humor depends on him remaining just that—a source of pure "garrulity" that is given meaning only when it is appropriated and interpreted in the service of the bachelor-author's benevolent agenda. As the narrator, Evergreen observes that Caesar's memories "could not have given [Langstaff] half the satisfaction, had he talked like a Cicero or a Solomon" (249). Caesar tells the tale, but Evergreen authors the sketch. *Salmagundi* in some ways works against the essentializing rhetoric of domesticity by mocking the performative virtue of the domestic housewife, and the homosocial alliances that the bachelor forms as a byproduct of these jokes consolidate a diversity of male interests and establish the bachelor as representative of an idealized masculinity.[42] Within this domestic space of homosocial consolidation, however, the need for a contrast between instinct and art remains.

BACHELOR AUTHORSHIP

Although *Salmagundi* parodies the overtly reformative function of eighteenth-century periodical culture, it also fully embraces and experiments with the potential for periodical reading to effectively communicate a reformative agenda that is conducive to the cycles of fashionable culture. As Dana recalls in the review that opened this essay, "[*Salmagundi*] had to do with the present and real, not the distant and ideal. It was exceedingly pleasant morning or after-dinner reading, never taking up too much of a gentleman's time from his business and pleasures, nor so exalted and spiritualized as to seem mystical to his far reaching vision. It was an excellent thing in the rests between cotillions, and pauses between games at cards" (334). The bachelors' method of reforming their readers "without their having the least suspicion of the reformation working within them" is achieved through editorial interruptions that keep the periodical's commentary "exceedingly pleasant" as it fills the "rests" and "pauses" of fashionable life. For example, Wizard's footnote at the end of Langstaff's nostalgic sketch describing his deceased Uncle John's failed attempts at courtship announces that "our publisher . . . has begged so hard that we will not overwhelm him with too much of a good thing, that we have, with Langstaff's approbation, cut short the residue of uncle John's amours" (200). Even as the story contrasts the beloved bachelor uncle's "antipathy *to doing things in a hurry*" with the frantic pace of the marriage market, the editorial footnote jerks the reflective reader back into the fashionable cycles from which it offered temporary relief. Uncle John's language of imaginative deferral ends the story—"*Tut, boys! I might have had her*"—but this potential for unending reverie is irreverently presented in the footnote as a digression that must be "cut short" (200). Repeatedly disrupting moments that might invite readerly reflection, the hostile relationship to its readers that has earned *Salmagundi* a place in narratives of Irving's protoromanticism manifests in an incessant tendency for the editors to insert themselves into the reader's private reveries.

These moments of editorial disruption are the most explicit way that the editors undermine their claims that they are uninterested in collaborating with their readers, as their eccentric interjections force readers to encounter authorial design. The eccentric whimsy that results from the bachelor-authors' domestic retreat and seduces readers into internalizing the production's reformative agenda also never lets readers forget that they are at the mercy of the editors' whim-whams. This strategy keeps *Salmagundi* invested in the collaborative periodical conventions that also tie it closely to the market pressures the Romantic author is supposed to find alienating.[43] *Salmagundi*'s use of editorial disruption to flaunt authorial control signals a skepticism towards the ethical possibilities of aesthetic retreat that are traditionally understood to inform the Romantic author's method. The editors go so far as to compare the pleasure they take in each "triumph over the spleen" to the pleasure their nemesis the partisan newspaper editor or "slang-whanger" takes "when he bathes his pen in the heart's-blood of a patron and factor; or sacrifices one more illustrious victim on the altar of *party animosity*" (229). Even authors who claim to be writing for the sake of pleasure are still writing with "mingled motives of selfishness and philanthropy" as they work to influence the reader. Although the slang-whangers find pleasure in party animosity, while the *Salmagundi* editors find pleasure in making their readers laugh, they both find pleasure in manipulating their readers. This connection between fiction and news is not only a critique of naive Enlightenment delusions—it also implicates the authors in the self-interested frenzy of the early national public sphere.

Salmagundi parodies the disingenuous nature of the performance of authorial retreat through the thwarted suitor convention of bachelor literature.[44] Will Wizard observes that the "posture of defence" taken up by old maids "was only to give the visitor a hint that they expected an attack," and observes "that the resistance of those ladies, who make the greatest noise and bustle, is most easily overcome" (305). Langstaff laments that this performative prudery is a sign of the "domestick innovations" that interfere with his nostalgia for a time when "women were more simple, more domestick, more lovely, and more true" (304). Even as Langstaff suggests that an excessive interest in performative virtue has made women less domestic than they were in "the good old times" of his boyhood, the old maids' performative prudery resembles the editors' own performance of hostility towards their readers. Langstaff's thwarted suitor performance more directly parodies authorial anxiety in his "Retrospect," where he concedes that the moral writer "often contemplates in silent disappointment his labours wasted on a barren soil, or the seed he has carefully sown, choaked by a redundancy of worthless weeds" (225). Given that the editors are choosing to discontinue their project despite its popularity, it seems clear that the editors deploy this fantasy of an unreceptive feminized reading public not only to arouse their readers' desire to differentiate themselves from the simultaneously barren and overproductive public they denigrate, but also to poke fun at the very position of alienation beginning to be cultivated by the celebrity author.[45]

The editors claim to be uninterested in fostering the collaboration that traditionally characterized the relationship between readers and editors in early national periodical culture. The editors not only announce that they "*care* not what the public think of us," but they also explicitly reject the reflexivity that print capitalist accounts of the eighteenth and nineteenth centuries have placed at the heart of the rise of the public sphere: "Perhaps the most fruitful source of mortification to a merry writer, who for the amusement of himself and the public, employs his leisure in sketching odd characters from imagination, is, that he cannot flourish his pen, but every Jack-pudding imagines it is pointed directly at himself" (87).[46] Despite the editors' pleas that readers refrain from taking the satire personally and "remember to bear in mind, that our characters are not individuals, but species" (80), Dana's review again demonstrates that readers couldn't help but imagine themselves as co-collaborators: "In the end, it took fast hold of people, through their vanity; for frequent use had made them so familiar with it as to look upon it as their own; and having retailed its good things so long, they began to run of the notion that they were all of their own making" (13). The final issue finds the editors reveling in the relationship they have developed with their readers: "One circumstance in particular, has tickled us mightily, as we jogged along; and that is, the astonishing secrecy with which we have been able to carry on our lucubrations! . . . Our grey-beard speculations have been most bountifully attributed to sundry smart young gentlemen, who, for aught we know, have not beards at all" (306). Insisting that those who doubt their identities as "merry old bachelors" have been corrupted by Old World novels, this not so subtle authorial wink acknowledges that readers are in on the joke.

Even if readers don't know the actual identities of the beardless "smart young gentlemen" who are responsible for *Salmagundi*, their recognition of the bachelor persona as a familiar literary type grants the editors the status of author.[47] Despite their skepticism toward the position of authorial disinterest or aesthetic retreat, the editors differentiate themselves from the corrosive political factionalism of the "slang-whangers" and the performative anxiety of the alienated author by celebrating the fictionality of their pseudonymous bachelor personas. An author-centered mode of reading must dismiss *Salmagundi*'s anonymous authorship as an obsolete convention of republican literary culture. For Paulding and the Irving brothers, who no longer have any faith in the possibility of civic disinterest, the playful conceit behind the editors' bachelor pseudonyms is a strategy for claiming authorship.[48] *Salmagundi* experiments with a form of authorship that does not fit comfortably into republican fantasies of consensus but is also far from celebrating a centralized literary marketplace organized by individual novelists. The success of the editors' authorial design depends on readers recognizing and laughing at the fiction behind a performance that is in turn dependent on a newly delineated private sphere. *Salmagundi*'s antiquated bachelor-authors stake their claim to the supposedly apolitical values of the private sphere while resisting the gender divide the rhetoric of domesticity worked to naturalize.[49] Adopting the personas of aristocratic bachelors, the authors reactively labor to control their reception in a liberal marketplace increasingly defined by but not yet reducible to gender difference. The editors advertise their performance as a sign of authorial prowess and expect readers to acknowledge and enjoy that performativity as a marker of fiction. This performance results in a realignment rather than a deconstruction of literary categories: as their performance unsettles the gendered homogeneity of domesticity, it also works to establish gender difference within the domestic space.

For the *Salmagundi* bachelors, domestic retreat becomes an important marker of dissenting literary genius, as they temporarily reject the benefits and obligations of public life. By attributing the source of their eccentric output to their bachelor domesticity, the editors insulate their romantic genius from the commodifying threat of their own popularity. For the *Salmagundi* editors, domestic retreat was not a right that could be universally claimed, and they repeatedly thematize the unimaginative nature of the servants and spinsters who serve as subjects for their sketches. The editors' defensive posturing can be understood as a reaction to an increasing association of domestic retreat with feminine literary genius. As we will see in the next chapter, even our approaches to women writers who reject the constraints of domestic fiction remain hampered by the limitations of a critical inheritance that primes us to read women's fiction as morally earnest rather than playfully skeptical. Turning to the early national frontier romance, the next chapter argues that Catharine Maria Sedgwick deftly manipulates the gender essentialism of early romantic historiography and domestic ideology to bolster her critique of nationalist fantasies of progressive history.

3
THE VOICE OF NATURE
Hope Leslie and Early American Romanticism

WE SAW IN THE LAST chapter how Washington Irving, once dismissed as a derivative imitator of British traditions, has been recontextualized within a transatlantic tradition of influence. I argued in my introduction that a recent interest in the speculative possibilities of the prose romance tradition in the early United States threatens to leave behind the poets of the early romantic movement who have been dismissed as somehow both embarrassingly derivative and blandly nationalist. This chapter picks up on that argument by repositioning Catharine Maria Sedgwick's historical romance novel *Hope Leslie; or, Early Times in the Massachusetts* within an early romantic poetic tradition. This might seem perverse, given that, of the authors covered so far, Sedgwick is most decidedly a novelist, but Sedgwick deliberately positions her novel within an early national romantic poetic tradition: the preface suggests the interchangeability of "historians or poets" and lines of British and American romantic poetry populate its chapter epigraphs.[1] In *Hope Leslie*, Sedgwick harnesses two defining aspects of early romantic poetry, the celebration of the feminine element as essential to literary genius and a desire to establish a "native" Anglo-American identity, to argue that feminine genius is best suited for channeling white indigeneity. While the *Salmagundi* editors defensively react to an increasing idealization of domestic labor as an aesthetic good by disentangling the generative literary possibilities of domestic retreat for the eccentric bachelor, *Hope Leslie* purposefully underscores the artfulness behind its transcription of the "voice of nature" to push back against attempts to domesticate women's literary output as effortless instinct (97, 310).

In the preface to his 1848 anthology *The Female Poets of America*, Rufus Wilmot Griswold proposes "feminine genius" as the answer to charges that Americans are "too much devoted to business and politics" to produce a national literature.[2] In the expanded preface to the second edition published four years later, Griswold illustrates the dynamic relationship between antebellum domesticity and Romantic historiography by turning to the frontier and its narrative of American progress to make his point: "it is in the West too where we look for what is most thoroughly native and essential in American character where we are struck with the number of youthful female voices that soften and enrich the tumult of enterprise, and action, by the interblended music of a calmer and loftier sphere."[3] Griswold's faith in the possibility of a national literature depends on feminine genius to represent Western expansion as a "native" instinct, even as the transcendent properties of that genius exclude women from the political rights earned by participation in the commercial enterprise of expansion. The rhetoric of domesticity established women as the source of private virtue that naturalized civic duty but that also excluded them from actually being considered citizens. Similarly, by establishing the frontier's wide open spaces as the source of national character that naturalized American expansion, Romantic historiography worked to preserve rather than assimilate nature's ever-receding possibilities. Amy Kaplan has compellingly analyzed the process by which "imperial domesticity" relies on the construction of uncivilized spaces to continue its "domesticating mission."[4] Reading Catharine Maria Sedgwick's frontier romance *Hope Leslie; or, Early Times in the Massachusetts* (1827) as an early Romantic experiment rather than as a straightforward precursor to mid-nineteenth-century domestic novels, this chapter traces a strain of antebellum discourse that romanticizes these uncivilized spaces as extrapolitical sources of national character. The logic of this rhetoric proposes the figures it imagines circulating in these spaces as working to naturalize culture rather than domesticate nature. I begin by situating Sedgwick in the early Romantic movement by arguing that early Romantic historiography called upon feminine genius to naturalize fantasies of progressive national history. I then argue that *Hope Leslie*'s cyclical concept of history poses a direct challenge to Romantic historiography's reliance on the essentializing rhetoric of domesticity. Although Sedgwick's experimental romanticism protests the artificial confines of domesticity, it can do so only by replacing the disenfranchised white woman of domestic fiction with the forsaken Indian woman of Romantic historiography as the figure who must remain the unassimilated source of the natural values that the United States claims for itself.[5]

EARLY AMERICAN ROMANTICISM AND WOMEN'S FICTION

Sedgwick's selection of poetry by Eliza Lee Cabot Follen, William Cullen Bryant, and Fitz-Greene Halleck for *Hope Leslie*'s title page and chapter epigraphs situates her novel in the context of the burgeoning New England Romantic movement. Most accounts of nineteenth-century literature would not categorize these authors within American Romanticism, primarily because their Old World metrical arrangements and didactic sentimentalism seem hopelessly opposed to the inventive aesthetics of midcentury American Renaissance authors.[6] Recent critical attention has begun to view early American Romanticism's transatlantic appropriations as revisionary rather than purely imitative, particularly by noting the nationalist agenda behind the movement's relationship with a specifically American landscape.[7] In their appropriation of Wordsworthian naturalism, early American Romantics preserved a jarring sense of eighteenth-century didacticism. A correspondence between the moral and natural worlds worked to naturalize expansion as an involuntary democratic impulse. Once we recognize the nationalist energies at work behind the moralizing naturalism of early American Romantic poetry, nineteenth-century literary culture realigns itself into new genealogies. The early Romantic movement troubles the false cultural divides that the American Renaissance established between postcolonial and imperial, masculine and feminine, and Romantic and sentimental literary culture.[8] Although the divide between feminine sentimentality and masculine romanticism has been challenged through a recognition of shared political and cultural work, the nationalist agenda behind early romanticism's dual investment in naturalistic retreat and sentimental didacticism remains underdeveloped, as does the movement's relationship to the explicitly nationalist agendas of antebellum historical romances.

Sedgwick and the historical romances of her time have recently been considered productively in relation to the fictional tradition of romance and its mode of conjectural history, a tradition I discussed in the first chapter of this book. Michelle Sizemore considers Sedgwick's historical romances as following from the tradition of romance inaugurated by Charles Brockden Brown that is marked by a sense of "uncertainty about historical knowledge."[9] Jeffrey Insko considers Sedgwick as a practitioner of "presentist historiography" that overtly attempts "to bring the past and present into relation, rather than to keep them apart."[10] Positioning Sedgwick in relation to the proliferating historical romances of the 1820s, Thomas Koenigs characterizes Sedgwick as thinking of fiction as "a qualifying supplement" to history that "allows us to imagine what has been elided from history."[11] While my own understanding of Sedgwick's historical romances accords with and is informed by these attentive analyses of how nineteenth-century romance writers trouble disciplinary distinctions between history and fiction, in this chapter I would like to position Sedgwick in relation to a more neglected tradition of romanticism, namely the British poetic tradition that Virginia Jackson has argued was appropriated by early national poets to transmute the unwieldy global colonial space of the early United States into an emphatically Anglo-American home.[12] Repositioning Sedgwick in relation to Bryant and Wordsworth rather than Hawthorne and Scott, my interest lies in how Sedgwick leverages domestic fiction and romantic historiography's shared investment in a naturalized morality to position women authors as uniquely equipped to create national literature. The speculative proximity between past and present that Sedgwick achieves in her historical romance is deeply informed by the early national poets Sedgwick cites who, through conventional fantasies of poetic genres like the first-person speaker of the lyric and the unifying primitive past of the ballad, labored to make American history and literature "simultaneously aboriginal and indomitably English."[13] In Sedgwick's fiction, the frontier takes on the symbolic importance of the home as the source of essential national character, and although it is an American girl's impulsive nature that makes her best suited for tapping this source of national character, Sedgwick also carefully distinguishes between her novel's secondhand indigenous romancer and its vanishing source material.

Early romanticism's exclusion from literary histories means that Sedgwick is most frequently positioned as an inaugural producer of domestic fiction rather than as a participant in the early romantic movement. *Hope Leslie*'s critical history in particular provides a snapshot of the conversations surrounding women's fiction that have developed over the last few decades; critics have argued that *Hope Leslie* typifies domestic fiction's refusal to engage with history, that it typifies domestic fiction's subversive potential to critique patriarchal discourses, and that it typifies domestic fiction's limited ability to negotiate racial difference.[14] The endpoint of this narrative is the critical impasse that characterizes analyses influenced by separate spheres ideology, as even arguments that emphasize the permeability of the spheres ultimately reify an oppositional relationship between masculine and feminine literary traditions.[15] Fully aware of the ways that its cultural moment exploits the falseness of this divide, *Hope Leslie*'s plot is driven by a mutually constitutive relationship between patriarchal authority and feminine reform. The novel's first volume develops a close relationship between Magawisca, the captured daughter of a Pequot chief, and Everell Fletcher, the novel's white hero. This relationship climaxes when Magawisca stops her father from executing Everell, losing her own arm in the process. The novel's eponymous white female lead then helps Magawisca's friend Nelema escape from the Puritan settlement where she has been convicted of practicing witchcraft. In return, Nelema makes Magawisca promise to arrange a meeting between Hope and her sister Faith, who was captured by Magawisca's father and has married Magawisca's brother. This meeting is interrupted by the Puritan authorities, who arrest Magawisca. Hope then frees Magawisca. This cycle of favors returned ends when Magawisca decides to leave the white settlement once and for all, despite Hope's promise that the settlers will soon grow past their prejudices.

Reading *Hope Leslie* within the context of the early romantic movement's progressive national histories allows us to recognize its cyclical concept of history as a skeptical critique rather than a failure of imagination. The end of the novel establishes that what makes Magawisca most vulnerable to Puritan violence is her friendship with Hope, whose liberal impulses make her a nearly irresistible force of reformative discipline. The novel's ambivalence about its white heroine's natural impulses unsettles the essentializing rhetoric of domesticity, but its preservation of the American Indian woman as a transcendent figure of exceptional national virtue upholds the fundamental logic of early American Romanticism's desire to naturalize national ideology. Rather than signifying the domestic novelist's failure to incorporate her Indian sister into a newly democratic community, this specific iteration of the Vanishing American nationalizes democratic virtue by locating it in the American wilderness.

Hope Leslie's preoccupation with who is able to heed "the voice of nature" directly aligns Sedgwick's project with the early Romantic movement (97, 310). William Cullen Bryant, a member of the same liberal New England community as the Sedgwick family, reviewed at least one of Sedgwick's novels in *North American Review*, and two poems from his 1824 collection *Poems*, "Monument Mountain" and "An Indian Story," appear as chapter epigraphs in *Hope Leslie*. The false cultural divide established by the American Renaissance limited Bryant as well as Sedgwick; it informs a critical approach that views incongruity between *Hope Leslie*'s tentative cultural relativism and its investment in the cult of the Vanishing American as a symptom of the inevitable failure of the domestic novelist's imagination. Similarly, this critical perspective sees the incongruity between Bryant's naturalism and his didacticism as a symptom of postcolonial conservatism. Although he was one of the most well-respected poets of the early nineteenth century, twentieth-century critics viewed Bryant's Shakespearean sonnets and Spenserian stanzas as U.S. literature at its most imitative and unoriginal, and the utilitarian claims he made for the aims of literature now seem hopelessly outdated.[16] As Jackson quips, "Bryant was not a Romantic, precisely because he imitated the British poets we still call 'the Romantics.'"[17] Jackson has brought Bryant's dubious reputation full circle. Whereas the twentieth-century nickname "the American Wordsworth" suggested Bryant was simply a pale imitator, an overcorrection that would rehabilitate Bryant within narratives of American exceptionalism misses the ways that Bryant deliberately aligns his verse with the British tradition to establish white Anglo-American indigeneity. Accordingly, Jackson argues that we should see Bryant's transatlantic adaptations as "racially identified rather than nationally competitive."[18] As I argue below, early American romanticism's aim of establishing white indigeneity appropriates theories of feminine genius to naturalize exceptional narratives of nationalist progress.

One thematic convention that makes early American Romanticism seem particularly divorced from the midcentury romanticism of Emerson and Melville is its moralizing tone. Bryant argued in his *Lectures on Poetry* that "it is the dominion of poetry over the feelings and passions of men that gives it its most important bearing upon the virtue and the welfare of society. Everything that affects our sensibilities is a part of our moral education, and the habit of being rightly affected by all the circumstances by which we are surrounded is the perfection of the moral character."[19] Bryant works to naturalize the moral utility of literature, claiming that poetry should avoid being "merely didactic" by "teaching truths which the mind instinctively acknowledges" (11). What makes Bryant's didacticism Romantic is its understanding of the close relationship between the moral and the natural world. For Bryant, "among the most remarkable of the influences of poetry is the exhibition of those analogies and correspondences which it beholds between the things of the moral and of the natural world" (19). He holds that these correspondences between the moral and natural world are universally recognized: "the simplicity and clearness of the truths with which [poetry] deals prevent any mistake in regard to their meanings or tendencies. They strike the mind by their own brightness and win its assent by their manifest and beautiful agreement with the lessons of our own experience" (19). This unmistakable clarity about a naturalized code of morals is not limited to lyric poetry—for Bryant it is the standard by which all literature should be judged. In his review of Sedgwick's 1824 novel *Redwood*, Bryant outlines his general views on the American novel and concludes by congratulating her for writing a novel, "the design of which is professedly to instruct," that manages to avoid being didactic:

> It is not enough to say of this novel, that the reader is relieved and refreshed at due intervals, by being let out from the instructions of the author into the great world about him, to amuse himself with what is going on there; and is then gently recalled to the lesson, which the author wishes to teach. It is doing it better justice to say, that the world itself is only then made to the reader, what it ought always to be, the great school and place of discipline, the experience and observation of which should form us to virtue.[20]

According to Bryant, *Redwood* is particularly successful in teaching its lesson because it trains readers to take their instruction from the world around them—rather than imposing its own artificial code, the novel teaches readers how to read for the lessons that already exist in the natural world.

Bryant's review seems only tangentially interested in Sedgwick's novel, and most of the essay is spent promoting his own theories about the formation of national literature. Although he praises the naturalness of *Redwood*'s instruction, he quickly commandeers nature's lessons and the successful literature they generate to support a narrative of American progress. According to Bryant, reading is a naturally democratic enterprise, and the simple character traits that all readers crave "are to be found abundantly in the characters of our countrymen, formed as they are under the influence of our free institutions, and shooting into a large and vigorous, though sometimes irregular luxuriance" (253). Like most critics of his day, Bryant argued that American history, landscape, and diversity provided ideal subjects for the novelist. Most inspiring for Bryant is the history of American progress:

> It is hardly possible that the rapid and continual growth and improvement of our country, a circumstance wonderfully exciting to the imagination, and altogether unlike anything witnessed in other countries, should not have some influence in forming our national character. At all events, it is a most fertile source of incident. . . . The hardy and sagacious native of the eastern states, settles himself in the wilderness by the side of the emigrant from the British isles . . . and then you see cornfields, and roads, and towns springing up as if by enchantment. In the mean time pleasant Indian villages, situated on the skirts of their hunting grounds, with their beautiful green plats for dances and martial exercises, are taken into the bosom of our extending population, while new states are settled and cities founded far beyond them. (254–255)

I cite this passage at length both because it is so typical of the early-nineteenth-century evaluations of U.S. literature that gave rise to historical romances like *Hope Leslie* and because it is such a clear statement of Romantic historicism. Anglo-American farms, roads, and towns appear "as if by enchantment," American Indians do not face removal policies but are "taken into the bosom of our extending population," and Anglo-American settlements exceed even indigenous claims to the land. Inevitable, exceptional, and already the stuff of romance, American progress is a source of both "national character" and literary "incident." In his poetry Bryant might mourn the Vanishing American and protest industrialization through pastoral nostalgia, but the theory underlying these sentiments is clear—indigenous people will disappear in the face of American progress, and literature is the best way to feel good about this disappearance.[21] In the same way that "a sense of the foreign is necessary to erect the boundaries that enclose the nation as home," the opportunity for "continual growth" provided by the frontier is necessary to inspire a national literature that will in turn naturalize the violence of this expansion through the "enchantment" of romance.[22]

Bryant's views on U.S. literature and history illustrate why Griswold refers to the West when introducing *The Female Poets of America*. If American values are rooted in the frontier's untouched wilderness, then the woman author's responsive relationship to nature makes her uniquely qualified to represent these values. Feminine genius provides an escape from the anxiety surrounding the corrupting forces of ownership that plague Bryant's own representations of the land, even as the act of publication threatened the idealization of women's writing as spiritual impulse.[23] Elizabeth Maddock Dillon argues that nineteenth-century sentimental discourse identifies women with a domestic space that "is also figured as determined by free will, love, and desire rather than by material need or compulsion"; the discourse thus constructs women's work as a "moral and aesthetic endeavor" divorced from the legal protections of the market.[24] *Hope Leslie*'s romanticism revises this construction by portraying the American wilderness rather than the home as a space of free will divorced from institutional demands.[25] Kinereth Meyer notes that nineteenth-century authors like Bryant struggled with dual conceptions of land as commodity and as "moral emblem."[26] The rhetoric of Indian removal policy was grounded in arguments that did not recognize tribal relationships to land as conforming to liberal notions of private property rights.[27] Doubly disenfranchised by a discourse of natural rights rooted in property ownership, the American Indian woman becomes a fantasy figure who provides the ultimate access to the spiritual resources of the land, untouched by the corrupting influence of the material world. In *Hope Leslie* the Indian woman rather than the white woman becomes the figure whose work—the nativizing of a new generation of Americans—is sanctioned by natural impulses that transcend both the limits and the protections of citizenship.

There is an additional context to consider when assessing the relationship between romantic historiography and the appeal of women writers. While liberal theory associates women with a prepolitical state of nature and uncivilized spaces provide the greatest potential for the work of domesticity, antebellum critics like Griswold also associated feminine genius with artless instinct rather than artful creation.[28] Bryant's privileging of Sedgwick's ability to record her "experience and observation" of the natural world is characteristic of a more general discourse that coded women's literary and domestic labor as natural, emotional impulses. While the gendered lyric tradition claims women as impulsively expressive poets, in the racialized ballad tradition, as Meredith Martin has established, the poem promises to re-create the lost "purer primitive poetics" of past civilizations.[29] In the preface to *Hope Leslie*, as Insko has noted, Sedgwick's narrator suggestively presents herself as serving as the surrogate historian-poet of a vanishing race: "In our histories, it was perhaps natural that they should be represented as 'surly dogs,' who preferred to die rather than live, from no other motives than a stupid or malignant obstinacy. Their own historians or poets, if they had such, would as naturally, and with more justice, have extolled their high–souled courage and patriotism."[30] This preface most certainly indicts Puritan histories as partisan and incomplete, but it also positions the novel that follows within a specific poetic tradition that claims to capture the primitive voices of a premodern race. In doing so, it presents the narrator as once removed from the Pequot versions of history she will relate to counter the prejudiced Puritan record. The secondhand nature of her translation presents Sedgwick's narrator as able to heed the purely expressive voices of this past and inventively mold them into a literary history for the present. Throughout the novel, Magawisca's instinctive understanding of natural law is appropriated to naturalize an authority that cannot imagine including her within its jurisdiction because it requires her to remain an unadulterated source of the natural law that justifies its own founding. As Colin Jager describes it, "second nature is culture naturalized and has the further advantage of always having been naturalized before one inherits it."[31] Even as Sedgwick's narrator aligns herself with Magawisca and occasionally distances herself from Hope Leslie's reformative prejudices, it is precisely this distancing that allows Magawisca's purely transgressive nature to serve as the unadulterated source of native Anglo-American national identity. Additionally, by relegating Magawisca to raw source material that can be tapped but not replicated by her white heroine, Sedgwick establishes the woman author's skill against critical narratives that idealize it as an impulse borne of domestic isolation.

I should clarify here that my aim is not to "censure" or "reprimand" Sedgwick for being "merely a product of her time."[32] As I discuss below, one reason why historical romances proliferated during the early national period is because there was little consensus about what the values of the time were. Nor do I claim to float above Sedgwick's revolutionary portrayal of Magawisca from a modern perspective I consider to be more progressive—I concur with critics like Sizemore and Insko who attend to the connections Sedgwick's novel invites between present and future readers. Rather, I argue that our readings of Sedgwick's fiction have been overly determined by the gendered assumptions about domestic fiction that are themselves products of nineteenth-century literary culture. In this sense, our own critical practices are products of Sedgwick's time. As I now argue, our understanding of women's fiction as morally earnest has led us to overlook the wryly skeptical narrative voice of Sedgwick's novel—a device she uses to undercut her period's use of fiction to naturalize national ideology and to showcase the design of her literary art.

HOPE LESLIE'S CRITIQUE OF GENRE

Although the occasion for Bryant to outline his theories about the relationship between U.S. fiction and history is his review of Sedgwick's novel *Redwood*, her next novel disrupts fiction's appropriation by the forces of nationalist history and challenges the generic expectations of women's fiction in the early nineteenth century. As Bryant's review of *Redwood* demonstrates, the primary purpose of antebellum history writing was to capture national essence, a principle supposedly privileged with much consensus following the War of 1812 and the bipartisan rhetoric of the Era of Good Feelings. As George Callcott explains, because "it was the purpose of history to strengthen society by supporting the basic principles in which men believed—society's concepts of morality, religion, and nationalism . . . it was not falsifying the past to select those facts which illustrated a particular principle, for principles were certain and the facts of history were not."[33] In the preface to *Hope Leslie*, Sedgwick's narrator tells the reader that although the novel is not "in any degree an historical narrative, . . . [r]eal characters and events are, however, alluded to . . . [in order to achieve the author's aim] to illustrate not the history, but the character of the times" (3). Like any good early national historian, Sedgwick selectively blends history and fiction to illustrate her idea of national character. Insko, one of the few critics to recognize the irony that characterizes Sedgwick's narrator, argues that the novel undermines historical authority by revealing its inherent fictionality: "in an extraordinary admission of historiographical partisanship, [the preface] frankly draws attention to the inevitable (often willful) blindnesses that always attend historical investigations, including the present one."[34] Given the fact that this "historiographical partisanship" was considered an important aim of early national history writing, Sedgwick's preface does not only challenge the authority of history; the shared goals of history and fiction in this period suggest that it also challenges the authority of fiction. If *Hope Leslie* seeks to undermine historical authority, it also works to undermine literature's authority as the mode best suited to appealing to the era's naturalized concept of national essence. Throughout the novel, the narrator's sarcastic interjections and manipulative plot devices never allow readers to forget that they are reading a work of fiction. If, as Lawrence Buell argues, "the utilitarian cast of American critical thought" meant "a strategic forgetting of the fictional element" in historical fiction, Sedgwick makes use of a heavy-handed, ironic narrator constantly to remind her readers of this fictional element.[35] By showcasing that what readers might think of as natural impulses are in fact generic conventions, the novel emphasizes the artful design behind literature that critics like Bryant praised for being merely expressive. Just as *Jane Talbot* withholds emotional affirmation from its marriage plot and *Salmagundi*'s irreverent editorial interjections disrupt its readers' sentimental reveries, *Hope Leslie* constantly disturbs readers with the knowledge that their readerly instincts can be misled.

Sedgwick's sarcastic narrator is her primary method for challenging the generic expectations of Romantic historiography. Sedgwick's novel invites readers to interpret its tale of the seventeenth-century Massachusetts Bay Colony through their own contemporary understanding of U.S. history, but it also undermines any confidence readers might feel in their modern superiority.[36] The novel first describes Hope through a comparison to its 1827 readers: "Nothing could be more unlike the authentic, 'thoroughly educated,' and thoroughly disciplined young ladies of the present day, than Hope Leslie; as unlike as a mountain rill to a canal—the one leaping over rocks and precipices, sportive, free, and beautiful, or stealing softly on, in unseen, unpraised loveliness; the other, formed by art, restrained, within prescribed and formal limits, and devoted to utility" (126). This description of the women of Sedgwick's present, characterized by artifice, discipline, and utility, hardly represents the progressive history that Bryant thought the native Anglo-American author should capture. The narrator's unfavorable comparison also alerts readers to the possibility that any claims she makes about the progressiveness of the present age might be disingenuous: "The character of man, and the institutions of society, are yet very far from their possible and destined perfection. Still, how far is the present age in advance of that which drove reformers to a dreary wilderness!—of that which hanged quakers!—of that which condemned to death, as witches, innocent, unoffending old women! But it is unnecessary to heighten the glory of our risen day by comparing it with 'the preceding twilight'" (15). Lucy Maddox cites this passage as evidence that Sedgwick accepts "without question the view that the intellectual and psychological narrowness of Puritan culture has given way to the enlightened liberalism of the nineteenth century."[37] Maddox's eagerness to contrast Sedgwick's "zeal for reform" unfavorably with Hawthorne's "skepticism about the validity of reform movements" misses the narrator's own skeptical parenthetical insertion two paragraphs later.[38] The narrator tells us that when William Fletcher decides to move his family from Boston to the isolated settlement at Springfield, "Mrs. Fletcher received his decision as all wives of that age of undisputed masculine supremacy (or most of those of our less passive age) would do, with meek submission" (15). This sarcastic comment makes it impossible to read the previous passage as a straightforward statement in support of American progress.

Hope Leslie does not encourage its readers to look back at the Puritans from a more progressive point in U.S. history. Although the novel's younger generation, represented by Hope, Magawisca, and Everell, is characterized by an increased understanding of the common humanity shared by men and women, whites and Indians, Magawisca's voluntary exile at the end of the novel reiterates the cyclical nature of history that Sedgwick is proposing—American Indians will not disappear for the first time with Andrew Jackson's 1830 Indian Removal Act; instead, they are disappearing yet again. This formulation is slightly different from the iteration of the Vanishing American that Lora Romero finds in James Fenimore Cooper's preface to *The Last of the Mohicans*: "The elegiac mode here performs the historical sleight of hand crucial to the topos of the doomed aboriginal: it represents the disappearance of the native not just as natural but as having already happened."[39] If the historical romances and romantic poetry about the decades of Indian removal policy portray the Indian's disappearance as "both spontaneous and ineluctable," by suggesting that Indian removal is a repetition, Sedgwick's version of the Vanishing American also presents Indian removal as a national character trait that has very little to do with modern progress and industry.[40]

The criticism leveled at Sedgwick for being unable to imagine a progressive ending for her revisionist history misses the fact that in 1827, history did not seem particularly progressive. Readers disappointed with the novel's ending for precluding the progressive possibilities at its beginning have missed the lesson its skeptical narrator points out over and over again: there is nothing progressive or exceptional about U.S. history. Despite *Hope Leslie*'s skepticism toward early

Romantic histories of American progress, literary historians place *Hope Leslie* squarely in a tradition of women's fiction that takes the possibility of progress as its founding tenet.[41] The palpable critical disappointment with Sedgwick's reliance on the Romantic convention of the Vanishing American to resolve her otherwise progressive novel demonstrates our conflicted investment in both the transgressive Otherness of women's fiction and its inevitable conventionality.[42] The ease with which this novel's contradictions are accounted for as symptomatic of the limits of domestic fiction suggests that our critical labor continues to naturalize a gendered divide in the antebellum literary canon. One example of this mode of reading comes in Ezra Tawil's *The Making of Racial Sentiment*, where an understanding of frontier romances as "anticipatory" of midcentury domestic fiction predetermines a reading of *Hope Leslie*.[43] Tawil argues that the racial logic of the novel excludes Magawisca from becoming a sentimental heroine because she is unable to adapt to the Fletcher household's domestic scene (124). The novel presents domesticity not as a positive but, rather, as a restrictive value that interferes with natural impulses. The difference between volume I and volume II of Sedgwick's novel can be characterized as a shift from the *vacuum domicilium* of the frontier to the "petty domiciliary tyranny" of the urban (131, 315). While the frontier's lack of domestic spaces allows Hope to act on her natural impulses, the Winthrops' civilized Boston "government-mansion," where Hope is sent after helping Nelema escape, forces its "inmates" to act according to the artificial codes of domesticity (149). Jennet and Mrs. Fletcher are the novel's two unpromising representatives of domesticity. Both die spectacular deaths that can be read as symptomatic of their relationship to the domestic; the silently submissive Mrs. Fletcher is killed in an Indian attack after refusing to remove her family to the fort until her husband returns home, and the aggressively tyrannical Jennet is killed in an explosion after trying to derail Everell and Hope's plan to liberate Magawisca. As Christopher Castiglia argues, *Hope Leslie* is an example of women's fiction that is hyperaware of domesticity's potential collusion with patriarchal conquest.[44]

Nineteenth-century reviews of *Hope Leslie* suggest that we have inherited our gendered critical impulses from the antebellum literary establishment. *North American Review* used its review of *Hope Leslie* as an excuse to welcome women to the realm of novel writing: "The purity and the goodness of women have here done their proper work. They are seen and felt in the elegant literature of the times. They have greatly contributed to chasten the morals of literature, and establish a code of laws, by which offences against decency are condemned as offences against taste."[45] The woman author, the review continues, "cannot be false to her nature. The cause of virtue must always find in her an advocate."[46] In a slightly different vein, the *Western Monthly Review* congratulates Sedgwick for recognizing her own limitations: "At present, the aim of all, who write for the imagination, is to produce an effect. The author cares not what established rules he violates, in making his book, if, by so doing, he can create a sensation in his readers. This mania does not seem to have touched our authoress. Her story presents a regular account of well regulated people, who figure only in still life."[47] According to this review, Sedgwick "was probably aware" that the "many powerful minds" who novelized the Puritan character before her left nothing new to say, and so she "confined herself" to reality, with the exception of her unrealistic portrayals of "the savage mind."[48] Although neither of these reviews should be considered the last word on how *Hope Leslie* was received by nineteenth-century readers, they both locate the success of women's fiction in its moral realism rather than in its imaginative potential.[49]

Hope Leslie's narrative playfulness challenges the limitations imposed on women's fiction by these reviews and reminds us, in Romero's words, "to exercise sufficient skepticism toward the antebellum period's narrative of itself."[50] The novel's most explicit rejection of these generic expectations occurs in the final chapter, when the narrator carelessly glosses over the details of Hope's hard-won domestic bliss: "We leave it to that large, and most indulgent class of our readers, the misses in their teens, to adjust, according to their own fancy, the ceremonial of our heroine's wedding" (369). If the marriage plot is one of the clearest markers of domestic fiction, this dismissal is a striking moment of genre confusion, as the narrator appears completely uninterested in the domestic portion of her tale.[51] In his review of *Redwood*, Bryant claimed that, unlike romances, when writing domestic novels, "it will not do to trust to the imagination of the reader to heighten the interest of such a narrative; if it ever attempts to fill up the sketch given by the writer, it is not often in a way calculated to increase its effect, for it is done with plain and sober hues, that color the tissue of our own lives" (247). Whether or not Sedgwick's decision to leave the details of Hope's wedding to "the imagination of the reader" is a tongue-in-cheek defiance of Bryant's instructions about writing domestic fiction, it is clear that as Magawisca disappears into "the deep, voiceless obscurity" of the "far western forests," the narrator loses interest in her tale (359). One might argue that Sedgwick rushes through the novel's final domestic details because once Magawisca disappears, Hope's marriage is beside the point, that what matters is that Magawisca's disappearance enables Hope and Everell's marriage. But the narrator's dismissive tone also corresponds to a growing skepticism toward the white heroine's natural impulses that directly challenges the rhetoric of domesticity's essentializing assumptions about women's moral natures. As Hope moves into a position of power in the newly democratic community, the secondhand nature of her limited moral impulses is precisely what allows her to replace Puritan patriarchs as the new force of American discipline. This coup, however, depends on preserving Magawisca outside the national enterprise as an unadulterated source of Hope's revolutionary dissent.

THE VOICE OF NATURE

As numerous critics have noted, *Hope Leslie* portrays Hope and Magawisca as sisters who share a spiritual connection to the American wilderness and act on a natural code of morals written on the heart.[52] This connection with the Pequot native seems to authorize the English settler with the crucial indigeneity sought by early Romanticists.[53] Magawisca's belief in the Great Spirit and Hope's own vague religious sentiments, "pure and disinterested" and unbound by "the contracted boundaries of sectarian faith," are conflated into the Romantic deism that finds expression in Bryant's theories of poetry (128). Critics frequently describe Magawisca and Hope's sisterhood as evidence that Sedgwick deliberately codes the novel's progressive, reformative values as feminine.[54] Although Magawisca and Hope both challenge the artificial laws enforced by Pequot and Puritan patriarchs, the ability to read for natural law seems determined by race at least as much as gender. Throughout the novel acts of transgression signify an unnatural, unjust system that can be subverted only by characters who listen to their natural impulses. *Hope Leslie* attempts to nationalize these transgressive, democratic impulses by linking them to the values of the American Revolution. Digby, a minor character who is a frequent enabler of Hope's schemes, responds to her self-consciousness that she has perhaps been "too headstrong in [her] own way" by telling her, "why this having our own way, is what every body likes; it's the privilege we came to this wilderness for" (235). Digby's rhetoric suggests that the spirit of revolution is somehow a natural resource of the American wilderness that will soon triumph over the "pretty tight rein" held by "the gentles up in town there, with the Governor at their head" (235). But it is also clear that the values claimed by the American revolutionaries did not descend from Puritans, but from Indians, as Sedgwick reverts to what by 1827 was an almost outdated conflation of American Indian with American rebellion.[55] As Insko observes, when Magawisca anticipates Patrick Henry and demands that Governor Winthrop grant her "death or liberty," "the fervor of the Revolutionary fathers, their oratorical authority, suddenly appears autochthonous, as if somehow *native* to the land itself, while the native Magawisca becomes a protonationalist, less an enemy than a source of founding principles."[56] Magawisca's "contagious" call for liberty leaves the Puritan audience feeling conflicted, "their reason, guided by the best lights they possessed, deciding against her—the voice of nature crying out for her" (310). National essence, it seems, can skip a generation. When Magawisca saves Everell at the sacrifice rock, this scene is doubled, but with an important difference. Before Magawisca intervenes, although there were "some whose hearts moved them to interpose to save the selected victim," like the Puritans who watch Magawisca's trial, "they were restrained by their interpretation of natural justice, as controlling to them as our artificial codes of laws to us" (95).

But after Magawisca sacrifices herself for Everell, "the voice of nature rose from every heart, and responding to the justice of Magawisca's claim, bade him 'God Speed!'" (97). Unlike the Puritans, the "savages" are able to act on their sense of natural justice (96–97). *Hope Leslie*'s romanticism anxiously circles around the white settlers' secondhand knowledge of natural law via a nostalgic pathos for a mythic time when natural law was the law of the land.

Representing a more progressive generation than the Puritan authorities they consistently disobey, Hope and Everell's natural impulses must be cultivated by someone indigenous to the land, and Magawisca serves as their conduit to the natural world and its lessons of personal freedom and cross-cultural understanding. When Hope argues with William Fletcher for Nelema's freedom, she uses a secondhand paraphrase of Magawisca's words: "I repeated what I had often heard, you, Everell, say, that Magawisca believed the mountain, and the valley, the air, the trees, every little rivulet, had their present invisible spirit—and that the good might hold discourse with them. 'Why not believe the one,' I asked, 'as well as the other?'" (111). Similarly, at the end of the novel, Hope can only accustom herself to her sister's marriage to Oneco after considering Magawisca's parting words: "the suggestions of Magawisca, combining with the dictates of her own heart, produced the conclusion that this was a case where 'God had joined together, and man might not put asunder'" (359). The novel ends reminding its readers that Hope must struggle to feel correctly, or as Magawisca dictates that she should.

By presenting Magawisca as the source of Hope's good feelings, the novel suggests that Hope's transgressive impulses might be second nature after all. Importantly, Hope is more conducive to Indian naturalism than Magawisca is to English domesticity. While Mrs. Fletcher despairs that one might as well "yoke a deer with an ox" as compel Magawisca to help Jennet with "the drudgery of domestic service," Hope takes naturally to the American wilderness (32). No scene implies Hope's natural affinity for Indian culture more than her theatrical entrance following the Bethel massacre. As Magawisca retreats into the forest with her father and his captives, Hope enters playing the part of Indian Princess: "Mr. Fletcher was attended by two Indians, who followed him, bearing on a litter, his favourite, Hope Leslie. When they came within sight of Bethel, they shouted the chorus of a native song. Hope inquired its meaning. They told her, and raising herself, and tossing back the bright curls that shaded her eyes, she clapped her hands, and accompanied them with the English words,—'The home!—the home!—the chieftain's home!'—'And my home too, is it not?' she said" (71). Hope, "who had left a palace in England," translates the "native song" as easily as she translates the isolated "rustic dwelling in the wilderness" into home (71). Unlike the Indian Princess of sixteenth- and seventeenth-century iconography that figured America as primitive, fertile, and available, Hope is an Indian-Columbian hybrid.[57] Bethany Schneider argues that Sedgwick's first novel *A New England Tale* (1822) "proposes that belonging to and being of this particular land is the prize for those white people who can read its special sacred status. . . . Indigeneity in a sacred landscape, like salvation, is conferred in a moment of passionate recognition."[58] Part of Schneider's point is that recognizing this strategy allows us to read an "Indianless novel as an Indian novel," but when Sedgwick employs a similar strategy in her explicitly Indian novel, Magawisca's original presence never fully allows Hope to achieve white indigeneity.[59] Although Hope easily becomes the novel's substitute for Magawisca, a move that subdues the threat of interracial marriage posed by Magawisca and Everell's adolescent attachment, this act of substitution also forever marks Hope as once removed from the natural law written on Magawisca's heart.[60]

Hope's triumphant entrance following the Bethel massacre marks the beginning of the end of the potential romantic attachment that the novel suggests has been developing between Magawisca and Everell. This potential attachment is one example of the ways that Sedgwick's narrator uses her readers' instincts against them through willful acts of diegetic misdirection.[61] The narrator first describes Everell and Magawisca together as "no unfit representatives of the people from whom they sprung" (22). Physically representing the best of their respective races, Everell and Magawisca appear to be a natural pair. This appearance is soon confirmed by the development of an intimate friendship that does not go unnoticed by their guardians. In one of the two letters included in the first volume, Mrs. Fletcher warns her husband: "two young plants that have sprung up in close neighbourhood, may be separated while young; but if disjoined after their fibres are all intertwined, one, or perchance both, may perish" (33). Given that Mrs. Fletcher's "vague forebodings" and "fearful thoughts" of Indian attacks are quickly fulfilled, her speculations about Everell and Magawisca also promise to come true. Later in the novel, Digby confirms the reader's initial impression by recalling that Everell and Magawisca were once "as good as mated" (224). Everell replies that he "might have loved her—might have forgotten that nature had put barriers between us" (224). An attachment that was once described as being as natural as two young plants joining fibers is later characterized as barred by nature.

Magawisca's friendship teaches Hope and Everell how to be American, and her timely disappearance at the end of the novel sanctions the democratic community founded by their union with a native blessing. What is less clear is why a novel that insists upon the morality of natural impulses would so deliberately mislead its readers' sympathetic instincts. In an era of historical writing defined by "a general consensus about essence, morality, progress, and national character," where "the most pervasive single assumption was the existence of moral law," what would it mean for a historical novel to make readers question their ability to read for this moral law, particularly when national identity is at stake in its recognition?[62] In his review of *Redwood*, Bryant argued that romances set in the past are easier to write than domestic tales set in the present: "In reading narratives of the romantic kind, our curiosity comes in aid of the author. We are eager to learn the issue of adventures so new to us. The imagination of the reader is also ready with its favorable offices. This faculty, always busiest when we are told of scenes and events out of the range of men's ordinary experience, expatiates at large upon the suggestions of the author, and, as we read, rapidly fills up the outline he gives with bright colors and deep shades of its own" (247). In *Hope Leslie*, readers' imaginations work against them, as the narrator's "outlines" and "suggestions" lead readers toward a fantasy of interracial marriage that is then emphatically described as unnatural. Readers are punished for the same desire they imagine Magawisca and Everell must feel for each other. Just as what happens on the frontier enables what can happen in the Winthrops' parlor, carefully disciplining readers' imaginations in the first volume prepares them to appreciate the necessity of Magawisca's disappearance in the second volume. But by using the conventions of romance writing to play with readers' feelings, the novel also denaturalizes appeals to sympathetic instincts by presenting the possibility that these appeals can be duplicitous rhetoric. If the historical romance gained legitimacy because of a national consensus about human nature, then Sedgwick's novel resists this standard by constantly undermining her readers' instincts about what is and is not natural.

Because Hope's arrival coincides with Magawisca's retreat, she becomes the figure who disciplines the reader's expectation that Everell and Magawisca are "as good as mated." Although Hope is a figure of unruly transgression, at the end of the novel, her transgressions have instituted a new order that seeks to banish figures like Jennet who do not have the appropriate natural impulses and to incorporate figures like Magawisca who do. Just as the American Revolution established a more natural government, by the end of the novel, Hope works to establish a democratic order founded in the good feelings of friendship and equality.[63] One of her final orders of business is to convince Magawisca to return to the white settlement. Hope once again tries to paraphrase Magawisca, promising "as you would say, Magawisca, we will walk in the same path, the same joys will shine on us, and, if need be that sorrows come over us, why, we will all sit under one shadow together" (349). In this final rhetorical battle of natural metaphor, Magawisca has the last word, replying "the Indian and the white man can no more mingle, and become one, than day and night" (349). Recognizing no difference between Puritan theocracy and Hope's democracy, Magawisca continues to resist efforts of inclusion that rest on assimilation. By refusing Hope's insistence that they can in fact "walk in the same path," Magawisca disrupts the process whereby sympathy naturalizes reformative discipline by making it appear to coincide with the reader's own feelings.[64] *Hope Leslie*'s opening premise that "the difference of character among the various races of the earth, arises mainly from difference of condition" is confirmed by the reader's sympathetic impulses but denied by the novel's resolution (4). According to Barnes, Sedgwick's novels are typical of the ways that antebellum domestic fiction domesticated the uncontrollable nature of sympathetic attachment that haunted early republican seduction novels: "Sympathy proves the golden rule of Sedgwick's domesticity . . . in converting the hapless protagonist of seduction fiction into a new and virtuous heroine, Sedgwick attempts to reform the role of sympathy itself—to teach by *positive* rather than by negative example."[65] In *Hope Leslie*, however, Hope's triumph over the authorities and her simultaneous adoption of their disciplinary language coincides with the narrator distancing herself from her heroine.

Magawisca's refusal of Hope's final request forces Hope to reveal the reformative agenda behind her appeal to good feelings, in turn reinforcing the novel's cyclical plot. Perhaps most troublingly, Hope, who once defended Magawisca's belief in the Great Spirit, now wishes "that a mind so disposed to religious impressions and affections, might enjoy the brighter light of Christian revelation—a revelation so much higher, nobler, and fuller, than that which proceeds from the voice of nature" (352). Hope also begins to speak the language of public good that she has resisted throughout the novel. When she asks Magawisca how she can win over her sister, still in captivity in the Winthrop mansion, Magawisca asks her "if any charm could win [her] affections from Everell Fletcher" (350). Hope, "summoning all her courage," "answered in a tolerably firm voice, 'yes—yes, Magawisca, if virtue, if duty to others required it, I trust in heaven I could command and direct my affections'" (350). Of course the reader knows that commanding and directing affections is precisely what Hope's attempt at disinterested matchmaking has demonstrated to be impossible. After Hope impulsively thrusts Esther and Everell together, although she is "exulting in her victory over herself," she actually has "put the happiness of all parties concerned in jeopardy," and Esther ends up feeling "cruelly, fatally injured" (225–226, 290). Hope's insistence that her sister should learn to "command and direct" her affections when "duty to others required it" sounds all too similar to the appeals to the greater good that throughout the novel have signaled the avoidance of superior moral claims. Governor Winthrop, for example, responds to Everell's outrage that Magawisca has been imprisoned with the reminder that "private feelings must yield to the public good" (245). When Hope meets her sister, the reader understands for the first time that the novel's heroine is capable of dishonesty. As Insko points out, Hope at last resorts to trying to bribe her sister with jewels, the same strategy employed by the villainous Sir Philip to persuade Magawisca to take Rosa into the wilderness.[66] This is not the first time in the novel Hope has acted the part of seducer. When Hope and Magawisca first meet, Hope zeroes in on Magawisca's primary vulnerability, her feelings for Everell. In turn Magawisca recognizes Hope as a force to be resisted: "'They tell me,' she said, 'that no one can look on you and deny you aught; that you can make old men's hearts soft, and mould them at your will'" (199). By coding Hope's persuasive charms first as the rhetoric of seduction, and then as the rhetoric of Puritan theocracy, Magawisca reveals the artifice behind Hope's benevolent democracy and disrupts the process of domestication that threatens to assimilate her.

Recognizing that Hope's appeals to sentiment at the end of the novel are in fact empty rhetoric—a symptom of her own secondhand knowledge of the natural law written on Magawisca's heart—allows us to read Magawisca's refusal to stay in the white settlement as resistance toward Hope's efforts to domesticate her rather than as evidence that she lacks the proper sentiment for domestication.[67] Hope tries to assimilate Magawisca by naturalizing consent through the good feelings of friendship, gratitude, and equality. By refusing Hope's invitation to join this new community, Magawisca insists upon a republican conception of citizenship grounded in consent, a concept that Hope's involuntary impulses work to erase.[68] In the years leading up to the Indian Removal Act, debates about American Indian citizenship reflected an anxiety about "the potentially anarchical implications of pure consensualism"; American Indians were denied citizenship not only because, like women, their lack of private property rendered them incapable of consenting to state protection, but also because of the dangerous implications of considering expatriation a natural right in a broader sense.[69] At stake in these debates were larger questions about national unity; as Priscilla Wald argues, "these cases call attention to the symbolic processes through which the United States constitutes subjects: how Americans are made."[70] Magawisca represents the right of individual dissent throughout the novel, as she refuses both the protection and the authority of English law. In her trial scene, for example, she declares, "I am your prisoner, and ye may slay me, but I deny your right to judge me" (302). Because we tend to read women's fiction as always making an argument on behalf of a liberal model of citizenship that argues for inclusion based on universal rights, it is easy to overlook moments when the assimilationist pressure of this citizenship is presented as a threat to be resisted.[71] As Lauren Berlant argues, "whether consensually or passively transmitted, national identity requires self-ablation."[72] For Magawisca, this "self-ablation" would mean assimilation. Magawisca's final farewell challenges the fantasy of belonging that is supposed to be at the center of the relationship between the sentimental novel and disenfranchised readers, as her insistence that "the Indian and the white man" are as fundamentally different as "day and night" resists the trajectory toward sameness that defines sympathetic identification.[73]

By constantly challenging its readers' sympathetic instincts, *Hope Leslie* critiques the cultural agendas disguised by the essentializing naturalism of discourses like domesticity and exceptionalism. Magawisca's decision to leave the settlement might force Hope's hand, exposing her as just another version of the Puritan patriarchs she eclipses, but it also forces Magawisca to serve as the source of the very values claimed by the American exceptionalism that romanticized Indian removal as essential to the development of national character. Even as *Hope Leslie* denaturalizes gender difference, it continues the Romantic project of naturalizing culture, as it promises that fundamental American values—"death or liberty"—have always been and always will be available on the frontier. By idealizing Magawisca as the source of Hope's Americanness, the novel positions the Indian woman, rather than the white woman, as the figure whose natural proclivity for forming a virtuous national character necessarily excludes her from the corrupting interests of Griswold's "business and politics." Magawisca's voluntary disappearance fulfills the conventions of the Vanishing American by erasing the historical violence of Indian removal, but there is an additional potential for irresolution that her disappearance enacts. Although "that which remains untold of [her] story is lost in the deep, voiceless obscurity of those unknown regions," the fact that an untold story remains prolongs the fantasy of discovery (359). The American historical romance novel works to domesticate human nature into a force of national cohesion, but this act of domestication functions through an exclusionary principle that conserves nature's possibilities rather than as a colonizing principle that works to assimilate them. By refusing assimilation, Magawisca's legacy becomes raw material for the construction of national character, a natural resource whose availability must be guaranteed by her disappearance.

4
EPICENE GENIUS IN THEODORE WINTHROP'S *CECIL DREEME*

I ARGUED IN THE introduction that considering domestic fiction's fantasies of self-determination alongside the speculative mode of the romance affords new insights into how the trope of domestic retreat functions as a site for imagining practices of dissent and reaffiliation that are informed by the costs and benefits of political and social recognition. This argument took shape in the previous chapter's repositioning of Catharine Maria Sedgwick as a bridge between the traditions of domestic fiction and American romanticism. *Hope Leslie* intervenes in attempts to establish gendered literary traditions by reimagining domestic retreat as natural retreat, as the symbolic function of the marriage plot of domestic fiction is performed by the Vanishing American of romantic historiography. Sedgwick's settler-colonist romance of an Indian princess who rejects the obligations of assimilative sentiment preserves the possibility of dissent that marks the future community led by the novel's prophetic Anglo-Americans as bound by voluntary affection. While previous chapters have considered the varied possibilities for domestic retreat that are imagined in the early decades of the nineteenth century, this chapter considers the transportability of domestic ideology across unexpected social arrangements once its conventions come to be firmly established in the mid-nineteenth century. While Sedgwick resists the constraints of these conventions, in this chapter, I turn to an author who claims them to structure a Gothic plot of triangulated desire between three men. I consider the transgender capacity of Theodore Winthrop's novel *Cecil Dreeme* within nineteenth-century theories of feminine genius that considered gender to be one of many reactive polar elements that structure relationships. By the mid-nineteenth century, domestic ideology's expansive portability allows the transmasculine artist at the center of the novel to tap the aesthetic generativity of domestic retreat without being constrained by the gender hierarchy that plagues Charles Brockden Brown's "self-dependent" Jane Talbot or succumbing to the defensive nostalgia of *Salmagundi*'s bachelor-editors. Paradoxically, as domestic ideology strengthens and congeals over the course of the nineteenth century, its protections become more accessible to those willing to conform to its structuring conventions. In turn, the retrospective narrative voice of *Cecil Dreeme* stages confrontations with an encroaching social sanction that renders the distinction between self-determination and social convention impossible to determine.

One of the first times I taught Theodore Winthrop's novel *Cecil Dreeme* (1861), a student recounted her experience of reading the final chapters. She was finishing the novel on a plane on her way home from a spring-break trip and "gasped aloud" when she read the novel's final plot twist. I was bemused by this response. To me, a reader well-indoctrinated in the codes, scripts, and genre conventions of nineteenth-century novels, there is nothing surprising about *Cecil Dreeme*'s ending. But the pleasure this student took in her surprise also made me wonder about the reading experiences the novel encourages. What possibilities had this reader remained open to that my own "expert" reading had shut down? The secret that is revealed at the end of *Cecil Dreeme* is that the main character, Robert Byng, has previously known the titular character as Clara Denman. For my student, this secret was both enabling and disappointing: because it is a secret, most of the novel reads as the undisguised story of a romantic relationship between two men, but when the "truth" of Dreeme's identity is revealed, those queer possibilities are potentially shut down, as Byng's attraction to a man is explained by the fact that Dreeme is a woman. But the novel is not particularly interested in hiding the "truth" behind Dreeme's identity. Hints are constantly dropped for the reader, and every character other than Byng immediately recognizes that Cecil used to be Clara. This renders the "reveal" at the end of the novel anticlimactic in the sense that not much changes in the relationship between Dreeme and Byng. Byng continues to refer to Clara as Cecil even as he professes that he "knew" Cecil was a woman all along. In other words, the reading experience of the novel does not mark either me or my student as a bad reader: "Clara Denman and Cecil Dreeme were one. This strange mystery was clear as day."[1] There is a "mystery," but it is a mystery that is "clear as day."

The previous chapter argued that our critical narratives of *Hope Leslie* have been determined by the expectations for moral earnestness Sedgwick's nineteenth-century contemporaries established for women's writing, a legacy that follows from early national projects like *Salmagundi* that defensively distinguished between termagant moralizing and bachelor whimsy. The association of femininity with genius the *Salmagundi* editors defensively reacted to relegates feminine genius to natural impulse and selectively establishes the imitation of the feminine as the marker of true genius.[2] In *Cecil Dreeme* we can see the generative effects of this appropriative availability of femininity. Rather than a repressed cause of anxiety, the nineteenth-century understanding of gender as performative is itself an appropriative yet generative reaction to the essentialist notion that women might have more direct access to genius. In *Cecil Dreeme*, even the supposed presentation of the material reality of the body does not overpower the trappings of gender: if "sex and its responsibilities" can be "restored" simply by "womanish drapery," then these surface trappings, and the genders they establish, can be repeatedly shed and restored (244). In turn, as femininity becomes firmly associated with performance, that performance is one that can be successfully or poorly performed by any body, including individuals who are expected to effortlessly perform what they already understand themselves to be. In this sense, domestic ideology's gender binarism is not reinforced but constrained by appeals to material embodiment that limit its universal applicability. In *Cecil Dreeme*, the separate spheres model has become so firmly entrenched that it organizes even Dreeme and Byng's queer domestic partnership: much like binary gender, the reductive simplicity of the separate spheres model is also its strength, as it can expand to accommodate any partnership willing to follow its rigorous conventions.[3] In *Cecil Dreeme*, an understanding of gender as a portable surface allows Dreeme to escape the conflation of medium and media that plagues the female artist. As a "strange" and "weird" woman "without beauty," Clara Denman's "so fair a soul" is trapped in a corrupted "medium"; as a man, the "somewhat epicene character" of Cecil Dreeme's work allows him to achieve "that fine something called Genius" (61, 4, 61, 206). Rather than a biological imperative, Dreeme's reclusive domestic retreat is seen as a symptom of his eccentric "artistic temperament," which "does not love to bustle about in the crowd, to shoulder and hustle for its facts" (145). This anonymity afforded by Dreeme's domestic retreat means his art is granted the status of original genius rather than being seen as autobiographically reflective.

By rendering the "strange mystery" at its center "clear as day," the novel encourages us to see Dreeme's history as private, but not secret. In turn, *Cecil Dreeme* places new demands on a reader accustomed to looking below and within for scandalous truths, particularly if the pursuit of that truth assumes that gender and sexuality are fixed traits that hold the key to identity. *Cecil Dreeme* opens with twenty-six-year-old Robert Byng newly returned to New York City after a ten-year sojourn in Europe. The impressionable orphan is immediately greeted with questions about his future from his friend Harry Stillfleet: "'Why then haven't you been five years at the bar, or ten years at the desk? Why are you not in command of a clipper ship, or in Congress, or driving an omnibus, or clearing a farm? Where is your door-plate? Where is your wife? What school does your eldest son go to? Where is your mark on the nineteenth century?'" (6) Although these questions are asked in a playful tone that mocks the pressures of Young Americanist reproductive futurity, the novel is written in the tradition of early national seduction novels, where the future of the young republic is tied allegorically to the marital choices of young, impressionable citizens. By the end of his first night on shore, Byng's "dual nature" is torn between two equally mysterious and magnetic men:

Densdeth, a villainous Wall Street speculator, and Dreeme, a virtuous and reclusive painter (43). Byng learns that his childhood companion Clara Denman has drowned on the eve of her forced marriage to Densdeth and eventually he half-heartedly begins a courtship with Clara's sister Emma. Although Winthrop is most often positioned in relation to "every queerly resonant text in the canon of white male authors of the later nineteenth century," the novel also follows from a broader tradition of domestic fiction's plots of young, impressionable protagonists, about to embark on period of social reproduction, torn between forces of corruption and virtue.[4] Like his literary predecessor Eliza Wharton of *The Coquette*, Byng's friends watch nervously as he ignores their warnings and insists that he can experiment with Densdeth without becoming ruined: "I let him bite, and clap on an antidote before the brain is benumbed" (147). The central villain of the novel, Densdeth is a blackmailer who gains power through the cynical assumption that everyone has something shameful to hide: "He revealed evil everywhere. That was at the core, according to him, however smooth the surface showed. Power over others consisted in finding that out" (127). Although Byng is tempted by the power Densdeth promises, he also attempts to resist the blackmailer's "riper cynicism" (39). A little more than halfway through the novel, Byng recalls his thoughts while observing the mysterious Cecil Dreeme: "And every moment fancies drift across my mind that I actually know his secret, and am blind, purposely blind to my knowledge, because I promised him when we first met that I would be so" (149). *Cecil Dreeme*'s retrospective first-person narrative structure attempts to create for the reader the opposite position of the blackmailer—the very specific position of refusing to know what you know. This tension accounts for the strange effects of Byng's retrospective narration, as his determination to remain "purposely blind" to Dreeme's history means the reader is provided with a similar opportunity to acknowledge Dreeme's history without allowing that history to determine their narrative expectations.

Cecil Dreeme's narrative logic shifts between a reflexive pursuit of knowledge and a kind of intimacy that does not require disclosure. These polar shifts do not mark either position as inevitable or stable, but as mutually reactive, and generative of the narrative movement between discovery and mystery.[5] Although *Cecil Dreeme* is a relatively understudied text, most scholarship attends to it as structured by the logic of paranoia that is traditionally associated with Gothic fiction.[6] Given that the central villain of the novel is a blackmailer, this approach makes sense. As Eve Kosofsky Sedgwick puts it in her influential account, "In the Gothic view . . . individual identity, including sexual identity, is social and relational rather than original or private; it is established only ex post facto, by recognition."[7] For Sedgwick, the relational understanding of identity leads to the homophobic panic that is fundamental to the Gothic genre: "blackmailability" is a symptom of the condition that "no man must be able to ascertain that he is not (that his bonds are not) homosexual."[8] In what follows, I argue that *Cecil Dreeme* borrows from the Gothic a "social and relational" understanding of identity but eschews the paranoia that accompanies this understanding. As a generic corollary to domestic fiction's use of the affectionate marriage plot to allegorize modern ideals of consent and individualism, the antiquated settings, depraved villains, and supernatural possibilities of the Gothic tradition are read as symptoms of repressed anxieties about the ways that tyranny and irrationality reinvent themselves in the enlightened world.[9] While domestic fiction is understood as underwriting modern individualism, Gothic fiction is understood as threatening the coherence of the individual. *Cecil Dreeme* attempts to reconcile a Gothic understanding of identity as "social and relational" with the desire for self-determined individualism that undergirds domestic fiction's affectionate marriage plots. Influenced by the dominant scientific and philosophical theories of its time, the novel thinks of these two seemingly irreconcilable positions as polar rather than oppositional. Even as the novel thinks of identity as reactive, it also sees this reactivity as a source of creative self-invention. Accordingly, it imagines a middle ground of public privacy as a retreat from the transactional publicity of the club and the imprisoning domesticity of the home, where a shared vulnerability to influence can be experienced as generative rather than a weakness to be exploited.

One of the most dominant strains of nineteenth-century philosophy and physical science, polarity understood the world to be composed out of the interaction of polar forces. For writers such as Julia Ward Howe and Margaret Fuller, polarity had particularly important implications for understanding gender. As Lara Saltz describes it, "using the magnet as a model, nineteenth-century writers believed that each pole of such opposing pairs as subject and object, masculinity and femininity must be understood as distinct, while at the same time indivisible from each other, for one implies and engenders the other."[10] This meant that all individuals had masculine and feminine tendencies within that were drawn out in proportion to interactions with other individuals. Because masculinity and femininity were distinct but equal qualities, gender hierarchy was the result of social convention rather than nature. *Cecil Dreeme*'s marriage plot is particularly unwieldy precisely because it imagines gender difference as one difference among many rather than the primary difference that determines and organizes relationships. *Cecil Dreeme* imagines individuals as repositories of potential tendencies—femininity and masculinity, evil and virtue, introversion and extroversion—that are activated proportionally through encounters with other individuals. While Brockden Brown struggles to consider how the marriage plot might resolve the seemingly incontrovertible hierarchy of sexual difference, *Cecil Dreeme* considers gender difference as one of many polar oppositions rather than a primary, fundamental difference. In this way, the novel imagines the viability of multiple combinations of characters across genders. These different relations include men and women being "imprisoned for life in matrimony," but also "opposites" who "neutralize each other"; an "explosive" kind of "repulsion," where the "weaker" is "utterly consumed away"; and the kind of "combinations" that reflect "the exquisite order and proportion" of Nature that Byng observes in his chemical laboratory (40, 133, 151).

At the beginning of *Cecil Dreeme*, the narrator claims affectionate marriage as a marker of a progressive, democratic society: "These are not the days of forced marriages" (5). By the end of the novel, he has learned his mentor's Foucauldian correction: "Moral pressure is more despotic than physical force" (5). What remains for self-determination once desires are shown to be activated externally? This knowledge brings with it the liberating subversiveness of the universalizing position. But for a subject like Byng who remains invested in affectionate marriage as a marker of a progressive democratic society, the sudden realization that an attraction you thought to be intimate, private, individualizing might in fact be perfectly conventional also threatens to bring with it a renewed interest in weaponizing identity as idiosyncratic, rooted within. As I discuss below, this tendency is brought to bear most punishingly on Emma Denman, who betrays the conventions of feminine virtue Byng idealizes in his partnership with Cecil Dreeme and dies a spectacularly Gothic death as a fallen woman. Although most existing criticism of *Cecil Dreeme* attends to it in the tradition of queer Gothic fiction, here I explicitly consider the transgender capacity of the novel, particularly in relation to the question of what room is left for self-determination in a polar understanding of identity. Transgender studies think of the body as a site of physical agency while remaining attentive to the limits of that agency. The body is not circumscribed by some kind of biological reality, but it is read and interpreted following social conventions.[11] In its conclusion, *Cecil Dreeme* offers a grim reminder of the fact that Byng's understanding of identity as activated relationally does not inevitably lead to a universal liberation from social convention. I will return to this insight below, as I consider how the novel uses race to police the moral boundaries of gender fluidity.

The novel's polar understanding of traits, including gender, as universal tendencies makes transgender studies particularly generative for considering the character of Cecil Dreeme.[12] David J. Getsy defines "transgender capacity" as "the ability or the potential for making visible, bringing into experience, or knowing genders as mutable, successive, and multiple." Much like the polar understanding of desire and attraction imagined in the novel, where individuals are repositories of competing desires that are activated in response to and in combination with other individuals, Getsy emphasizes that "capacity" is aligned with "potentiality," something that "may lie in wait to be activated." For Getsy, the potential for transgender capacity to "be an unintended effect" that "may emerge at any site where dimorphic and static understandings of gender are revealed as arbitrary and inadequate" is useful for countering charges of anachronism from those who seek to erase transgender lives from the historical record.[13] This definition complements early American approaches to gender and sexuality that highlight the contingent and relational understanding of these concepts in the eighteenth century before the imposition of sexology at the end of the nineteenth century would congeal sexual practices and gender identities into the heteronormative taxonomies we recognize today.[14] As critics of *Cecil Dreeme* frequently note, the novel might be read as melancholically mourning this looming foreclosure of possibilities through Byng's ambivalent reaction to Cecil Dreeme being exposed as Clara Denman.[15] Notably, however, the novel is not structured around the narrative convention of the "reveal" that often "regulates and corrects gender noncompliance." As Danielle M. Seid puts it, "Structuring an audience's knowledge of a character's transgender status as a reveal can contribute to the perception that living a transgender life involves concealing 'the truth' of sexed bodies."[16] But because Cecil Dreeme's history as Clara Denman is an open secret in the novel, the moment when Cecil is "revealed" to be Clara does not use "shock and revulsion" to confirm that Cecil is "really" Clara. Instead, Byng continues to refer to Cecil and to use masculine pronouns through the final pages of the novel. Counterintuitively, out of the novel's understanding of gender as one of many in a collection of universal polar tendencies emerges an understanding of gender as a trait that remains stable within relational units, unaffected by the trappings of dress or public address. Because polarity is a logic of binarism, the novel reproduces the gendered structure of domestic ideology, but because it understands individuals themselves to be governed from within by this binarism, masculinity and femininity are understood as universally held and socially reactive potentialities.

OTRANTOISH: THE PUBLIC PRIVACY OF CHRYSALIS COLLEGE

A novel that opens with the exclamation "Home!" is an apt novel for a project on domestic retreat (1). This first "Home!" refers to the United States, as Byng returns from his prolonged absence in Europe, and the contrast between the domestic and the foreign is reiterated as Byng embraces his native "vernacular" rather than continuing the imported "idioms" of other affected travelers.[17] The novel's opening chapters are characteristic of the novel as a whole in its swings between paranoia, the comic deflation of that paranoia, and the sinking recognition that paranoia was perhaps justified after all. When the hotel servant announces he has a visitor, Byng immediately wonders if it is Densdeth: "Not Densdeth already! . . . I fear I should think it a little ominous if he appeared at the threshold of my home life, as my first friend in America. Bah! Why should I have superstitions about Densdeth? Our intimacy on board will not continue on shore" (2–3). This suggestive inner monologue immediately alerts the reader to an ongoing "intimacy" with Densdeth that is only feebly assured to be over now that they have arrived back in the United States. But the next exchange also presents a strikingly comic adaption of the "paranoid Gothic" convention of mental transparency Sedgwick has identified.[18] After considering the possibility of Densdeth's appearance, Byng next wonders if his visitor is his friend Henry Stillfleet: "He cannot help being wide-awake. He used to wear his beard *a la* three-moustache mode. His appearance as my first friend would be a capital omen" (2). The visitor is indeed Stillfleet, who announces himself as though he has read Byng's mind: "'Here is he, wide-awake, three moustaches, first friend, capital omen.'" In this exchange, Byng's thoughts seem to be immediately accessible and readable, but this transparency is a sign of friendly intimacy rather than vulnerability.

The next few chapters involve Byng securing his lodging in Chrysalis College, a financially precarious institution that has started renting rooms to "several artists, a brace of young doctors, one or two quiet men about town" (11). The novel's descriptions of Chrysalis College—"sham convent, sham castle, modern-antique affair"—continue the opening scene's oscillation between Gothic foreboding and a modern mocking of Gothic conventions (10). Stillfleet tells Byng not to be misled by its "grimmish aspect": it is "not a jail" and it is "not an Asylum" (10). But he also can't help but suggest there are mysterious secrets harbored within: "No lunatics, *that I know of*, kept there, nor anything mysterious, guilty, or out of the way" (my emphasis). He offers a similarly suggestive answer to Byng's questions about a bolted door in the back of his chambers that leads to an "Otrantoish" "dark room." The door, it turns out, leads to a room kept by Densdeth:

> "Densdeth," I repeated, aware of a slight uneasiness. "What use has he for a dark room?—here, too, in this public privacy of Chrysalis?"
>
> "The publicity makes privacy. Densdeth says it is his store-room for books and furniture."
>
> "Well, why not? You speak incredulously."
>
> "Because there is a faint suspicion that he lies. The last janitor, an ex-servant of Densdeth's, is dead. None now is allowed to enter there except the owner's own man, a horrid black creature. He opens the door cautiously, and a curtain appears. He closes the door before he lifts it. Densdeth may pestle poisons, grind stilettos, sweat eagles, revel by gaslight there. What do I know?"
>
> "You are not inquisitive, then, in Chrysalis."
>
> "No. We have no *concierge* by the street-door to spy ourselves or our visitors. We can live here in completer privacy than anywhere in Christendom. Daggeroni, De Bogus, or Mademoiselle des Mollets might rendezvous with my neighbor, and I never be the wiser."
>
> "Well, if Densdeth is well bolted out of my quarters, I will not pry into his." (16–17)

This conversation introduces Byng to the principle that informs the homosocial domestic space of Chrysalis College, as Stillfleet enflames the very suspicion he claims the tenants are protected from. Professing a respect for privacy, Stillfleet can only imagine nefarious activities being protected by that privacy, and he conjures into being a Gothic space of illicit depths where all are vulnerable to exposure. For Stillfleet, a respect for privacy is a euphemism for an internalized paranoia that is projected suspiciously onto others.

Although there is a teasing undertone to Stillfleet's suggestive hints, as he characterizes Byng as a heroine in a Gothic novel—"What are you afraid of, Byng?" "Your voice certainly trembled"—as we learn in the final chapter of the novel, Densdeth's dark room is indeed a space of terror, as it becomes the scene of Emma Denman's ruin and suicide, a tragedy that Dreeme, looking back, wishes he could have averted by asking "what use Densdeth made of his dark room" (15, 231). But Chrysalis College is also a space of homosocial pleasures, of "mild orgie[s]" and sexual puns, oyster roasts and collaborative studios (105, 110). The "public privacy" of Chrysalis College is a hybrid space of multiple affordances: it is public in the sense that it is not a fully enclosed home, but rather a series of "den[s]" housed within a private institution (9, 15, 44, 75, 111, 252). The men who rent these rooms do not perform domestic labor; they either go out for meals or have them sent up by the janitor's wife. It is a more private space then, say, the cruise-y Chuzzlewit Inn where Byng is plied with drinks or the club where Densdeth gossips over billiards, but it is also a space where residents might be "lurking" and "leering" "through the key-hole" (196). Still, the individual privacy of each resident of Chrysalis College is mutually assured by all of the other residents, and this "public privacy" allows for a kind of domestic community. The isolation Byng might otherwise face is made clear by the comically dismal listings of temporary residences available to single men in the city:

> Lodgings for a single gentleman of pious habits.
>
> Fine suite of apartments to let. N. B. Dodsley's Band practices next door, and can be heard *free of expense*, at all hours of day or night.
>
> Parlor and bedroom over Dr. Toothaker's office in Bond Street. Murderers, Coroners, Banjoists, and District Attorneys need not apply. (23)

Unlike these miserable alternatives, Chrysalis College offers comfort rather than shame, to invoke Michael Warner's description of queer counterpublics: men in danger of starvation are rescued by concerned neighbors; artists whose studios have flooded are provided temporary work spaces; those who have been corrupted by the blackmailer's cynicism can find a redeeming sociality.[19] Although Byng, contemplating the "wretched" "mean" "dreary" public square in front of the college concludes, "Outdoor life offers no temptation. I am forced inward to indoor duties and pleasures," those indoor pleasures are the "people" within (30–31). As I consider in my next section, rather than a "middle distance of male homosocial desire" that reactively attracts the forces of detection, it is more useful to think of Chrysalis College as a space characterized by what Elizabeth Maddock Dillon has called "open sociality," by which she means "a space for the creative configuration of subjectivity."[20] The "public privacy" of Chrysalis College is not a space that shores up and protects an authentic, immutable, private identity, but a space where those private identities are formed and re-formed in relation to public encounters.

A POSSIBLE COUNTERBLAST

The opening descriptions of the domestic space of Chrysalis College allows for a distinction to be drawn between sociable intimacy and shameful secrecy. That this distinction is always on the verge of collapse is reinforced by Byng's attraction to both Densdeth, the unscrupulous blackmailer, and Dreeme, the virtuous recluse. Describing both of their effects on him as "magnetic" (the novel uses a variant of the word "magnet" eleven times), Byng's desire for Dreeme and Densdeth is charged by his relationship with each's counterpart: Densdeth brings out Byng's "cynical side" and "rotten spots" that in turn need Dreeme as a virtuous and reformative "counterblast" (2, 35, 27, 29). During Byng's first day on shore, even before meeting Dreeme, upon simply viewing his nameplate on the door to his rooms in Chrysalis College, Byng fantasizes about him as a "possible counterblast to Densdeth." At dinner that same evening, as Byng is again lost in a speculative reverie aroused by Dreeme's nameplate, Densdeth's "faithless and cruel" laugh interrupts and "seemed to strike at the romantic interest I had felt in the name Cecil Dreeme" (39). When Byng first meets Dreeme later in the evening following his encounter with Densdeth at dinner, he indeed serves as the "counterblast" Byng imagined: "Instantly the wound of Densdeth's cynicism was healed" (109). Byng's competing attraction to Densdeth and Dreeme is sustained throughout the novel, until Densdeth is finally murdered by one of his victims at the end of the novel. Mournfully pondering Densdeth's beautiful corpse, Byng is overcome by "a strange sense of indolence," as he faces a life without the struggle and uncertainty that he understands to be the very "business of life" (240). When Byng mournfully considers Densdeth's corpse, he says the quiet part out loud, eulogizing Densdeth as a "quiet form" possessed by an "unrestful spirit," "a being who to every other man was the personification of that man's own worst ideal of himself" (241). Here the sodomite blackmailer is declared to be an empty form wholly constituted by other men's fears about themselves. Articulating the very knowledge the Gothic is traditionally assumed to repress, Byng's self-conscious understanding of the panic exploited by the blackmailer also allows him to develop alternative responses. Although the blackmailer thrives on the threat of exposing private secrets that would irrevocably fix identity, the blackmailer also highlights the constructed nature of this public knowledge, as public exposure is what threatens to determine identity, not the secret itself. The cynical blackmailer recognizes the universal potential for sin and thrives on the paranoia this universal potential generates. This Gothic structure has other affordances, however, particularly for a chemist like Byng, well versed in nineteenth-century theories of polarity that understand individuals to be constituted by the same polar logic that organizes the natural and the social world.

Byng's movement between Dreeme and Densdeth, and the narrative inertia following Densdeth's death, suggest that rather than a one-directional model where the sexual possibilities of Chrysalis College are the repressed cause of a paranoid reaction, the domestic retreat shared by Byng and Dreeme is also created in response to the blackmailer as a space to counteract the isolating paranoia that only enables the paralyzing threat of publicity. At first the Densdeth plot seems to map itself cleanly onto Sedgwick's theory of Gothic sexual panic and the paranoid reading practices it engenders. At dinner his first night on shore, Byng has dinner at the Chuzzlewit Inn, where he is plied with drinks from men who have offered him employment. Soon Densdeth also sends a drink and watches him with a look that Byng "interpret[s]" as saying "'Young man, I saw on the steamer that you were worth buying, worth perverting . . . How much more have I to pay'" (35)? As Byng stares into the drink Densdeth has sent, which has become "symbolic" of whether he will "resist" and remain his "own man" or "yield and become "Densdeth's," he ponders Densdeth's strange power over him: "When his eyes are upon me, I feel something stir in my heart, saying, 'Be Densdeth's! He knows the mystery of life.' I begin to dread him. Will he master my will? . . . Why has he been trying to turn me inside out all the voyage? Why has he kept touching the raw spots and rotten spots in my nature?" As critics have noted, it is certainly useful to read this fear that his "rotten spots" are immediately accessible by Densdeth as sexual panic.[21] But rather than succumbing to the panic Densdeth engenders with homophobic repression and heteronormative policing, Byng attempts throughout the novel to resist Densdeth's cynicism by remaining "purposely blind" to the secrets of others, particularly Cecil Dreeme.

Following this fraught dinner at the Chuzzlewit, Byng finally meets the man behind the doorplate and has the opportunity to practice a kind of domestic care that counters the fear of intrusion Densdeth inspires. When Byng first encounters Dreeme, he is dying from a lack of domestic care. When the college janitor, Locksley, tells Byng he has not heard from Dreeme all day, after a lengthy debate about when an invasion of privacy might be justified, they decide, as it is a "a case of life and death," they will "break in" (74). As Locksley and Byng travel through Chrysalis College to Dreeme's apartment, the institution takes on its full Gothic potential: what seemed "unreal and incongruous" "by daylight" has become "an actual place, not mere theatrical scenery," and "Chrysalis passed very well for a murky old castle of the era of plots, masks, poisons, and vendetta" (82). For Byng and Locksley, the suspense of what they might find as they "stole into the tacit chamber" with "unlawful noise" is directly linked to the gravity of invading Dreeme's highly prized privacy (84). Once they enter the apartment to find not a corpse but a neighbor in need of food and warmth, domestic comfort banishes the Gothic potential of the scene back into the realm of theater. This shift from Gothic suspense to domestic comfort parallels Byng's determination that he "was not committing the impertinence of trying to force a man to live who had wished to kill himself" but instead was rescuing Dreeme from "unwholesome solitude" (89). In this respect, Dreeme's "determined withdrawal from the world" shifts from being a right to be respected at any cost to a damaging obsession. Byng returns to his apartment for more supplies and is amused to think of himself as a "walking tableau," "with my antique branch of six lighted candles on one hand, the mass of shining drapery on my arm, and in the other hand the glass, flashing with the red glimmers of its wine" (95). Byng's perspective of himself as a character in a Gothic drama has shifted to something comical, easily dispatched with an earnest sociability.

While Gothic fiction, particularly the tradition of the female Gothic, is understood as reimagining the domestic as a space of imprisonment and terror, *Cecil Dreeme* domesticates the Otrantoish institution of Chrysalis College into a space of neighborly care and sociability.[22] Byng's decision to invade Dreeme's private chambers becomes an opportunity to investigate the mysterious artist's inner character by studying his face while he is unconscious. Byng's drawn-out account of his first glimpse of Dreeme's face continues the novel's preoccupation with privacy and publicity. The ambivalence Byng feels toward the power he holds over Dreeme as he examines his face links this moment to physiognomy, the influential nineteenth-century pseudoscientific discourse of surface and depth. Even as the United States understood itself as progressing away from arbitrary aristocratic hierarchies to a mobile society of self-determining individuals, there was also a regulatory interest in reading innate character traits on the body (a regulatory interest that, as we will see in the next chapter, was firmly grounded in racist essentialism). As Christopher Lukasik has established, the study of physiognomy in the early United States ultimately worked to relocate character away from "the voluntary performances of an individual to the involuntary and immediately visible features of the face."[23] Domestic fiction explicitly invites considerations of interiority, not only through its preoccupation with the private home but also because its affectionate marriage plots encourage readers to evaluate characters by their inner virtues. Physiognomy simultaneously carries both domestic fiction's promise that what is most authentic lies within and Gothic fiction's terror that this inner truth can be read on the surface—that the "rotten spots" of the soul are immediately legible to those like Densdeth who traffic in unseemly secrets.

A seeming adherent to the tenants of physiognomy, Byng, when he is first left alone with the vulnerable and unconscious Cecil Dreeme, claims to be unable to "doctor [Dreeme] intelligently without feeling the pulse of his soul by studying his face" (89). But this recognition that the soul can be read on the face also leaves Byng wary of crossing the line from care to trespass. Left alone with the unconscious Dreeme, Byng "stopped intentionally short of a thorough analysis of his countenance": "Curiosity urged me to study the face more in detail. But that seemed disloyal to the sleeper. . . . He was not dead, that I should dissect him. While a face can protect itself by the eye,—which is shield to ward, to parry, and point to assail,—one feels not much scruple in staring. But what right had I to profit by this chance lifting of the visor of a disarmed man, who wished to do his battle of life unknown?" (90). Here Byng registers the potential for the face to be a site of both deliberately dissembling performance and inadvertently transparent authenticity. He also imagines an alternative to the options of looking away and intrusive detecting, as he determines to observe but not dissect.[24] Although Byng claims he resists his curiosity and leaves Dreeme undissected, he goes on to draw a distinction between "a thorough analysis" and "general impressions": "It is error to waste the first look and the first few moments, if one wishes to comprehend a face,—to see into it. No after observations are so sharp and so unprejudiced." Byng describes Dreeme's face, but only so far as to relay his initial impression that "this was a man of another order, not easy to classify" (91). Dreeme's mysterious face only points to the existence of more mystery within. This moment dramatizes what Lukasik has termed the "physiognomic fallacy": in practice, physiognomy "created the very faces it claimed to interpret."[25] Here, however, physiognomy's circular logic, which uses physical features to substantiate preexisting suppositions, is used only to affirm Byng's desire to allow Dreeme to remain a mystery. Byng does not overcome the physiognomic fallacy, but he uses its discourse to deny its classificatory schemes. As Lukasik puts it, "Instead of discerning character from the face, [physiognomy] merely collapsed the difference between the two." Similarly, Byng concludes "the face and the facts were consistent, and both faithful to their mystery." Byng borrows from physiognomy the power it grants the viewer to invent the face that conforms to preexisting determinations of character, but only to preserve the mystery of Dreeme's history. Rather than immobilizing Dreeme as a particular type, the "impression" Byng relays is of simultaneity and movement, "of a vigorous mind, controlling varied and perhaps discordant elements of character into unison" (90).

Byng examines Dreeme's unconscious face only long enough to determine that Dreeme's mysterious face reflects a mysterious interior, which Byng chooses to let remain a mystery: "I resolved never to open my eyes, to shut them even to any flash of suspicion of his secret that any circumstance might reveal" (111). Although the promise of mystery attracts and encourages detection, the novel avoids this kind of tantalizing suspense by rendering Dreeme's secret so obvious.

Byng reads Dreeme in the same way he reads his nameplate, as "not precisely evading, but certainly not inviting notice" (30). Byng's determination to look away from what he might already know about Dreeme does not mark this history as a shameful secret. We might see Dreeme's gender transitivity as simply a plot device that allows the novel to safely express Byng's repressed desire for men.[26] Once Dreeme's "true identity" is "revealed," Byng's attraction to him can be explained by the fact that he was a woman all along. In this reading, gender works with the logic of repression, as its strategic performance temporarily enables the safe expression of hidden queer desires. Alternatively, remaining open to the transgender capacity of the novel allows us to see that Byng's determination to remain "purposely blind" to Cecil's history does not only need to be read as a symptom of his own repressed desires. Rather than not wanting to see Cecil as Clara because of his own repressed desire for men, we might also understand Byng's refusal to recognize Cecil as Clara as simply accepting that Clara is Cecil. Even as physiognomy's character studies deemphasized "voluntary performances" in favor of "involuntary and immediately visible" physical features and can thus be aligned with so-called gender critical perspectives that claim the "truth" of biological sex will always tell, it is precisely in granting the power to determine character to the prejudiced viewer that physiognomy also must acknowledge the fabricated nature of the features it claims to read.[27]

Disrupting the paranoid logic of the Gothic tradition in queer studies, this understanding of vulnerability to social readings as a universally shared condition rather than an effect of idiosyncratic dishonesty or illicit secrecy allows Byng to remain open to examination himself. Dreeme regains consciousness as Byng is kneeling at his feet covering him with a satin robe. Remarkably, Byng allows himself to be examined in the same way that he tried to resist examining Dreeme: "All at once, as, kneeling, I was arranging this robe of state about Dreeme's feet, I became conscious, by I know not what magnetism, that he had opened his eyes, and was earnestly looking at me. . . . I kept my head bent down, and let him examine me, as I felt that he was doing, with hollow, melancholy eyes" (95). Despite the unsettling effects of Densdeth's probing magnetism during dinner earlier that evening, Byng allows himself to remain vulnerable to Dreeme's examination. Counteracting the transactional publicity of the dining room at the Chuzzlewit Inn, the domestic retreat of Chrysalis College affords a different kind of intimacy. Although Byng, unlike Dreeme, is conscious for this examination and has some agency over how he will be recognized—"as a friend, at a friend's work"—this attempt to equalize vulnerability leads to its own pleasures. While we might certainly locate the novel's most explicit sexual energies in Byng's "perverse" desire to be "dominate[d]" and "conquered" by Densdeth, it is equally true that he seeks Dreeme when he needs to be "aroused and healed" (147, 160).[28] The final chapter detailing Byng's first encounter with Dreeme is titled "A Mild Orgie," and describes the oysters Locksley brings back to roast over the fire. This "mild orgie" is as suggestive as one might think, but both the overtness and the mildness of their restorative revelry also pokes fun at the reader who aims to uncover scandal, as Byng reminds Locksley that Stillfleet once teasingly warned the janitor about the orgies the new tenant, indoctrinated into corrupt European practices, might introduce to Chrysalis College (21). Locksley and Byng's entry into Dreeme's apartment is presented as an act of neighborly care rather than intrusion. The five chapters that describe their intervention celebrate the affordances of privacy while maintaining a distinction between privacy and secrecy. The most immediate affordance is the indeterminate nature of the sex acts and gender identities involved in this "mild orgie." The jumbled imagery of Locksley presenting Dreeme with an oyster's "calcined lips, invitingly parted" that has been "done to a bulge" augments Byng and Dreeme's reciprocal gender ambiguity (107).[29] Even as Dreeme is described as "a man of another order, not easy to classify," Dreeme thanks Providence for sending him Byng, "a gentleman whose touch to mind and body is fine and gentle as a woman's" (103). Thus Dreeme's gender does not necessarily register as a symptom of the novel's repressed queer desires—instead, Dreeme's gender is no more mutable or mysterious than any other character's gender.

IN-DOOR MEN

The question of how to read the character of Cecil Dreeme in this novel is complex, in part because of the expansive ways people living in the mid-nineteenth century understood gender and sexuality. As Jen Manion's research into the so-called female husbands of the transatlantic world of the eighteenth and nineteenth centuries demonstrates, it is difficult to determine the precise motives behind people who were assigned female at birth who came to live as husbands in partnerships with women.[30] Clara Denman is described from the start of the novel as gender nonconforming, so the novel does tentatively imagine that acts of cross-dressing and gender transitivity do not only stem from pragmatic concerns like economic or political opportunity but also from what readers today might refer to as gender identity. *Cecil Dreeme* does not neatly conform to the looming imposition of twentieth-century sexology that associates gender nonconformity with same-sex desire.[31] It is never implied that Clara desires women—it is more accurate to say that Clara begins to live as a man and as another man's wife. Rather than a female husband, Cecil is a male wife. Eventually, Dreeme and Byng fall into a relationship structured by the private-public divide of domestic ideology, with Dreeme serving as the private moral corrective to Byng's public life.[32] Dreeme lives as both a man and as another man's wife, as Byng assigns Dreeme the "unmasculine office" of being his "in-door man":

> "I often feel, now, as I stir about among men, collecting my budget of daily facts, that I only get them for the pleasure of hearing your remarks when I unpack in the evening." . . .
>
> "Yes, Dreeme, your fresh, brave, earnest character I begin to regard as my guardian influence. With you I escape from the mean ambitions, the disloyal rivalries, the mercenary friendships of men,—from the coarseness, baseness, and foulness of the world. You neutralize to me all the evil powers." (146–147)

The transgender capacity of the novel expands beyond Dreeme to characterize Byng as well: although when he is in public, his interactions with Densdeth position Byng as an ingenue in danger of being seduced, when he is with Dreeme, Byng takes on the role of a world-weary husband in need of recuperative domesticity.[33]

Although Byng's description of his relationship with Dreeme reproduces the typical gender roles of domestic ideology, Dreeme's virtue is not seen as linked to his sex, but to his artistic genius. Dreeme's position as the private, moral corrective to Byng's public life is directly tied to what Dreeme characterizes as his own "artistic temperament," which "does not love to bustle about in the crowd, to shoulder and hustle for its facts" (145). As a man, Dreeme's domestic retreat is portrayed as an eccentric choice rather than a biological or social imperative, just as his profession of painter authorizes his femininity and renders it nonsuspect. In turn, Dreeme's artistry is granted the status of genius precisely because his femininity is seen as a primary but partial element of his character: "the feminine element is largely developed in you, as a poetic artist" (171–172). In previous chapters we have seen that because nineteenth-century theories of romantic genius understood the feminine to be an essential element of genius, women's aesthetic production was relegated to natural impulse. For men, however, the imitation of the feminine was seen as a crucial aspect of their genius. As Rufus Wilmot Griswold puts it in his anthology *The Female Poets of America* (1848), "It does not follow, because the most essential genius in men is marked by qualities which we may call feminine, that such qualities when found in female writers have any certain or just relation to mental superiority."[34] As Eliza Richards notes, "by naturalizing the feminine to the domain of the woman's body—her womanliness—Griswold neutralizes its potential to fuel genius." In turn, nineteenth-century romantic poets—Poe being the primary exemplar—theorized that "male poets must transform themselves into theatrical women if they wish to be geniuses" (39).[35] Although *Cecil Dreeme*'s art of choice is visual rather than lyric, its careful consideration of the aesthetic generativity of gender performance is clearly informed by the theories of romantic lyric that Richards discusses. Even before meeting Dreeme, Byng reads the nameplate on his door and speculates about the kind of artist his neighbor will turn out to be: "a man in force, but with the feminine insight,—one whose labor is love, one whose every work is a poem and a prayer?" (30) The ideology that aestheticizes women's domestic labor as loving impulse is here reconstituted to account for Dreeme's artistic production. Domestic ideology's expansive portability allows Dreeme to achieve the autonomous pleasures of domestic retreat without being constrained by the gender hierarchy that plagues Charles Brockden Brown's "Literary Wife." Additionally, it is only as a man that Dreeme's "feminine insight" grants him the status of genius, as this feminine proximity to genius is seen as artful performance rather than natural impulse.

Clearly preoccupied with the aesthetic potential of domestic retreat and the feminine element of aesthetic production, the novel returns repeatedly to descriptions of the art that the reclusive Dreeme produces and its usefulness as a means of revealing the inner self, particularly when that inner self is understood to be indistinguishable from gender. A conversation among a group of artists who happen to view one of Dreeme's sketches continues the novel's interest in debating the expressive and performative aspects of private identity. The artists first discuss more generally the potential for a portrait to capture a subject's true self. Even as portraiture has the potential to capture someone's "immortal soul," sitting for a portrait is also akin to being "probed and flayed": if a subject has something "to be ashamed of lurking in my heart," the artist "would drag it out, and set it inexorably in full view" (204–205). This conversation seems to align portraiture with the blackmailer's ability to see straight through to his victim's "rotten spots." Much like physiognomy, nineteenth-century theories of portraiture allow for the possibility that external appearances are expressive of a subject's authentic and fixed inner self. But as Sarah Blackwood demonstrates in her study of nineteenth-century portraiture and psychology, nineteenth-century literary portrayals of portraiture are equally preoccupied with the potential for aesthetic representations of external appearance to create rather than express interiority: in their "recursive" as well as their "revelatory" potential.[36] It is precisely this recursive potential that is dramatized when the artists turn to a sketch by Dreeme that Byng has accidentally left "exposed" and only "half covered" (205). The sketch, set in a French chateau, portrays a "dark-haired lady" "with her back to the spectator" sitting at a table with Densdeth styled as "that demon" Robespierre, while figures resembling Byng and Locksley look on (153). It is obvious to the reader that the "dark-haired lady" in the sketch (who also happens to wear a yellow satin garment that resembles the coverlet Byng brought to Dreeme on the night he rescued him) is Dreeme, and given the conversation that has preceded the artists viewing Dreeme's sketch, the reader is primed to understand that this portrait will in fact reveal the "truth" of Dreeme's identity:

> "It is a new hand," said I, "what do you think of it?"
>
> "She has great power, as well as delicacy," said Pensal,—the others waiting for him to speak.

> "She! Who?" I asked.
>
> "The artist."
>
> "Odd fancy of yours! It is a man."
>
> "What! and paint only a back view of a woman? I supposed that being a woman, as the general handling too suggests, she took less interest in her own sex; or, on the other hand, fancied that she could not represent it worthily."
>
> "O no!" said I. "He had no female model."
>
> "Probably," said Towers, "he is too young to have a woman's image in his brain, which fevers him until he wreaks it on a canvas." (206)

Although the earlier conversation focused on what could be gleaned about a subject's interiority from a portrait, while this conversation focuses on what can be learned about the artist, the reader understands that the sketch is a self-portrait: in discussing the artist, the critics are in fact discussing the subject. This complex framing confirms the reader's knowledge of Dreeme's secret, but the conversation among the artists only serves to highlight the multiple interpretive possibilities that follow from a recursive understanding of physical expression. Notably, the artists' heteronormative assumption about the artist's gender does not follow from an examination of the subject's face as studies of nineteenth-century portraiture and physiognomy would lead us to expect, but instead is inferred from the fact that the subject's face is *not* visible. Unlike the opening conversation among the artists, which theorizes portraiture as discovering and revealing an inner truth, the conversation about Dreeme's sketch demonstrates that in practice, portraiture, and the interpretive practices it encourages, produce this inner truth. As Blackwood puts it in her reading of Hepzibah's famous scowl in Nathaniel Hawthorne's contemporary novel *House of the Seven Gables*, "the external appearance . . . calls the inner state into being. The scowl emphasizes the recursive nature of expression, and indeed, of inner life itself: the way in which psychology is made, not found or expressed."[37] The conversation among the artists takes this recursive understanding of portraiture one step farther: unlike Hepzibah's scowl, which is a physical symptom of her chronic nearsightedness that is *given* expressive meaning, here the artists don't even require physical features to read the expression of gender. Just as the novel plays with physiognomy's tendency to invent the features it claims to interpret as evidence of inner character, here it similarly adapts the conventions surrounding portraiture to dramatically draw out the assignment of interiority as a social process of invention.

Even as gender is considered to be fundamental to the identity of the artist and to the work the artist produces, the determination of the artist's gender is imposed onto the painting entirely from without, as the absence of a woman's face leads the critics to determine that the artist is a woman. At first it seems that Dreeme's attempt to hide his identity has only led the artists to uncover exactly what he has tried to hide—sex will always tell—but Byng, as he does consistently throughout the novel, deflates the import of this "discovery" by simply dismissing the notion that Dreeme is anyone other than who he claims to be as an "odd fancy." At first the conversation moves away from considering the painting itself to heteronormative speculations about the artist's method (he had no female model) and biography (he is sexually inexperienced). Thus the rigid system of binary gender easily transposes itself to resolve the initial gender confusion and explain why the painting does not objectify a feminine subject. But the conversation concludes with the lead artist proclaiming, "Man or woman . . . and I confess it seems to me to have a somewhat epicene character, it is a very promising work" and determining that "Fame waits him. Here is that fine something called Genius." Even as the scene confirms what any introductory gender studies class will teach, that gender identity, rather than being expressive of an authentic inner self, is a social imposition, by returning to the idea that the portrait has an "epicene character," the conversation among the artists also uses nineteenth-century theories of genius to praise art that expresses an ideal of gender indeterminacy. Readers who have heeded Byng's descriptions of Dreeme understand that rather than acquisitively claiming access to the feminine, Dreeme's art achieves genius because it expresses an inner self that is only ever "of another order, not easy to classify." The conversation concludes reiterating an expressive notion of gender, but the gender that is expressed is one that enables multiple interpretive possibilities.

It is precisely the looming threat of "Fame" that leads to the novel's frenzied conclusion. In the novel's final chapters, Byng is not so much forced to confront the "truth" about Dreeme in a conventionally regulatory conclusion as to reckon in public with his knowledge of Dreeme's history. The final five chapters move at breakneck speed as Byng races to rescue Cecil, who Densdeth has recognized as Clara and holds captive in an asylum. Although this final chase and rescue scene might be read as devolving into a kind of hyperheterosexual camp, even in these final chapters that would appear to discipline the novel's unwieldy queerness, Byng musters only tenderness and regret toward the murdered Densdeth, and despite learning the "truth" about Clara Denman, he continues to refer to "Dreeme—for so I must call him" through the final scene of the novel (246). Although "each of us felt the awkwardness of our position," there seems to be a quiet adjusting to how this new knowledge will affect their relationship, a movement toward "this strange new joy" (245). During the carriage ride back to Chrysalis College, Byng and Dreeme move back and forth between intimacy and withdrawal:

> Thinking thus, I let fall Cecil's hand, and drew apart a little. . . .
>
> But thinking of what might start up between Cecil Dreeme and me, and part us, I let fall the hand I held.

> "No, Robert!" said Cecil, reaching out that slight hand again, and taking mine. . . .
>
> . . . She would have withdrawn her hand. I held it closer than before. (253–256)

As they reenter Byng's room in Chrysalis College, Byng "smiled to notice the masculine effect of her crisp curling black hair. She perceived my feeling, and smiled also. A quiet domestic feeling seemed to grow up between us. I busied myself in reviving the fire from its ashes. Cecil sat silent. Neither was yet at home in our new relation" (258). This newfound domestic quietude is also a scene of potential and adjustment: a "new relation," a fire revived, a home in need of reinvention.

As the domestic ideal expands to incorporate Byng and Dreeme, their world potentially shrinks to accommodate its encroachment. Byng has loved his friend "as one loves a woman," but "now that the friend proved a woman," Byng worries that his love is forced, externally imposed, doubting, and incomplete: "Every moment it came to me more distinctly that Cecil Dreeme and I could never be Damon and Pythias again. Ignorantly I had loved my friend as one loves a woman only. This was love,—unforced, self-created, undoubting, complete. And now that the friend proved a woman, a great gulf opened between us" (253). The paranoia engendered by the blackmailer is precisely what has rendered Byng's "blindness" a purposeful choice. Once Densdeth and the exposure he threatens has been dispatched, Byng's virtuous life with Dreeme is no longer an eccentric alternative, but a conventional certainty. Byng's discomposure is the same that unsettles our critical reading—we, like Byng, are unsure if his desires have been informed by convention all along.[38] As we shall see, a polar understanding of masculinity and femininity as distinct yet indivisible does not render gender conventions any less powerful, as the same structuring conventions that lead Byng and Dreeme to domestic quietude lead Emma Denman, Cecil Dreeme's sister, to her death. However, Byng's retrospective narration also allows him to reconstitute Emma as his own double rather than a poor substitute for the queer partnerships he desires. Reinforcing only the perversity of compulsory heteronormativity, Emma's spectacular fall also functions to highlight the affectionate virtue of Byng and Dreeme's newly conventional partnership.

"SHE WHOM I SHOULD HAVE LOVED"

Following Dreeme and Byng's moment of domestic quietude, the novel has one last monster waiting in the wings. The Gothic returns in a doubling of the Mild Orgie, as Byng, belatedly receiving a suicide note from Emma Denman confessing her involvement with Densdeth, grabs a mace, "a terrible weapon, with its head studded with spikes, and rusty with old stains" from "a suit of ancient armor," and breaks down the door to Densdeth's dark room (262). This time around Byng's intrusion into private chambers does indeed unearth a corpse, the "pale, dead face" of Emma Denman (263). The Gothic collides with the domestic in spectacular fashion, as the final line of the novel finds Byng and Dreeme committing to "their life together" in front of Emma's corpse. In this final scene, the rigid price the portability of domestic ideology exacts within the Gothic genre becomes clear, as Emma is violently expelled for betraying its strict standards of feminine virtue. The relational notion of gender identity the novel develops out of its interest in polarity and magnetism allows for queer domestic partnerships and feminine geniuses, but it also highlights the interdependence of evil and virtue, paranoia and blindness, cynicism and naivety. For the virtuous Dreeme, domestic gender ideology's correlative properties of rigidity and portability are saving and generative. For Emma, who expertly wields the power of knowledge and publicity Densdeth offers, the correlative nature of these properties is lethal. Emma's confession and death in Densdeth's dark room confirms Byng's reluctance to marry her as a correct choice—in death, the fallen woman serves as the Gothic guarantor of a right to self-determination that is only ever withheld from her.

Byng's determination to resist what the novel repeatedly characterizes as the seductive cynicism of the blackmailer prolongs the pleasures of his domestic partnership with Dreeme and attempts to maintain a distinction between privacy and secrecy, vigilance and paranoia, security and shame, witnessing and surveilling. These distinctions, of course, are always on the verge of collapse. In keeping with Byng's characterization of himself as "susceptible to every touch and breath of influence," "of identifying myself with others," his perspective as a narrator and the interpretive lessons he draws are not always consistent (23, 78). Although Byng's retrospective narration re-creates his determination to remain "purposely blind" to Dreeme's history, he has a more difficult time resisting the suspicion he feels towards Emma Denman. Emma's character consolidates the confusion the novel expresses about the impossible distinction between convention and individuality, as Byng tortuously laments, "It was she whom I felt that I did not love, and yet ought to love" (160). When a family friend of the Denman sisters implies that Emma is doomed to a life of sin because her mother's soul was corrupted when she was born, Byng resists the "old dead dogma of original sin" (58). But Emma does indeed fulfill this prophecy, as she dies a fallen woman. Although Emma, from birth to death, serves to establish the individual autonomy of others, her own fate is predetermined by an inheritance she is born into.[39] In this way, Emma remains a grim reminder of the fact that Byng's understanding of identity as activated relationally does not inevitably lead to a universal liberation from social convention.

Emma potentially comes to serve the function of what Sedgwick has called the "the sexually pitiable or contemptible female figure," as Byng projects panic about his queer desires onto her.[40] Emma's father quickly makes it known that he would like to have Byng as a son-in-law. But Byng struggles to feel as he should for Emma, held back by a vague "suspicion" that he in turn attributes to Densdeth's cynical influence:

> My heart was free from any love of woman.
>
> And my doubt was based on a suspicion.
>
> A suspicion! Of what?
>
> If I at all stated to myself, however faintly, what, it seemed to me such disloyalty that I despised myself for entertaining the unwholesome thought.
>
> "You are not fit," I said, "for the society of a pure woman! Densdeth has spoilt you." (168)

This passage, of course, clearly demonstrates that Byng's reluctance to pursue Emma is coded with his own illicit desire, from the winking claim "my heart was free from any love of *woman*" to its tentative and impenetrable style. After much hesitation, Byng finally decides to "perversely" "do violence to an unerring instinct" to prove that he remains unaffected by Densdeth's "doctrine, that women and men only wait opportunity to be base" (160–161). Just as Byng's fate is about to be irrevocably determined with a proposal, he catches Emma and Densdeth sharing "a laugh and a look":

> I cannot describe this look of hers. I do not wish to. It is enough to say that it told me of a dishonorable secret between the two. It told me that at this moment, however it might be in a mood of stronger self-possession, she felt no compunction, no remorse, no agony, that such a secret existed,—nothing but an indolent acquiescence in the treason.
>
> And this was the interpretation of so much mystery. This justified my instinctive suspicions. This punished my generosity and my resolve to quell the warnings of nature. This explained the inexplicable. (188)

From this look, Byng concludes that his worst suspicions of Emma are correct, and his "suspicions" are reconstituted as "instinctive" "warnings of nature," as his "inexplicable" lack of desire for Emma is explained and justified by her moral corruption. In turn, Byng's desires for Dreeme are naturalized by aligning them with the very instincts that warn him away from Emma, instincts that he "perversely" tries to ignore (161).

Byng seems to have internalized the blackmailer's cynicism, as he immediately assumes that the secret between Emma and Densdeth is "dishonourable." But here again the retrospective perspective is important: just as looking back allows Byng to demonstrate his determination to remain "purposely blind" to Dreeme's history, it also allows him to question the uneven deployment of this purposeful blindness, as he comes to remember Emma as a victim of convention, much like himself. Byng belatedly determines that Emma attempted to resist the pressure to make a match at least as much as he does: "With me she seemed always eagerly striving that I should not misapprehend her, always protesting against some possibility of a false impression" (164). We can also see that a mutual attraction to Densdeth positions Emma as Robert's double rather than Densdeth's poor substitute. Both Byng and Emma are described as being torn between the illicit pleasures promised by Densdeth and a more virtuous and conventional option. Byng describes his own interest in Densdeth as being motivated by a desire for knowledge for "the perilous as well as the safe among my race. . . . I find Densdeth a most valuable preceptor. He has sounded every man's heart, in life or history, and can state the depth of evil there in fathoms, feet, and inches" (147). He also cautions us "I was to pay a price for my knowledge. . . . My danger with evil personified, in such a man as Densdeth, was to sear into me a profound and saving horror of evil" (127). This language mirrors his impression of Emma: "I was terrified sometimes by her keenness of insight into bad motives, her comprehension of the labyrinthine causes of bad acts. It is a perilous knowledge. We must pay price for power. How had she bought this unerring perception of the laws of evil?" (167). Rather than simply confirming that Emma is unsuitable for Byng because of her sinful nature, the novel suggests that Emma and Byng are elementally similar in their desire for the knowledge and power Densdeth promises. Imagining repulsion as a prospect for people of different genders but similar characters, the novel's polar logic hypothesizes that if gender difference is one of many differences rather than a primary difference, then it is also not a strong enough difference to organize all relationships.

Domestic fiction is traditionally understood to construct heteronormative desire as a site of agency through affectionate marriage plots between individuals of similar moral characters. Byng's retrospective narration disrupts this aim, but the novel's emphasis on character also risks eliminating sexual desire entirely. Byng attributes his reluctance to marry Emma to a problem of character and attributes his affection for Dreeme to their perfectly complementary masculine and feminine tendencies. The novel celebrates Dreeme and Byng's chaste domestic partnership and portrays Densdeth, the primary force of physical desire in the novel, as a deviant temptation to be resisted. In turn, the conventions of domestic gender ideology appear to repeatedly surpass embodied presentation. The dramatic irony of Byng wistfully imagining Emma as "her own sister self" or that his relationship with Dreeme might be sanctioned by a marriage to his sister renders the virtuous Dreeme more divinely feminine than his sister Emma (160, 172). While Dreeme is "angelized" by gender indeterminacy, gender transgression leaves Emma a Gothic monster (159). These inconsistencies turn on the novel's fixation with race as an expressive trait that falls outside of its polar logic of reactive and transformational identities. The novel consistently returns to the body to establish racial difference. Densdeth's face is characterized by an "olive complexion," an "aquiline" nose, and "Oriental hues"; his voice by a "delicate lisp" and "Spanish softness"; and the "conscious air" of his dress betrays that he "desired to be flagrant" (41–43). Each of these physical racial markers highlights Densdeth's sexual deviance—his elegance, his lisp, his love of adornment. Nowhere is this highlighted more clearly than the novel's description of Densdeth's servant as an external reflection of Densdeth's own inner character: "He was an Afreet creature, this servant, black, ugly, and brutal as the real Mumbo Jumbo. Yet sometimes, as he stood by his master, I could not avoid perceiving a resemblance, and fancying him a misbegotten repetition of the other. And at the moments when I mistrusted Densdeth, I felt that the Afreet's repulsive appearance more fitly interpreted his master's soul than the body by which it acted" (34). As Travis Foster notes, even descriptions of the corrupted Emma's coloring, hair, and temperament are marked with racial indeterminacy. In this way, "whiteness lends social sanction to queer desire and gender indeterminacy."[41] In *Cecil Dreeme*'s use of racial contrast to establish the inviolate virtue of Byng and Dreeme's domestic retreat we see the more damaging affordances of the inevitably subjective and self-interested impulses behind Byng's descriptions of Dreeme's face, as Densdeth's villainy is not attributed to an inner sexual deviance but to a racial indeterminacy that will always reveal itself through external features. The novel's self-conscious use of discourses of surface and depth suggests that even though physical features will always "tell," what they tell is preexisting determinations of character. While this logic is used to counter readings of Dreeme that watch for involuntary signs expressive of an authentic inner gender, it is used to establish race as an immutable and expressive trait.

Shawn Michelle Smith has shown that nineteenth-century discourses of visual representation, like the portraiture and physiognomy that *Cecil Dreeme* repeatedly returns to, worked in concert with domestic ideology to imagine racialized interiority. Building on studies of domestic fiction that establish that gender comes to replace class, as affectionate marriage plots encourage readers to consider interior character rather than superficial lineage, Smith connects domestic ideology and nineteenth-century visual culture's shared preoccupation with interiority to argue that the middle-class woman idealized by domestic ideology comes to stand in for a kind of racial purity that mimics the very aristocratic bloodlines domestic fiction originally reimagined as gendered differences of character.[42] Whereas *Cecil Dreeme* uncertainly negotiates the encroaching expectations a socially legible domestic partnership imposes, in the next chapter, we will see Harriet E. Wilson take this ambivalent critique one step further. Wilson's experimental novel-narrative *Our Nig: Sketches from the Life of a Free Black* (1859) highlights the fragile nature of the authority separate spheres ideology claimed to grant women who performed domestic gentility and the ways that this ideal relied on the racialization of domestic labor. Rather than calling for a future when a transcendent domestic ideal is universally inclusive, Wilson explicitly takes up domestic retreat as a position that appeals to interiority only to shore up whiteness.

5
TRACKING HARRIET E. WILSON'S SPIRITUALIST VISIONS

THROUGHOUT THESE CHAPTERS we have seen authors experiment with the possibilities and constraints of an aesthetic theory that locates the source of genius within a domestic scene increasingly being imagined as feminine. For Charles Brockden Brown, who is writing during the transition when this ideal is being uncertainly established, a contractual hierarchy founded on feminine dependence troubles the fantasy of autonomy promised by domestic retreat. This unease leads Brown to experiment with literary genres that are not defined by narrative resolution or nationalist consolidation. The gendered literary conventions that emerge out of the attribution of aesthetic genius to domestic retreat lead Washington Irving and Catharine Maria Sedgwick to defensively showcase the artfulness behind the seemingly contradictory positions of masculine domesticity and feminine romanticism. As the binary conventions of domestic ideology become more established, they also become more transportable: by the mid-nineteenth century, Theodore Winthrop claims domestic retreat as a site of transgender capacity that can be sustained by the proper balance of gender polarity. In this final chapter I return to the question of labor that has proved so difficult for many of these authors to reconcile with the aesthetic promise of domestic retreat. It is precisely the pastoralization of household labor that leads to the idealization of domestic retreat as a position of intellectual and aesthetic freedom. Some authors, such as Brown, tentatively critique this conflation of the material and the spiritual as a means of concealing the artificial inequality of the sexual contract; others, such as Irving and Sedgwick, selectively position their own art against the unthinking conformity of termagant spinsters and Puritan housewives whose imaginations are confined to household management. As I now argue in this final chapter, there is a third alternative to these strategies of conflation and division that understands domestic and intellectual labor to be distinct but not antithetical. This third position is most forthrightly claimed by the subject of this final chapter, Harriet E.

Wilson's radically experimental novel-narrative *Our Nig; or, Sketches from the Life of a Free Black* (1859).

The previous chapter argued that Theodore Winthrop's novel *Cecil Dreeme* asks questions about what to *do* with knowledge, namely closely held secrets that seem to hold the key to private identities. The novel's retrospective narrative circles around the question of when the pursuit of knowledge becomes suspicion and when looking away becomes quietism. When does vigilance become cynicism, and when does a resistance to suspicion become willful ignorance? Are the sensual and aesthetic pleasures of domestic retreat a sufficient antidote to the dangers that must be ignored next door? In this final chapter we will see Harriet E. Wilson force readers to confront the question of when the position of not knowing is a purposeful and damaging fiction. Wilson repeatedly insists that readers who misinterpret her project as working to expose the violence of domestic retreat disingenuously protect a damaging fiction of an inviolate private sphere.

Wilson's novel tells the story of Frado, an indentured servant in New England. The daughter of a white woman and a Black man, Frado is abandoned by her parents out of financial necessity at the home of the Bellmont family when she is six years old. Frado is subjected to horrific physical abuse by Mrs. Bellmont and her daughter Mary and to the sympathetic but ineffectual interventions of Mr. Bellmont, the other children Jack, James, and Jane, and Mr. Bellmont's sister Aunt Abby. By the time her servitude ends, Frado is too physically weakened to support herself by her own labor. Following the rediscovery of the novel in 1982 by Henry Louis Gates Jr. and his authentication of Wilson's authorship, Barbara White confirmed many of the details in the text as autobiographical, including that Wilson spent her childhood working for the Haywards, a family in New Hampshire with ties to the abolitionist movement. Following the novel's publication, Wilson's son, who is named in the preface as Wilson's reason for writing, died in a poor house. Although *Our Nig* was not a financial success, Wilson goes on after its publication to be a successful entrepreneur and to advocate for improved labor practices and children's education through the spiritualist movement.

In the third chapter we saw that critical narratives of Catharine Maria Sedgwick's frontier romance *Hope Leslie* (1827) have been determined by the expectations for moral earnestness Sedgwick's nineteenth-century contemporaries established for women's writing. Expectations for authenticity are heightened for authors who approach slave narratives through the conventions of sentimental domestic fiction, a characterization that has traditionally been applied to Wilson's semiautobiographical novel.[1] Denied the protections of white womanhood, Wilson is free to conceive of imaginative production as a form of material labor and to reject the conventions of domestic and romantic fiction that require a performative discomfort with the financial implications of publishing. Wilson's preface immediately introduces her text as a financial experiment: "Deserted by kindred, disabled by failing health, I am forced to some experiment which shall aid me in maintaining myself and child without extinguishing this feeble life" (3). Although this financial endeavor is qualified as a means to support her child, the preface explicitly characterizes antislavery autobiography as a financial transaction: "I sincerely appeal to my colored brethren universally for patronage." This "conviction that writing was work" Hazel Carby identifies in the preface does not mean that Wilson does not challenge her readers: Wilson's text is not only a financial experiment, but a formal one as well.[2] Rejecting the expectations of realism placed on both domestic writing and slave narratives, the text that follows is a series of loosely connected sketches characterized by disorienting shifts in perspective and genre from which certain facts have been "purposely omitted." Wilson's preface points to the demands placed on autobiographical writing by the antislavery public sphere: assuring her potential patrons that she does not intend to undermine their fight against Southern slavery "by disclosures of its appurtenances North," Wilson claims to have "purposely omitted what would most provoke shame in our good anti-slavery friends at home." Wilson's emphasis on purposeful omissions does not call into question the truth claims of antislavery autobiographies, but instead recognizes their artful inventiveness.[3] The overt connection Wilson's preface draws between the material and the aesthetic emerges in carefully staged scenes that flaunt the creative artifice behind the transparent authenticity expected by consumers of slave narratives and women's writing.

Wilson's novel is part of a much larger constellation of Black authors who self-consciously negotiate the demands for authenticity and confession expected of them by nineteenth-century readers. While the conversion experience of sentimental fiction depended on readers imagining themselves as characters in pain, the slave narrative genre consistently returns to the question of how sentimental readers consume the experiences of enslaved people and how successfully sentimental reading bridges the gap between experiencing and witnessing. For example, in his *Interesting Narrative* (1789), a text foundational to the nineteenth-century slave narrative genre, Olaudah Equiano sharply transitions from listing the horrors he has witnessed in the West Indies to considering the accumulative effects of this description on his readers:

> In the preceding chapter I have set before the reader a few of those many instances of oppression, extortion, and cruelty, which I have been a witness to in the West Indies: but, were I to enumerate them all, the catalogue would be tedious and disgusting. The punishments of the slaves on every trifling occasion are so frequent, and so well known, together with the different instruments with which they are tortured, that it cannot any longer afford novelty to recite them; and they are too shocking to yield delight either to the writer or the reader. I shall therefore hereafter only mention such as incidentally befel myself in the course of my adventures.[4]

Equiano's address to his reader accomplishes three things we see adopted by Wilson in her novel decades later. First, just as Wilson suggestively alludes in her preface to "purposeful omissions," Equiano notes here that his narrative is editorially capturing only a fraction of the overwhelming racial terror taking place in the Atlantic world. Second, Equiano notes that these terrors he has documented are so "well known," the reader does not actually need his testimony to add to their store of knowledge. As I argue below, Wilson carefully documents the many knowing witnesses to her abuse who have remained silent but who certainly did not require her firsthand narrative to provide them with testimony. Third, Equiano calls out the reader's self-absorbed reactions to the accounts of violence that became a staple of the slave narrative genre: these accounts are both too "tedious" to afford any "novelty" and "too shocking to yield delight." These expectations of novelty and delight position Equiano's readers as passive consumers rather than the potential activists the slave narrative genre aimed to convert. It is precisely this failure of sentimental reading that Wilson makes her subject decades later, as she cautions her readers against expecting to take any "pleasure" from her "crude narrations" and presents the sympathetic characters her readers might align themselves with as complicit witnesses to her abuse.

Decades later, expert practitioners of the slave narrative genre like Frederick Douglass and Harriet Jacobs follow Equiano in questioning if the conventions of sentimental reading can lead to understanding. Douglass notes that he is "frequently asked how I felt when I found myself in a free State. I have never been able to answer the question with any satisfaction to myself."[5] At first Douglass seems confident in the connection between experience and imagination: "to understand it, one must needs experience it, or imagine himself in similar circumstances" (88). Inviting the reader to imagine themselves in increasingly fantastic situations, Douglass concludes his famous list of anaphoric similes with one final impossible condition: "let him be placed in this most trying situation,—the situation in which I was placed,—then, and not till then, will he fully appreciate the hardships of, and know how to sympathize with, the toil-worn and whip-scarred fugitive slave." Douglass characterizes sympathy not as a natural impulse, but as a response that must be carefully taught. Even as he holds out the possibility that his reader will "know how to sympathize," he also makes those conditions of knowledge impossible: only when the reader is placed in "the situation in which I was placed" will he "know." Harriet Jacobs prefaces her *Incidents in the Life of a Slave Girl* (1861) with a similar contradiction between her goal and what she knows to be possible: "I want to add my testimony to that of abler pens to convince the people of the Free States what Slavery really is. Only by experience can any one realize how deep, and dark, and foul is that pit of abominations."[6] While she aims to "convince" her readers of "what Slavery really is," the only condition that will lead to that understanding is "experience."[7] Following Equiano's characterization of his reader as desiring novelty and pleasure from his firsthand account of the horrors of Atlantic world slavery, Douglass and Jacobs hold open a gap between sympathy and knowledge, insistently withholding an element of their experiences from the reader's acquisitive appetite.

I spend some time on Equiano, Douglass, and Jacobs to highlight that Wilson is part of a much larger tradition of African American literature that purposefully considers the limitations of autobiographical writing and the exploitative tendencies of sentimental reading. While Equiano, Douglass, and Jacobs each negotiate these limitations and conventions from within their firsthand accounts, I argue that Wilson tries a different strategy—recognizing the artful craft that has always characterized the slave autobiography's rhetorical appeals, Wilson uses the overtly fictional convention of a third-person narrator to make the sentimental witness rather than her own suffering the subject of her narrative. Wilson's project is a complex one, as she offers a metacommentary on both Black women's authorship and white sentimental readership. Wilson turns her history with an abusive abolitionist family in New England into an allegory of sentimental readers. Making the sentimental reader the subject of her novel allows Wilson to spin free of the limiting expectations for Black authorship that are tethered to firsthand testimonials written to be consumed by white readers. Wilson does not use fiction to disavow her particularized history of physical abuse and racial terror, as she argues that only someone in her raced and gendered position could be a witness for the story she tells. But rather than making her interiority reading material to be consumed, Wilson turns the tables and makes her readers the subject of her narrative. Wilson claims a position of distinctly embodied authorship that does not transactionally grant readers access to her own interiority, but instead puts their own sentimental reading practices in uncomfortable proximity to the abusive members of the Bellmont household.

Despite the autobiographical elements of *Our Nig*, it is most often referred to as a novel. Wilson's text is a generic hybrid and includes elements of slave narratives, Gothic fiction, sentimental fiction, and seduction novels.[8] Although Wilson's protagonist, Frado, is an indentured servant living in New England, the terms of her servitude are dubious at best, and the narrative uses conventions of the slave narrative genre to criticize Northern labor practices and the racism of white abolitionists. As Carby argues, Wilson's text "can be most usefully regarded as an allegory of a slave narrative, a 'slave' narrative set in the 'free' North" (43). Cindy Weinstein has historicized the romantic critique of allegory within contemporary debates about labor and industrialization. As nineteenth-century literary culture was increasingly associated with a space of leisure insulated from the mechanizing labor of the factory, the allegorical mode was criticized for calling attention to the labor behind literary production. Wilson, of course, immediately challenges this expectation by explicitly presenting her novel as labor undertaken out of financial need. She also allegorizes sentimental reading practices that were most determined to erase the labor of fiction writing.[9] Wilson is uninterested in a literary mode that hides her own labor or that makes reading itself a labor-free experience. Foregrounding the labor behind sentimental conventions that allowed readers to maintain a position of innocent unknowing, Wilson makes visible the literary contrivance behind conventions read as authentic and transparent and in turn presents her own labor as valuable and skillful craft. Weinstein establishes that critiques of allegorical contrivance were often made using bodily imagery; discomfort with the allegorical mode was also discomfort with signs of an authorial body. Wilson contests these expectations by explicitly highlighting the financial motivation for her writing labor, making her authorial presence felt through jarring shifts in perspective, and locating both her own authorship and her protagonist's potential liberation in a distinctly embodied personal history.

Initially, criticism of Wilson's text was dominated by questions of how the combination of autobiography and fiction enables or hinders the achievement of authorial control and narrative coherence, terms that are often conflated with Wilson's own sense of self. In his introduction to the text, Gates argues that Wilson is "able to gain control over her materials more readily than her fellow black novelists of that decade precisely by adhering closely to the painful details of suffering that were part of her experience."[10] For critics such as Gates, there is an authentic self behind the narrative's dissembling fictionality, a self whose politics can be glimpsed both in the text's "silences and lacunae" and in moments of direct address when Wilson "abandons the mask of the storyteller."[11] I read *Our Nig* as challenging precisely this mode of reading that locates truth in an authentic interiority. The novel weaponizes Wilson's alienation from the protections and constraints of domesticity's fraught cultural power by fostering alliances through public performance rather than private confession.[12]

Critical projects that grant Wilson some authorial distance from her protagonist tend to portray the abjection of her fictional self as a trade-off—Wilson publicly exposes the violence of sentimental domesticity and gains the status of author by capitulating to sentimental reading conventions that commodify her own suffering.[13] In these readings, Wilson's project is compromised from the very beginning, as she is granted authorial creativity and inventiveness by trafficking in conventions that require an abstraction she can only achieve by distancing herself from the private and embodied suffering of her fictional self. Given that the text makes explicit that Mrs. Bellmont's reputation as a "right she-devil" is a matter of public knowledge in the community, it seems clear that Wilson does not simply seek to expose the violence enacted in the privacy of white houses (12). Crucially, the novel emphasizes that the violence of the Bellmont kitchen is an open secret within the family and the neighborhood. Rather than exposing the hidden violence of the Bellmont home's "kitchen scenes," the novel instead focuses on what the characters around Frado *do* with their knowledge of her suffering (37).[14] The text suggests that exposure cannot be the end goal and argues that "slavery's shadows" will continue to haunt a movement bolstered by disingenuous reading practices that consume matters of public record as private confessions (1). The final chapters present Frado as dependent on a community that is fully cognizant of her history with the Bellmont family: neighbors who curiously gossip about "the opinions Mrs. Bellmont would express" upon learning of Frado's conversion, the "watchful and friendly" Mrs. Smith, the doctor who notes that Frado's illness "commenced" under her time with the Bellmonts, the "two maidens, (old,)" who take Frado in for pay when it becomes necessary for "the public must pay the expense" of caring for her, and Mrs. Moore, whose husband had been "defrauded of his last means by a branch of the Bellmont family" (57–58; 64–68). All of these community members are knowing witnesses to the violence that has rendered Frado chronically ill and dependent on public assistance. In the penultimate paragraph the narrator sharply tells the reader that although "some part of her history is unknown," "enough has been unrolled to demand your sympathy and aid" (72). Rather than expressing a desire to keep veiled a shameful personal history, this jab at the sentimental appetite for intimate details and graphic violence is the final and most overt statement of a narrative strategy that redirects the reader's attention away from Frado's interiority to their own investment in confession and exposure. Suggesting that a method primarily motivated by exposure potentially obfuscates a rather obvious connection between violence and sentimental domesticity, Wilson's novel asks what new modes of protest and persuasion can be imagined that don't hinge on scenes of suffering or require us to continue looking below the surface to confirm what we already know.

KITCHEN SCENES

Unflinchingly describing the home as a scene of violent coercion and debilitating physical labor, Wilson's text disrupts liberalism's fetishization of privacy as the grounds for consensual citizenship and calls into question the kind of freedom that it supports, as the Bellmont family is morally bankrupted and disempowered by their indoctrination in the cult of domesticity. If sentimental domesticity functioned to "produce the freedom of the liberal subject through affective abundance and nonutilitarianism," Wilson's text shows that this nonutilitarianism also emerges as unconstrained socially unproductive power, as the "manifest enjoyment" Mrs. Bellmont takes in physical abuse renders Frado too weak to work and uninterested in Christian reform (37).[15] One of the most jarring effects of Wilson's combined use of slave narrative and domestic fiction is the physical violence that Frado endures in Mrs. Bellmont's kitchen. Traditionally domestic ideology has been understood as complicit in modern forms of discipline that emphasize self-regulation as part of a larger shift away from corporal punishment that in turn sets the Northern home apart from the Southern plantation. As Richard Brodhead argues in his Foucauldian account of "disciplinary intimacy," slave narratives, most famously represented by Frederick Douglass's, present whipping as "the scene of initiation into slavery."[16] Frado, however, is initiated into New England domestic servitude through whipping, as Mrs. Bellmont responds to Frado's tears of loneliness and exhaustion "by applying a raw-hide, always at hand in the kitchen" (18). The novel repeatedly demonstrates that the desire to maintain a private domestic sphere enables violence, as Frado is subjected to Mrs. Bellmont's physical and sexual abuse in the Bellmont's home, particularly the kitchen, and Mr. Bellmont is unwilling to intervene in his wife's domestic terror.[17] Presenting the man of the house as a cowardly sentimental operative and the woman of the house as a rapacious sexual predator, the novel flips the gender conventions of antislavery arguments that appeal to the sanctity of the domestic and refutes the underlying assumption of domestic ideology that if "women rule the earth, and all in it," the world would be a more just and moral place (25).[18]

The text formally questions the illusion of privacy through the narrative device of an autobiographical third-person narrator. Wilson shifts between the first and the third person, but predominantly writes about Frado in the third person. Wilson introduces her text as a partial recounting of events from "my own life," and the first three chapter headings are in the first person: "Mag Smith, My Mother," "My Father's Death," and "A New Home for Me," but the text itself, beginning with the first chapter, is written in the third person (3). The fourth chapter heading, "A Friend for Nig," adopts Wilson's own ironic pseudonym, "Our Nig," the name that is given to Frado by the Bellmont family. In the final chapter, the first-person returns, but the distance between narrator and Frado is maintained, as the narrator refers to "my narrative" and "Frado" within consecutive sentences (70). This device is most certainly an effort to counteract the ways that the antislavery public sphere commodified the private experiences of authors of slave narratives. Most accounts of Wilson's third-person autobiographical perspective focus on its implications for Wilson's relationship to her fictional self and her ability to gain control and authority over her personal history; I argue that this device actually redirects the reader's attention away from Frado's interiority to the reactions of those around her.[19] Wilson not only invents a fictionalized version of herself in the character of Frado but also a frequently omniscient narrator to tell Frado's story. The third-person narrator allows Wilson to imaginatively speak for other characters in her story, as she invents conversations and internal dialogue she would have no way of knowing if writing a purely autobiographical narrative.

One example of this redirection from victim to witness comes after Frado has been brutally beaten with rawhide and repeatedly kicked by Mrs. Bellmont.

The text does not detail Frado's reaction, but the reaction of the ineffectual sentimental witnesses of the household:

> As she expected, Mrs. Bellmont, enraged, approached her, and kicked her so forcibly as to throw her upon the floor. Before she could rise, another foiled the attempt, and then followed kick after kick in quick succession and power, till she reached the door. Mr. Bellmont and Aunt Abby, hearing the noise, rushed in, just in time to see the last of the performance. Nig jumped up, and rushed from the house, out of sight.
>
> Aunt Abby returned to her apartment, followed by John, who was muttering to himself.
>
> "What were you saying?" asked Aunt Abby.
>
> "I said I hoped the child never would come into the house again."
>
> "What would become of her? You cannot mean THAT," continued his sister.
>
> "I do mean it. The child does as much work as a woman ought to; and just see how she is kicked about!"
>
> "Why do you have it so, John?" asked his sister.
>
> "How am I to help it? Women rule the earth, and all in it."
>
> "I think I should rule my own house, John,"—
>
> "And live in hell meantime," added Mr. Bellmont.
>
> John now sauntered out to the barn to await the quieting of the storm. (25)

If Frado has "rushed from the house, out of sight," then the conversation that follows is Wilson's invention. This scene is most certainly a damning indictment of the cultural power accorded to white women through sentimental domestic ideology, as Mr. Bellmont refuses to interfere in his wife's domestic reign, power that is only granted as a trade-off for Mrs. Bellmont's powerlessness in the public sphere. Frequently gagging Frado so that her sympathetic allies in the household cannot hear her cries, the text enacts a perversely literal scene of the feminist rhetoric of the nineteenth century that conflated the silent slave with the disenfranchised white woman.[20]

As this scene makes clear, however, Mr. Bellmont is perfectly aware of Frado's suffering; it is only his investment in the ideology of separate spheres that keeps him from acting. Mrs. Bellmont's methods of binding and gagging allow Mr. Bellmont the illusion of maintaining a home characterized by consent rather than coercion, as he only infrequently and reluctantly asserts his power as the head of the household, power that threatens the fantasy of the domestic woman's authority and threatens to render visible the immense labor required to maintain a household.[21] The novel carefully ties Mrs. Bellmont's violence to the performative leisure required by domestic ideology, as her only domestic labor appears to be asserting her power over Frado: "It was her favorite exercise to enter the apartment noisily, vociferate orders, give a few sudden blows to quicken Nig's pace, then return to the sitting room with SUCH a satisfied expression, congratulating herself upon her thorough house-keeping qualities" (37). Additionally, the compartmentalizing and silencing enforced by Mrs. Bellmont allows Mr. Bellmont to pretend that he is powerless to stop acts that happen outside of his purview, as he "saunter[s] out to the barn" or, in another scene,

> left the house, as he usually did when a tempest threatened to envelop him. No sooner was he out of sight than Mrs. B. and Mary commenced beating [Frado] inhumanly; then propping her mouth open with a piece of wood, shut her up in a dark room, without any supper. For employment, while the tempest raged within, Mr. Bellmont went for the cows, a task belonging to Frado, and thus unintentionally prolonged her pain. (25, 20)

The casual violence of Mr. Bellmont's unintentionality is reiterated when he returns: "Just then Mr. Bellmont entered, and asked if Frado was 'shut up yet'" (21). It is not lack of knowledge that prevents Mr. Bellmont from acting, as Jack, who protests about Frado's treatment to his father, discovers: "He then imparted her situation to his father, who seemed untouched, till a glance at Jack exposed a tearful eye." Carefully portraying Mr. Bellmont's knowing sentiment as what must be "exposed," the scene suggests that the true secret to be revealed is not Mrs. Bellmont's domestic violence but the knowledge that informs Mr. Bellmont's policy of domestic nonintervention.

The Bellmont home is, of course, a direct critique of the fantasy of domesticity as imagined in Harriet Beecher Stowe's blockbuster novel *Uncle Tom's Cabin* (1852). Stowe's prevailing argument is that the domestic shelters a kind of transcendent morality and that the women who inhabit that realm might wield this private virtue to reform an unjust political sphere. This is presented most clearly in the chapter detailing the Bird household, "In Which It Appears a Senator Is But a Man," where what Lauren Berlant has called the "juxtapolitical" nature of sentimental culture is precisely demonstrated.[22] In this chapter, Mrs. Bird, who rarely "trouble[s] her head with what was going on in the house of the state" and rules her household "more by entreaty and persuasion than by command or argument" confronts her husband, Senator Bird, about his vote in favor of the Fugitive Slave Act.[23] Mrs. Bird, who only cares whether a law is "right and Christian" is rebuffed by her husband, who asserts, "'Your feelings are all quite right, dear, and interesting, and I love you for them; but, then, dear, we mustn't suffer our feelings to run away with our judgment; you must consider it's a matter of private feeling,—there are great public interests involved,—there is such a state of public agitation rising, that we must put aside our private feelings'" (69). Senator Bird's confidence in the distinction between public duty and private feeling is immediately thrown into crisis upon the arrival of Eliza Harris, fresh off her daring escape across the frozen Ohio River. Upon hearing Eliza's story, the senator, like his wife, children, and servants, can't help but surreptitiously shed a tear: "Our senator was a statesman, and of course could not be expected to cry, like other mortals; and so he turned his back to the company, and looked out of the window, and seemed particularly busy in clearing his throat and wiping his spectacle-glasses, occasionally blowing his nose in a manner that was calculated to excite suspicion, had any one been in a state to observe critically" (73). Unlike Mr. Bellmont, whose secret tear marks him as privately sympathetic but unmoved to act, Senator Bird immediately breaks the law he has just voted for and transports Eliza to safety, even going so far as to suggest that Mrs. Bird give Eliza's son the clothes of their own recently deceased child. In the world of Stowe's novel, witnessing Eliza's pain converts Senator Bird from someone who "scouted all sentimental weakness" in his support of "state interests" to someone who actively breaks the laws of the state to accord with the laws of his heart (77). Like magic, witnessing Eliza's pain makes a theoretical fugitive real: "The magic of the real presence of distress,—the imploring human eye, the frail, trembling human hand, the despairing appeal of helpless agony,—these he had never tried." The directness with which Wilson revises this scene is remarkable. The Bellmont home is an incubator for violence and abuse rather than sympathy and right feelings, where the man of the house uses the model of separate spheres not to patronizingly pretend that his wife's feelings are irrelevant to politics, but to permit himself to ignore his own private feelings toward the suffering taking place in his home. Rather than being converted by witnessing suffering, Mr. Bellmont simply leaves. Where Senator Bird needs to see Eliza's suffering to understand the harm of the Fugitive Slave Act, Mr. Bellmont has all the information he needs, but simply refuses to act.

Whereas the conceit of Stowe's novel is that readers simply do not know, Wilson's novel asserts that this lack of knowledge is a pretense. Tellingly, James claims "Mother pretends to think she don't know enough to sorrow for anything; but if she could see her as I have, when she supposed herself entirely alone, except her little dog Fido, lamenting her loneliness and complexion, she would retract" (42). Even as James tries to set his sentimental perspective apart from Mrs. Bellmont's based on his recognition of Frado's interiority, an interiority that Mrs. Bellmont "pretends" not to recognize, his characterization of Mrs. Bellmont's attitude as pretense admits that the recognition of Frado's suffering does not prevent violence, and in fact seems to provoke it, as Mrs. Bellmont's abuse frequently follows Frado's displays of emotion. For example, following James's death, "the tears rolled down [Frado's] dark face, soon followed by sobs, and then losing all control of herself, she wept aloud. This was an act of disobedience. Her mistress grasping her raw-hide, caused a longer flow of tears, and wounded a spirit that was craving healing mercies" (56). In this sense, the novel offers a resounding affirmation of Saidiya Hartman's challenge to "suppose that the recognition of humanity held out the promise not of liberating the flesh or redeeming one's suffering but rather intensifying it."[24] Frado is endangered not only by Mrs. Bellmont's explicit abuse but also by Mr. Bellmont's withholding of protection, given that he can only advise Frado that "when she was SURE she did not deserve a whipping, to avoid it if she could" (58). Mr. Bellmont spends the entire novel negotiating his patriarchal attachment to the fantasy of domesticity and his knowledge of the abuse that paradoxically destroys and is symptomatic of this fantasy. In this sense, Wilson's revision of the Bird household ingeniously positions the man of the house as the female complainant, whose address is characterized by "the conditions of bargaining that allow people to maintain both their critical knowledge and their attachments to what disappoints."[25] Wilson continues this gendered revision of sentimental domesticity by rewriting Stowe's Little Eva as James Bellmont, the sentimental interlocutor who begins the work of Frado's Christian conversion but dies before fulfilling his intention of removing Frado from Mrs. Bellmont's abuse.[26] By seamlessly rewriting Stowe's classic examples of feminine morality and disempowerment as men, Wilson wields the formally generic nature of these essentialist fantasies of feminine address to highlight the insufficiency of their promises: even when spoken by the enfranchised and the powerful, a sentimental attachment to the home as providing "*relief from the political*" makes its vision of social justice impossible to attain and limits its didactic instruction to adaptation rather than transformation.[27] Recognizing the socially constructed nature of the private confessions the sentimental collects as evidence for its critique, Wilson turns her readers' attention to the literary craft behind the elements of sentimental fiction its readers would have prized as most authentic and consumed most tearfully.

It is in the scenes with James where Wilson uses the third-person autobiographical narrator to offer the most complex meditation on the authenticity that sentimental witnessing equates with suffering and private expression. While Mrs. Bellmont is provoked by Frado's humanizing sorrow and Mr. Bellmont responds by weaponizing the attribution of self-determination, James, who refuses to "excuse or palliate Nig's impudence," signals his acceptance of her humanity with the rhetoric of Christian reform (40). In one particularly tricky moment of sentimental witnessing, the text describes James describing to Aunt Abby his experience of overhearing Frado "lamenting her loneliness and her complexion": "'Oh! Oh!' I heard, 'why was I made? Why can't I die? Oh, what have I to live for? No one cares for me only to get my work. And I feel sick; who cares for that? Work as long as I can stand, and then fall down and lay there till I can get up. No mother, father, brother or sister to care for me, and then it is, You lazy nigger, lazy nigger—all because I am black! Oh, if I could die!'" (42). The didactic force of this embedded dialogue depends on the assumption that Frado thinks she is alone, thus her outpouring of grief can be read as an impulsive emotional response that serves as a blank slate for James to appropriate to establish his own position as sentimental auditor. James's own witnessing of this moment also requires an audience, as he can only position himself as a sentimental witness by imparting the story and its lessons to Aunt Abby during a conversation that the narrator allows the reader to overhear, one of many where James and Aunt Abby share "unseen glories, and heart-experiences" and debate "the prevalent opinion of the public, that people of color are really inferior; incapable of cultivation and refinement" (41). It is notably unclear whether Frado is physically present for these conversations or is merely a topic of interest: "In these confidential interviews, Frado was never omitted." Providing James's secondhand transcription of Frado's thoughts rather than Frado's first-person perspective, the text suggests that it is precisely this slippage between participant and object that characterizes the perspective of the sentimental witness. Using this moment to argue for "the finer feelings" of Frado's "people," James's sentimental authority—both over Frado ("She has such confidence in me that she will do just as I tell her") and as a public testifier—depends on the availability of Frado's passive and readable interiority (41–42). James enters public discourse by granting Frado what Christopher Castiglia has called "civil interiority."[28] The very presumption of privacy—"when she supposed herself entirely alone"—that allows James to argue for Frado's authentic expression of "finer feelings" is precisely what is violated by James's own intrusion, an intrusion that not only establishes James's sentimental credentials but also grants Wilson's sentimental reader access to Frado's private expressions of suffering.

I have argued that the third-person narrator redirects our attention from Frado to the other characters in the novel, a formal innovation that demonstrates how the identities of the sentimental witnesses and violent tormentors of the Bellmont home are dependent on their appropriative constructions of Frado's interiority. I'd now like to suggest an alternative: if we do indeed follow the directives of the autobiographical claims of the preface, then we might also grant Frado a keen sense of audience.[29] When Frado tricks a willful sheep into jumping into the river, Mr. Bellmont and his "laborers" can only watch "in breathless silence" because they assume they are "unseen by Frado" and worry they "might startle her" (31). In retelling this story, Wilson focuses on the ways that the witnesses' breathless silence and convulsive laughter depend on their assumption that Frado believes she is not being watched. Even in public, Frado's actions are interpreted as pure impulse. The alliances that Frado forms with sentimental auditors and fellow laborers ("the men on the farm were always glad to hear her prattle; she was a great favorite with them") depend precisely on this assumption of artlessness (21). Although the autobiographical claims of the preface cater to the expectations for authenticity demanded by the antislavery public sphere, they also provide an opening to question both James's assumption that Frado "supposed herself entirely alone" and the laborers' assumption that they are "unseen by

Frado." Manipulating reading conventions that place a premium on a lack of artifice, Wilson flaunts the literary craft behind the scenes of authenticity valued by the nineteenth-century literary public sphere and interrogates reading practices that measure her success against expectations of authenticity.

So far I have argued that Wilson's novel challenges liberalism's location of freedom in a transcendent private sphere both thematically, as the idealization of domestic retreat is characterized as enabling violent abuse and coerced labor, and formally, as a third-person autobiographical narrator confirms that publicity constructs privacy. I now turn to how this critique invests figures like Frado who are alienated from both the rights of public life and the consolation prize of domestic authority with a kind of autonomy that reverses the traditional liberal hierarchy of public abstraction and private embodiment. One of the most jarring elements of Wilson's text is the disjunction between the detailed descriptions of Frado's suffering and her "exuberance of spirit almost beyond restraint" (11). The narrator draws our attention to this uncomfortable contrast: "strange, one spark of playfulness could remain" (31). Frado's "jollity was not to be quenched by whipping or scolding," and the alliances she forms with schoolmates, who "enjoyed her antics so fully that any of them would wrongly suffer to keep open the avenues of mirth," allow her to "venture far beyond propriety, thus shielded and countenanced" (22). This aptitude for "sly prank[s]" is notably at odds with James's description of Frado's self-conception as "unpitied, friendless, and utterly despised" (42). The majority of criticism either ignores Frado's "exuberance," "playfulness," and "jollity" or dismisses her "antics" as minstrelsy performed for the enjoyment of white spectators. Focusing on suffering because that is what is deemed most private, while play is assumed to be a superficial performance that belies a deeper and more true suffering, these readings risk repeating the sentimental witness's selective recognition of suffering as interiority.[30] As I now argue, Wilson reimagines the mutability of surface not as a sign of deception but as enabling inventive alternatives to the cyclical discourse of sentimental interiority that grants humanity according to terms that will only ever restrict her access to the public sphere and its material freedoms.

HEARTS AND SKINS

Wilson's critique of sentimental reading practices and domestic ideology follows from a long tradition of ambivalence towards these generic values and strategies from Black and working-class women. As Berlant puts it, "Insofar as these writers were writing from *within* a sphere of address and demanding revision of its terms of recognition they were writing as critical members of an intimate public to demand its reorganization."[31] Rather than promoting domesticity as an ideal that is not yet attainable to all, Wilson consistently and overtly rejects the promises of patriarchal domestic life that organizes this tradition of women's fiction. More to the point, Wilson deploys Frado's exceptional and inescapable embodiment to highlight the passive freedom granted to those who accept the abstracting terms of liberal recognition. Frado's triumph over the sheep occurs in the middle of a chapter that is primarily concerned with the marriage plot of Jane Bellmont, as she negotiates the advances of two suitors and her mother's self-interested machinations. The arrangements of Jane's marriage follow a description of Frado's physical feats outside of the home. Frado, who must "do the work of a boy, could one be procured to endure the tirades of Mrs. Bellmont," manages to occasionally "utter some funny thing for Jack's benefit, while she was waiting on the table, provoking a sharp look from his mother, or expulsion from the room." Expulsion becomes escape as, following one of these domestic scenes, she is found "mounted in high glee" playing on the roof of the barn. Again, the novel turns to the reactions of those watching: "Mr. Bellmont called sternly for her to come down; poor Jane nearly fainted from fear. Mrs. B. and Mary did not care if she 'broke her neck' while Jack and the men laughed at her fearlessness" (30–31).[32] Following this description of Frado's "high glee" on the barn roof and her bold prank on the sheep, the narrator abruptly writes, "But to return" and provides the details of James's and Jane's marriages, suggesting that Frado's play has provided temporary relief from the predictable domestic plot that determines the future of "poor Jane." Mrs. Bellmont attempts to force Jane to marry a wealthy but morally unsuitable suitor she does not love. Mr. Bellmont finally intervenes, declaring that "he would see that she was not compelled to violate her free choice in so important a transaction. He then sought the two young men; told them he could not as a father see his child compelled to an uncongenial union; a free, voluntary choice was of such importance to one of her health. She must be left free to her own choice" (34). The emphasis in this passage on free choice (repeated three times) is striking, particularly given the contrast between the freedom Mr. Bellmont feels he owes Jane "as a father" and the bondage he allows Frado to endure. But given that the novel has so explicitly disabused the reader of the fantasy of the home as a space of consent, Mr. Bellmont's characterization of marriage as how Jane will express her freedom of choice rings hollow.[33] Later in the novel when Jane and Jack have left home, this connection between the promised freedom of Jane's household and the coerced labor and violence that undergirds Mrs. Bellmont's domestic autonomy is reiterated: "Jane begged [Frado] to follow her so soon as she should be released; but so wearied out was she by her mistress, she felt disposed to flee from any and every one having her similitude of name or feature" (61).

The embodied freedom Frado repeatedly if temporarily achieves outside of the home highlights through contrast the anemic freedom the rhetoric of domesticity accorded to middle-class white women through its emphasis on spiritual authority over political power.[34] Jane's courtship plot is a classic example of domestic ideology's emphasis on depth of character over the superficial trappings of wealth and class.[35] This privileging of interiority over surface collides in sentimental antislavery fiction with the "terrified sense that the body is inescapable," a tension that is resolved through "a moral, emotional, and fundamentally spiritual code that devalues bodily constraints to focus on the soul."[36] Frado's own marriage plot, which is recounted in six short paragraphs in the final chapter, expertly condenses both the fragile freedom accorded to women through domestic dependence and the confused relationship in sentimental antislavery discourse between bodily surface and soulful depth. After a brief courtship, Frado marries a "dark brother," one of the "professed fugitives from slavery, who recounted their personal experience in homely phrase" for New England abolitionists (70). Samuel "never spoke of his enslavement to her when alone, but she felt that, like her own oppression, it was painful to disturb oftener than was needful." The narrator describes his physical appearance: "He was a fine, straight negro, whose back showed no marks of the lash, erect as if it never crouched beneath a burden." This lack of physical signs of enslavement turns out to be a true warning sign. Frequently deserting her to "'lecture,'" "compell[ing]" Frado to "again" "resort" to her "self-dependence," Samuel finally confesses that "he had never seen the South, and that his illiterate harangues were humbugs for hungry abolitionists" (70–71). Samuel's "illiterate harangues" are performances for abolitionists like James who are "hungry" to consume the "personal experience" and transcribe the "homely phrase" that in turn renders the fugitive unfit for civic life.

The fact that Samuel's body does in fact contain clues to his "true" history operates as a devastatingly ironic critique of the professed logic of sentimental antislavery fiction that universal sympathies trump physical differences. Co-opting the language of proslavery discourse that rooted the naturalness of slavery in bodily signs, Samuel's lack of scars and erect posture, linked in the next sentence to "a silent sympathy which Frado felt attracted her," are in fact provided as cautionary clues that he has never been enslaved.[37] Rather than surface being the artificial layer that must be bypassed to access what is true, this moment points to the ease with which the body's truths are misread, forced into inventive alignment with politically convenient constructions of interiority, in this case an understanding of "pain and disgrace" as the only recognizable signs of Black "civic righteousness."[38] Even as sentimental antislavery fiction appealed to supposedly universal emotions, both pro- and antislavery forces became increasingly preoccupied with essentializing and differentiating racial interiority in ways that emphasized Black Americans' unfitness for the rights and duties of citizenship.[39] This romantic racialism emerges in sentimental antislavery novels like *Uncle Tom's Cabin*, where Stowe portrays people of African descent as ideal Christians because of an innate docility and dependency. Even as sentimental antislavery fiction imagines that universal feelings can transcend physical difference, it also obsessively details how essentialist conceptions of Black interiority can be read on the body. For example, in Lydia Maria Child's short story "The Quadroons" (1842), the African ancestry of the nearly white Xarifa is betrayed by the shape of her eye, which is then immediately linked to a typological docility: "The iris of her large, dark eye had the melting, mezzotinto outline, which remains the last vestige of African ancestry, and gives that plaintive expression, so often observed, and so appropriate to that docile and injured race."[40] Wilson challenges this generic romantic racialism through Samuel, who calls the bluff on a liberal narrative that grants publicity through a supposedly equalizing abstraction that will only ever reiterate his own particularized embodiment.[41]

Frado's attempts as a child to understand racial difference and her own physical appearance and social position are constant indicators of the confused relationship between abstraction and embodiment in liberal narratives of publicity. Frado's skepticism toward a God who would make the evil Mrs. Bellmont white and herself Black, if to be Black is to be "kicked and whipped," and her gleeful speculation following Mary's death that should Mary go to hell, "she'll be as black as I am," relate a child's understanding that the conditions of whiteness and Blackness are as relational and shifting as the power dynamics that determine them (28, 59). As Peterson notes, Frado herself challenges both legal and literary conventions of race and gender: "Frado follows the condition, not of her mother, but of her 'free' father, and becomes Our Nig, an appellation that calls attention to her blackness and erases her mother's whiteness."[42] Frado's father, Jim, convinces her mother to marry him by arguing "'I's black outside, I know, but I's got a white heart inside. Which you rather have, a black heart in a white skin, or a white heart in a black one?'" (9) In a twist that points to the arbitrary enforcement of legal definitions of race, because Frado's own racial identity is determined to follow her father's condition rather than her mother's, she has inherited not only his Black skin but also his white heart. On one hand, Jim's ironic distinction between white hearts and Black skins co-opts sentimental rhetoric that proclaims to see past racial surfaces, even as it thinks of race as an interior character trait, rooted within.[43] But the novel does more than confirm that race is socially constructed, as it repeatedly returns to physical markers: skin, hair, posture. Mrs. Bellmont anxiously attempts to darken Frado's skin to decrease a troubling similarity between Frado and Mary and cuts her curls to force a correspondence between the labor that masculinizes Frado and her appearance. The novel challenges the logic of racial interiority not by imagining that Frado might leave her abused and particularized body behind to achieve the abstracted and speculative equality promised by narratives of both liberalism and Christian reform, but by repeatedly showing the ways that embodiment, the very thing that is supposed to permanently imprison Black Americans, is precisely what is rendered most malleable by racial discourse—a malleability that can entrap but that can also be wielded in inventive and unpredictable ways.

Frado's body, like Samuel's, is a material signifier of the mutability of the body denied by deceptive sentimental reading practices. The penultimate chapter of the narrative concludes with Frado living with "a plain, poor, simple woman, who could see merit beneath a dark skin." Recommitting herself to "book information" and "self-improvement," the chapter ends claiming that Frado's "devout and Christian exterior invited confidence from the villagers" (68–69). The contradictory logic between these two formulations of interior and exterior is worth fleshing out. Seeing "merit beneath a dark skin" suggests that what is true and valuable exists underneath the surface and can only be seen by those who are able to look past Frado's skin, which, though dangerously similar to the white skin of Mary Bellmont, is read as "dark" by those who know her history. This is precisely the logic that will only ever particularize Frado, as only those categorized as not white possess skin that must be actively disregarded. This logic is contradicted by the claim that Frado has achieved a "Christian exterior" that "invited confidence." What does it mean to think of Christianity as surface rather than depth? What does Christianity look like? For most of the novel, a Christian exterior has meant whiteness: "Frado pondered; her mistress was a professor of religion; was SHE going to heaven? then she did not wish to go. If she should be near James, even, she could not be happy with those fiery eyes watching her ascending path. She resolved to give over all thought of the future world, and strove daily to put her anxiety from her" (58). Rather than a veiled reference to a performative or hypocritical Christianity, Wilson's description of Christianity as exteriority is representative of a larger narrative strategy that imagines the possibilities of embodiment, and thus links speculative spiritual outcomes to material realities.[44]

Even as Wilson foregrounds the ways that discourses of interiority like sentimental conversion and Christian reform deceptively construct racialized surfaces, within the novel this insight functions less as a truth to be exposed and corrected than an inevitability that might nevertheless be put to unpredictable ends. Wilson concludes her novel positioning Frado as a spiritual medium. Having been denied a place in heaven by Mrs. Bellmont, at the end of the narrative Frado is left in the position to resurrect her former tormentor. As I conclude in the final section, Frado's position as a distinctly embodied medium is precisely what grants her access to the spiritual domain that allows her to speak for the Bellmont family in public. The position of medium allows Wilson to bring together the autobiographical and fictional elements of her narrative—not in a failure that suggests she has lost narrative control over the personal but in a way that allows Wilson to locate her inventive genius within her exceptional material circumstances.

WILSON'S SPIRITUALIST VISION

Once again redirecting her reader's attention from what remains "unknown" about Frado's "history" to what is known about the Bellmont family, it is particularly apposite that Wilson deploys the rhetoric of the spiritualist movement in the final line of her text: "Frado has passed from [the Bellmont's] memories, as Joseph from the butler's, but she will never cease to track them till beyond mortal vision" (72).[45] Although we don't have records of Wilson participating in the spiritualist movement until after *Our Nig* is published, this final image of supernatural vision anticipates her success as a medium in the next decades and allows Frado to remain empowered through embodiment, despite her chronic physical weakness following her indentured servitude. An emphatic investment in the material and the embodied accompanies the spiritualist movement's aim of contacting the spiritual world. Spiritualism granted those whose race and gender made it difficult to achieve abstraction a mode of speaking in public, even as the disembodiment the medium achieved by speaking for others was granted through essentialist stereotypes that only reiterated the medium's particularity.[46]

Mediumship and authorship are often conflated in *Our Nig* criticism, in the sense of the mature Wilson giving voice to her past self's unspeakable trauma. For some critics, because the first sentence of the final chapter of the novel includes the phrase "within the compass of my narrative," the first-person autobiographical returns only to disrupt the authoritative distance Wilson has gained over her personal history, suggesting that Wilson has failed to maintain a cohesive narrative perspective or to tell a fulfilling and complete story (70).[47] It is, however, just as possible to attribute the possessor of "my narrative" to the third-person narrator, who is staking a claim to the story she has created rather than the experiences she has recounted. These readings risk suggesting that Wilson must wait for future readers to rewrite her literary failure into a legacy that more enlightened readers can appreciate.[48] Entering the literary public sphere without suffering the ghostly abstraction that would subsume the material circumstances of her history, Wilson does more than claim the position of the transcendent "editor-medium" who translates "voice into text."[49] Wilson concludes by rendering the Bellmont family disembodied spirits who are granted legibility through Frado's tracking, as she weaponizes rather than reverses what Russ Castronovo has described as the "parasitic relationship of white spirit and black body."[50] Although the final paragraph suggests that justice is to be found in death, as Mrs. Bellmont suffers "an agony in death unspeakable" and Aunt Abby and Jack "rest in heaven," thus enacting a sentimental logic that defers justice to a spiritual afterlife, the dead are left silently dependent on the distinctly embodied Frado to speak for them. The final positioning of Frado as a medium once again redirects our attention to the abusive members of the Bellmont household, as Frado speaks from a perspective that once again surpasses the autobiographical. Frado is not the illegible self Wilson speaks for; rather, the Bellmonts are the ghostly spirits Frado promises to track. Rather than failing to fully achieve an abstracting distance from her own particularized circumstances that would signal her ascension as a liberal subject, this positioning shows Wilson harnessing the incoherent fantasies of biological racialism for her own creative purposes.

Wilson's conclusion maintains a complementary distinction between the material and the spiritual that allows her to enter public discourse without participating in a print capitalist logic of abstraction that would require an impossible shedding of her own material circumstances. Rather than seeing embodiment as an impediment to the abstracting demands of public discourse, her particularized body is precisely what grants her access to the spiritual domain that allows her to speak for the Bellmont family in public. The implications of surveillance in Frado's promise to "track" the Bellmont family have led critics to characterize her continuing interest as vengeful obsession that imagines Frado as occupying the position of domestic overseer.[51] Eliza Richards's research on spiritualist poetics helps us to see an alternative to this reading of surveillance and its implications of one-directional relation. On the one hand, because mediums were "not considered to be the authors of the information they conveyed," when Wilson speaks for the Bellmonts, the dialogue she imagines is granted the truth status of spiritual testimony. On the other hand, because the relationship between spirit and medium is not a possession that results in a loss of agency but one that allows for both "the originality of receptivity and the individuality of the spirit-medium," the Bellmont family becomes the raw source material for Wilson's creative genius.[52] We've seen in previous chapters how fictional figures of exceptional virtue—Caesar for the *Salmagundi* editors and Magawisca in *Hope Leslie*—are reduced to source material whose imaginative potential is only generated by their relegation to the home or the frontier, two spaces that serve the same structural function in constituting the nationalist public sphere. Wilson deploys the logic of the spiritualist movement to reverse engineer the logic that silences and disappears these figures, so that her protagonist's white tormentors become the abstracted and silenced material for her own embodied creative genius. Wilson uses the language of a movement that celebrated receptivity to assert her own formative role in the Bellmont's understanding of themselves. Although Frado has been forgotten by the Bellmont family—a necessary elision given that her coerced labor has served to maintain the illusion of their own domestic retreat and to establish their self-perceptions of autonomy—the narrative has testified to her central role in their public identities.[53] Unlike the Victorian poetesses that Richards examines, however, who see lyric poetry as the mode that comes closest to transcending the materiality of language, Wilson does not suggest that her printed text is a pale imitation of the spiritual communications it transcribes—a logic that would extend to her own physical body as corrupted vessel rather than fundamental medium for her literary production. Wilson's text reconciles the confusion between the spiritual and the material that plagues romantic notions of feminine genius not by pastoralizing her creative labor as spiritual impulse, thus participating in a mode of authorship that would erase the coercive history of her material circumstances, but by insisting on the material dimensions of her literary production. Untethered from fantasies of domestic retreat, Wilson advertises her aesthetic labor's inseparability from her position as a gendered and raced subject, but not in a way that essentializes her literary production as natural impulse. Instead, Wilson registers her literary labor on a formal level, as she invites readers into familiar conventions of domestic fiction—the seduced woman, the abusive mistress, the dying martyr—only to denaturalize the reading practices they have come to understand as expressing their own private sentiments.

CODA

#WFH

I STARTED DRAFTING the introduction to this book in the early weeks of the COVID-19 pandemic, when many employers began encouraging their employees to "work from home." Quickly earning the Twitter-friendly hashtag WFH, tips for how to manage productivity and mental health while working from home soon appeared on social media and online periodicals. But given that the home has always been a space of labor, what did the W in WFH mean, exactly? One implication is that the work we do to maintain our domestic comfort is imagined as loving impulse rather than material labor. At first, for those unaccustomed to the daily grind of domestic labor, tasks such as organizing the pantry and baking bread were presented as pleasurable distractions from the real Work we were supposed to be doing. Even as it quickly became apparent that the pleasures of domestic retreat are unevenly distributed—students were suddenly expected to learn from homes that were not spaces of plenitude or security, and women quickly realized they would bear the brunt of increased caretaking responsibilities—the proliferation of work-from-home advice implied that we continue to find something counterintuitive about thinking about Home as a space of Work.[1]

As an academic, many of my days are spent working from home—grading, writing, researching, and preparing for class. Advice for those of us who work from home has always encouraged a careful compartmentalizing of this work to preserve it from the encroachments of domestic labor. How many of us have traded stories of the so-called virtuous procrastination we are guilty of when we clean our workspace before buckling down to write reader reports or grade student essays? Some of this sheepishness has to do with the kind of work we do at home—namely, intellectual labor—and perhaps its uneasy correspondence to the "labor that is not labor" that is traditionally understood to take place in the domestic sphere.[2] Even as academics are encouraged to maintain strict boundaries between intellectual and domestic labor, both kinds of work are idealized as being motivated by something loftier than material gain. By the time I was finalizing this manuscript, the

Twitter of #WFH no longer existed, but a labor movement given life by the 2016 National Labor Relations Board decision affirming that graduate students at private universities are employees was making history with a record-breaking number of strikes in 2022 and the largest strike in the history of education in the United States taking place in the University of California system in 2023. In part, it is the romanticization of intellectual labor that this recent rise in labor organization has challenged, as organizers demand that academic institutions recognize the labor of graduate-student employees and provide institutional support and living wages commensurate with that labor.[3]

I've just gestured to two different but related notions of domestic labor that inform this book's present moment. In the first, a distinction is made between the material obligations of work typically performed outside the home and the labors of love performed within the home. In the second, a distinction is made within the home between the material obligations of domestic labor and the intellectual work that is understood as an idiosyncratic choice to pursue a life of the mind, insulated from both economic motivation and protection. We can understand both attitudes as outgrowths of the significant shift this book has traced in concepts of the home from a space of labor to a space of retreat. Overdetermining an antithetical relationship between material and intellectual labor has a potentially chilling effect on who feels authorized or able to do scholarly work. Equally true, however, is that in a time of dwindling job prospects and research support in the humanities, the so-called life of the mind risks becoming the very luxury of the elite it is caricatured to be in antilabor reform circles. As nineteenth-century theories of romantic genius worked to conflate pastoralized domestic labor with a naturalized theory of feminine genius, figures like Charles Brockden Brown and Harriet E. Wilson who resist this conflation become historical allies in the struggle over conditions of intellectual labor in a time of increasing resource scarcity.

As we emerge out of a period of renewed scrutiny toward the incoherent boundaries drawn between domestic and professional labor, there has also been a reinvestment in a nostalgic fantasy of domestic retreat. Sarah Mesle and Koritha Mitchell remind us that this nostalgia erases the immediately contested nature and unexpected outcomes of the ideal of domestic retreat, exemplified in this project through critics of domestic ideology like Catharine Maria Sedgwick and Harriet E. Wilson.[4] The text that opens this book, Charles Brocken Brown's "A Literary Wife," is especially resonant in this book's contemporary moment of reckoning with the immediate aftershocks of COVID-19 quarantine. While Brown's narrator laments the conditions that require women to give up their intellectual pursuits following marriage, during the COVID-19 pandemic, a stunning number of women left the workforce, many of them attributing the move to the need to provide childcare for their household.[5] This connection should not overlook the complex developments in ideas of the private home and labor over the course of the last two centuries.

Undoubtedly, this immediate publication context will quickly feel distant to future readers. I draw this connection between this book's source material and the working conditions out of which it emerged to highlight the ongoing availability of the fantasy of domestic retreat and a cycle of reactivity between moments that render the coercive conditions of domestic labor hypervisible and a reinvestment in the illusion that pastoralizes this labor. As this book has reconstructed, the fantasy of domestic retreat newly popularized by so-called Momfluencers on social media also overlooks the unsettled aspirations this ideal first served as it emerged out of the market revolution of the late eighteenth century. Authorizing itself through selectively interpretive nostalgia, the conservative ideology that often accompanies this contemporary iteration of domestic fantasy would not recognize the sensuous household of Brown's creole refugees, the socially unproductive whims of *Salmagundi*'s bachelors, or the partnership between Cecil Dreeme and Robert Byng as being equally invested in domestic retreat as a position of dissent from which to actively negotiate the demands and limits of social recognition. From Brown's curiosity about how the ideal of domestic retreat might allow for feminine self-dependence to Irving's territorial claims to Winthrop's re-creation of domestic ideology for a virtuous queer partnership, this book's archive has traced surprising investments in the ideal of domestic retreat that upend our gendered assumptions about the literary culture of the nineteenth century.

Imagined as a prepolitical space of affective bonds, the domestic becomes a powerful site for contesting and authorizing the artificial impositions of an experimental theory of consensual citizenship that unevenly evolves during a period of coverture, settler colonialism, and slavery.[6] The ideal of domestic retreat was undoubtedly an important supporting structure for the increasingly restrictive understandings of citizenship that developed over the first half of the nineteenth century. The logic that imagined domestic fiction's marriage plots as allegories of consensual citizenship supported an illusion of an inviolate home that could only be established through relational contrast to the institution of slavery; the protective paternalism that determined who was capable and incapable of consent was replicated in U.S. policy toward Native people; and a generic shift from superficial class hierarchy to internal character traits morphed into the sentimental romantic racialism that linked self-determination to whiteness. Still, the history of domestic retreat, like the theories of citizenship it supported, also preserves a spectrum of alternative precedents, from Charles Brockden Brown's erotic and cosmopolitan domestic scenes to Harriet E. Wilson's critique of domestic racial terror and affirmation of the literary labor behind Black feminine genius. The literary tradition that emerges out of these decades—one that aligns creative genius with domestic retreat—reminds us that a politics that authorizes itself through appeals to private feeling must also reckon with the inventive and divergent visions of labor, kinship, and reform that are proposed in exchange for the sanction of affiliation.

ACKNOWLEDGMENTS

Many years ago, Virginia Jackson and Elizabeth Maddock Dillon served as advisors on my dissertation committee and wrote letters in support of several rounds of job and fellowship applications. Their influence as scholars can be seen throughout this book. Their generosity as advisors is less visible but equally as meaningful and an even greater rarity, and I have tried my best to pay it forward in my own teaching and advising. Many more years ago, Bethany Schneider started me on my way by advising my senior thesis and supporting my applications to graduate school. Many of the books I now teach, some held together with binder clips, still have marginalia from Professor Schneider's classes and are reminders of transformative first encounters with what would become my field of study. Even many more years ago, I was a public-school kid in West Virginia, and I thank my teachers for creating my first sense of intellectual community.

I am grateful to be part of an exceptionally collegial department of first-rate teacher-scholars at the University of Massachusetts Dartmouth. Despite demanding teaching loads and service commitments, my colleagues in the Department of English and Communication continue to produce top-notch scholarship and support their students with dedication and warmth. You will not find harder working students than the students at UMass Dartmouth; I am inspired every day by their curiosity and determination. The reading lists of several undergraduate courses helped shape this book's archive, and I am grateful to the many students who thought alongside me. This book has benefitted from funding from the Provost's Office and the Office of the Dean of the College of Arts and Sciences at the University of Massachusetts Dartmouth, including grants for conference travel and one semester of sabbatical leave. This book was also supported by a UMass Dartmouth Subvention Grant awarded by the Office of the Dean of the College of Arts and Sciences.

Looking back on the years spent thinking about this book, I can trace a constellation of small moments of revitalizing fellowship that sparked forward momentum and provided an antidote to isolation and uncertainty. Duncan Faherty and Elizabeth Hewitt welcomed me into the Charles Brockden Brown Society, a community that has provided sustaining friendship and meaningful professional support. The convivial Constance Fenimore Woolson Society took a chance on a paper on Washington Irving. Jeffrey Insko doesn't know this, but years ago at ICR, his enthusiasm converted me from someone who dreaded conferences to someone who understands their worth. And Karen Weyler once intervened at a crucial moment to insist I take a nap. Sections of this book have been discussed along the way at many additional conferences and I thank the organizers for their crucial service to the profession, particularly the members of C19: The Society of Nineteenth-Century Americanists and SEA: The Society of Early Americanists. Many people have been generous readers of bits and pieces of this book, including Jacob Crane, Elizabeth Hewitt, Helen Hunt, Thomas Koenigs, Alex Moskowitz, Elizabeth Neiman, and Jay Zysk. I thank them for heartening exchanges and for sharing their time and expertise.

I benefitted enormously from the camaraderie of graduate students at Tufts University who have gone on to do extraordinary things. A shout-out to Maik Stanitzke, fast friend since we entered the program together, for helping so many of us pass our German reading exam. Nino X. Testa has taught me the importance of ritual, transportable across friendships and writing practices. I am proud to be a lifelong member of BALOT and TEGPA. Caroline Gelmi has read every word of this book, from start to finish, in countless iterations. She is an ideal reader and one of my favorite writers. Capacious in her knowledge, perceptive in her critique, she has un-stuck me more times than I can count. I consider it a cosmic stroke of luck that our lives remain parallel. With one phone call Nicole Flynn once rescued me, a very lonely first-year doctoral candidate, and taught me how to take myself seriously as a scholar and what it means to be a friend. Her friendship is that rarest of things that stays true yet welcomes change, and everyone who is fortunate enough to be in her orbit is the better for it. She continues to be an unwavering pulse of assurance that makes me feel like I can do anything, including write a book.

Suzanne Guiod at Bucknell University Press responded with prompt enthusiasm and fruitful suggestions when I first approached her about this book, and this initial response kept me going when finishing seemed impossible. I thank her for believing in this project and shepherding it to completion. I am deeply grateful to the anonymous manuscript readers for their attentive and insightful reports. Their labor undoubtedly made this a better book. Many thanks to the editors of the *Transits* series for including this book among such fine company.

A version of chapter 2 previously appeared in *Nineteenth-Century Literature*, published by the University of California Press. I thank the anonymous readers for helping to make this section of the book stronger and UC Press for permitting republication. A version of chapter 3 previously appeared in *Legacy: A Journal of Women Writers*, published by the University of Nebraska Press. I thank the editor at the time, Jennifer Tuttle, and the anonymous readers, for their feedback and editorial guidance, and the UNP for permitting republication.

The semester-long sabbatical I was supposed to spend finishing this book was the infamous spring of 2020. Quarantined at home with a six-month-old, any writing I accomplished can be attributed to our nanny, Jessica Young, who spent many hours walking our sleep-averse daughter around the neighborhood. I thank her for trusting us to take care of one another during those months. I am also deeply grateful for the excellent care my daughter has received from her daycare and preschool teachers while I have been writing this book.

This book is dedicated to my parents, Joseph and Virginia Hankins. The most fulfilling parts of my life have come from following their example. Their faith in me was never something I felt I had to earn, and that has been a formative and steadying gift. Meredith Hankins is the bravest person I know and has helped me see old books in new ways.

The members of my own domestic scene deserve unending thanks for enduring bouts of grouchy preoccupation with patience and good cheer. Wally Dog offered solidarity with impeccably timed sighs. My daughter, Josephine, has grown along with this book. As it goes to print, she goes to kindergarten. Memories of her first five years are bound up with every page. No one is better at celebrations than my husband, Austen Farrell, who has understood and sympathized with all fits and starts but never once indulged self-doubt. His steadfast partnership is my greatest fortune. His expansive generosity to friends and neighbors enriches our home. Ours is my favorite marriage plot.

NOTES

INTRODUCTION

1. "A Literary Wife," *The Literary Magazine and American Register* 3, no. 18 (March 1805): 195, Charles Brockden Brown Electronic Archive and Scholarly Edition. Hereafter referred to parenthetically. On the editorial practices of the Charles Brockden Brown Electronic Archive, see Mark L. Kamrath et al., "The Charles Brockden Brown Electronic Archive: Mapping Archival Access and Metadata," *Archive Journal* 4 (April 2014): http://www.archivejournal.net/essays/the-charles-brockden-brown-electronic-archive-mapping-archival-access-and-metadata/. On the challenge of authorial attribution in the early national magazine in relation to Brown specifically, see Matthew Pethers and Len von Morzé, "Early American Magazine Writing in and out of the Charles Brockden Brown Canon," *Early American Literature* 57, no. 2 (2022): 555–562, Project Muse. On early national collaborative and hybrid authorship in relation to Brown's periodical writing, see Karen A. Weyler, "Reader-Centered Periodicals and the Literary Commons," *Early American Literature* 57, no. 2 (2022): 543–548, Project Muse.
2. "A Literary Wife," 196. All translations are mine, unless otherwise noted.
3. For a representative overview of "the sexual division of individualism within domesticity" and how individualism and domesticity are understood as "distinct and oppositional trajectories" in our literary histories of the nineteenth century, see Gillian Brown, *Domestic Individualism: Imagining Self in Nineteenth-Century America* (Berkeley: University of California Press, 1990), 4–5.
4. Nancy F. Cott, *The Bonds of Womanhood: "Woman's Sphere" in New England, 1780–1835*, 2nd ed. (New Haven: Yale University Press, 1997), 57.
5. Amy Dru Stanley, *From Bondage to Contract: Wage Labor, Marriage, and the Market in the Age of Slave Emancipation* (Cambridge: Cambridge University Press, 1998), 138.
6. Stanley, *From Bondage to Contract*, 10–11.
7. Anne McClintock, "Imperial Leather: Race, Cross-Dressing and the Cult of Domesticity," in *Feminist Postcolonial Theory: A Reader*, ed. Reina Lewis and Sara Mills (New York: Routledge, 2003), 650–653.
8. Cott, *The Bonds of Womanhood*, 56; Stanley, *From Bondage to Contract*, 29–34.
9. See Brown, *Domestic Individualism*, 4–5, and Elizabeth Maddock Dillon, *The Gender of Freedom: Fictions of Liberalism and the Literary Public Sphere* (Stanford: Stanford University Press, 2004). Dillon argues that the private sphere is not protected from public interests but is in fact produced in public to undergird notions of the autonomous liberal subject.
10. Cott, *Bonds of Womanhood*, 57.
11. On the link between the pastoralized domestic labor and aesthetic production, see Elizabeth Maddock Dillon, "Sentimental Aesthetics," *American Literature* 76, no. 3 (2004): 509–511. EBSCO. On "the romantic commonplace that poetic accomplishment in men arose from their feminine aspect," see Eliza Richards, *Gender and the Poetics of Reception in Poe's Circle* (Cambridge: Cambridge University Press, 2004), 38.
12. Rufus Wilmot Griswold, preface to *The Female Poets of America* (Philadelphia: Carey and Hart, 1848), 8.

13. Rufus Wilmot Griswold, preface to *The Female Poets of America*, 2nd ed. (Philadelphia: Henry C. Baird, 1852), 8.
14. I consider these theories in more detail throughout this project, particularly in chapter 4. For an overview of nineteenth-century theories of polarity and gender, see Laura Saltz, "'Rather Both Than Neither': The Polarity of Gender in Howe's *Hermaphrodite*," in *Philosophies of Sex: Critical Essays on* The Hermaphrodite, ed. Renée Bergland and Gary Williams (Columbus: The Ohio State University Press, 2012), 72–92. On capacious eighteenth-century theories of gender more generally, see Greta LaFleur, "Sex and 'Unsex'": Histories of Gender Trouble in Eighteenth-Century North America," *Early American Studies: An Interdisciplinary Journal* 12, no. 2 (Fall 2014): 469–499.
15. Griswold, *Female Poets of America*, 7.
16. Richards, *Gender and the Poetics of Reception*, 38–39. Although Richards is making a point about lyric poetry specifically and its distinct association with "unmediated personal expression," her research "has the potential to expand and revise understandings of the function, location, and limitations of gendered forms of literary expression in the nineteenth-century public sphere" more broadly (*Gender and the Poetics of Reception*, 6). Given how saturated nineteenth-century literary culture was with poetry, throughout this project I find Richards's argument that romantic theories of the lyric hold open a gap between gender conventions and the gender of an author useful and generative for considering the novelists and periodicals that were informed by these theories.
17. For the traditional distinction between the literary and the aesthetic, see Charles Alteri, afterword to *American Literature's Aesthetic Dimensions*, ed. Cindy Weinstein and Christopher Looby (New York: Columbia University Press, 2012), 393–404.
18. Dillon, "Sentimental Aesthetics," 509–511.
19. For the contradictions in our literary histories of American Romanticism, see Virginia Jackson, "American Romanticism, Again," *Studies in Romanticism* 55 (Fall 2016): 320.
20. The fundamental text for this tradition remains Nancy Armstrong, *Desire and Domestic Fiction: A Political History of the Novel* (New York: Oxford University Press, 1987), 36–42. Armstrong argues that the political logic of the social contract is imported into the narrative logic of the sexual contract that organizes domestic fiction, a rhetorical move that serves to naturalize fictions of consent and self-determination and to establish gender rather than class as society's primary organizing principle. Building off Armstrong's analysis of the British domestic novel, Dillon notes that because the aristocratic hierarchy this social reorganization replaced did not exist in the United States, "the narrative of heterosexual desire in the early Republic often looked more ominous and fractured than in English fiction" (*Gender of Freedom*, 141).
21. Studies of the early American novel see both disciplinary and subversive potential in its use of sentiment. For Cathy Davidson, who primarily sees the early American novel as Federalism's unruly other, it is in "the disjunctions between the conventional and the radical readings of the plot—that the early American sentimental novel flourishes." See Cathy N. Davidson, *Revolution and the Word: The Rise of the Novel in America*, 2nd ed. (Oxford: Oxford University Press, 2004), 230. On connections between the sentimental politics of the early national period and the rhetorical strategies of the early national seduction novel, see Elizabeth Barnes, *States of Sympathy: Seduction and Democracy in the American Novel* (New York: Columbia University Press, 1997). On how sympathy in the early American novel functions to memorialize expansive social possibilities in the process of being foreclosed by post-Revolution politics, see Julia A. Stern, *The Plight of Feeling: Sympathy and Dissent in the Early American Novel* (Chicago: University of Chicago Press, 1997). My argument here is most crucially informed by Dillon's understanding of the early national marriage plot less as an allegory of consensual citizenship, where public and private are united, than as a convention that registers dissent and confusion as private desires are newly expected to align with normative ideas of social legibility (*Gender of Freedom*, 135–136).

22. Arguing against the conflation of these terms, Marion Rust asserts that the use of sentiment in early American women's fiction cannot be contained by the conventions of domestic ideology. See Marion Rust, "'Into the House of an Entire Stranger': Why Sentimental Doesn't Equal Domestic in Early American Fiction," *Early American Literature* 37, no. 2 (2002): 283. I discuss Rust's important intervention in more detail in my first chapter, where I invert Rust's proposal, arguing that Charles Brockden Brown writes domestic but not sentimental fiction.
23. Rogers Smith explains that during the 1790s Federalists increasingly embraced a position "that American citizenship was rightfully as much a matter of birth, heritage, and natural allegiance as of choice." See *Civic Ideals: Conflicting Visions of Citizenship in U.S. History* (New Haven: Yale University Press, 1997), 153. Although consensual citizenship had always denied citizenship to populations deemed incapable of consenting to the social contract, either because of a perceived essential inferiority or a lack of private property, this newly ascriptive position continued to restrict citizenship on the basis of race, gender, and immigration status and arbitrary naturalization policies but was also equipped to counter the "rights of expatriation" that were becoming "convenient vehicles for disavowing duties to the new national regime." Recognizing "the potentially anarchical implications of pure consensualism," this shift is as much about enforcing conformity to the obligations of citizenship as it is about limiting citizenship (153–159). See also Carrie Hyde, *Civic Longing: The Speculative Origins of U.S. Citizenship* (Cambridge, MA: Harvard University Press, 2018), 32–35.
24. Barnes, *States of Sympathy*, 9.
25. Hyde, *Civic Longing*, 18–39. Hyde goes on to argue that the literary autonomy claimed by the romance author is linked to "the belated and contentious idealization of an artificial form of allegiance that was subject to dissolution and revision" (14). I return to this claim in my first chapter, where I consider domestic retreat in relation to this tradition of romantic disaffiliation.
26. On the recursive rather than linear temporality of the liberal subject's movement between the private and the public sphere, see Dillon, *Gender of Freedom*, 24–25.
27. Cindy Weinstein and Christopher Looby, introduction to *American Literature's Aesthetic Dimensions*, ed. Cindy Weinstein and Christopher Looby (New York: Columbia University Press, 2012), 9.
28. As Gillian Brown puts it in her study of the Lockean legacy in early American fiction, "In the act of consenting to government, individuals choose and accept constraints upon themselves. Individuals in the act of consent freely determine their lives, forming states, contracts, and alliances; by these practices, they also simultaneously exemplify their subjection to cultural authority" (*The Consent of the Governed: The Lockean Legacy in Early American Culture* [Cambridge, MA: Harvard University Press, 2001], 124). This "paradoxical condition of consent" Brown identifies is mirrored in early national aesthetic theory. As Eric Slauter puts it, early national aesthetic debates "addressed a central political problem, especially for governments based on the consent of the governed. How . . . could the subjective judgments of individuals be reconciled with or even subordinated to the authority of experts?" See *The State as a Work of Art: The Cultural Origins of the Constitution* (Chicago: University of Chicago Press, 2009), 87. Tensions between the subjective autonomy of individuals and community standards of taste captured what Edward Cahill calls the "dialectic of liberty in aesthetic theory" (*Liberty of the Imagination: Aesthetic Theory, Literary Form, and Politics in the Early United States* [Philadelphia: University of Pennsylvania Press, 2012], 4–5).
29. Eve Kosofsky Sedgwick, "Paranoid Reading and Reparative Reading, or, You're So Paranoid, You Probably Think This Essay Is About You," in *Touching Feeling* (Durham, NC: Duke University Press, 2003), 123–151.
30. See Heather Love, "Truth and Consequences: On Paranoid Reading and Reparative Reading," *Criticism* 52, no. 2 (Spring 2010): 235–241; Eva Cherniavsky, "Cultural Studies

Revisited: Determinate Conditions and the Depressive Position," *American Literary History* 34, no. 1 (Spring 2022), 54–66; Jennifer L. Fleissner "Romancing the Real: Bruno Latour, Ian McEwan, and Postcritical Monism" in *Critique and Postcritique*, eds. Elizabeth S. Anker and Rita Felski (Durham, NC: Duke University Press, 2017), 99–126.

31. For Christopher Castiglia, romanticism's "aesthetic counteractuality" provides an alternative to the historicist suspicion of aesthetic surfaces that has prioritized realism as an object of study ("Aesthetics Beyond the Actual: *The Marble Faun* and Romantic Sociality," in *American Literature's Aesthetic Dimensions*, ed. Cindy Weinstein and Christopher Looby [New York: Columbia University Press, 2012], 118). See also Hyde, who considers the political significance of "romantic fictionality" as an alternative to the more familiar assumption that "the political force of literature depends on a degree of realism—and the interpretive investment in restoring this lost 'reality' through referential interpretive paradigms like historical contextualization" (*Civic Longing*, 119). On what the self-consciously conjectural, speculative early national romance can add to critical traditions that have privileged the realist novel, see Gretchen J. Woertendyke, *Hemispheric Regionalism: Romance and the Geography of Genre* (Oxford: Oxford University Press, 2016), 4–7, and, to our historicist methods, see Michelle Sizemore, *American Enchantment: Rituals of the People in the Post-Revolutionary World* (Oxford: Oxford University Press, 2018), 166–170.
32. On becoming "disenchanted with disenchantment" see Nancy Bentley, "Warped Conjunctions: Jacques Rancière and African American Twoness," in *American Literature's Aesthetic Dimensions*, ed. Cindy Weinstein and Christopher Looby (New York: Columbia University Press, 2012), 291.
33. Here and throughout, *Woldwinite*, a term coined by Philip Barnard and Stephen Shapiro, refers to the Wollstonecraft-Godwin circle that was such a crucial network of influence for Brown (Philip Barnard and Stephen Shapiro, introduction to *Arthur Mervyn; or, Memoirs of the Year 1793*, by Charles Brockden Brown, ed. Philip Barnard and Stephen Shapiro [Indianapolis: Hackett Publishing Company, 2008], xv). On paranoia as anticipatory, see Sedgwick, "Paranoid Reading and Reparative Reading," 130–133. Sedgwick goes on to link the paranoid mode's "faith in exposure" to the production of narrative (138).
34. Sedgwick, "Paranoid Reading and Reparative Reading," 138–143. As Justine Murison notes, because historically adjacent modes like romance, sentimentalism, and realism share an investment in authenticity and the private self, critical approaches to the nineteenth-century novel share with their "objects of study" an investment in exposure (*Faith in Exposure: Privacy and Secularism in the Nineteenth-Century United States* [Philadelphia: University of Pennsylvania Press, 2023], 15). I read these early national texts as structured by dialogue and oscillation between positions we might label as paranoid or reparative reading and their various offshoots that aim for, in the words of Stephen Best and Sharon Marcus, "receptiveness and fidelity to the text's surfaces, as opposed to suspicious and aggressive attacks on its concealed depths" ("Surface Reading: An Introduction," *Representations* 108, no. 1 [Fall 2009]: 10–11, JSTOR).
35. Theodore Winthrop, *Cecil Dreeme*, ed. Peter Coviello (New York: Washington Mews Books, 2016), 244. Hereafter referred to parenthetically.
36. Eve Kosofsky Sedgwick, "The Character in the Veil: Imagery of the Surface in the Gothic Novel," *PMLA* 96, no. 2 (March 1981): 256. This understanding of the Gothic genre is characteristic of Sedgwick's earlier work, which establishes many of the paranoid reading practices reconsidered in later essays.
37. The novel thus registers the distinction between secrecy and privacy: "If privacy is publicly oriented, then its opposite is not publicity but sinful secrecy" (Murison, *Faith in Exposure*, 11).
38. Christopher Castiglia, "Hope for Critique?" in *Critique and Postcritique*, ed. Elizabeth S. Anker and Rita Felski (Durham, NC: Duke University Press, 2017), 211–212.
39. Addressing the recent turn away from historicist critique, Caleb Smith holds out the possibility that "people might be enchanted not only into submission but also into other

postures—into protest, for example or into dissent." See "From the Critique of Power to the Poetics of Justice," *J19: The Journal of Nineteenth-Century Americanists* 1, no. 1 (2013): 161.

40. Michael T. Gilmore, *American Romanticism and the Marketplace* (Chicago: University of Chicago Press, 1985), 12.
41. Lora Romero, *Home Fronts: Domesticity and Its Critics in the Antebellum United States* (Durham, NC: Duke University Press, 1997), 105. Examples of critics who treat these positions as "textual productions" abound. See, for example, Meredith McGill, who argues that Nathaniel Hawthorne self-consciously cultivates a "fiction of obscurity" to "control the terms of his reception" as a national novelist by distancing himself from a successful early career as a writer of short magazine fiction (*American Literature and the Culture of Reprinting, 1834–1853* [Philadelphia: University of Pennsylvania Press, 2003], 218–222) and Theresa Goddu, who argues that Louisa May Alcott "had to disguise her mercenary motives under the pretense of disseminating the feminine values of the private sphere" (*Gothic America: Narrative, History, and Nation* [New York: Columbia University Press, 1997], 118).
42. Jane Tompkins, *Sensational Designs: The Cultural Work of American Fiction 1790–1860* (New York: Oxford University Press, 1985), 124.
43. For Richard Brodhead, when "placed in the somber light of Foucault's magisterial *Discipline and Punish*," domestic fiction emerges as "another agent of discipline through love" (*Cultures of Letters: Scenes of Reading and Writing in Nineteenth-Century America* [Chicago: University of Chicago Press, 1993], 16, 47). Laura Wexler reveals the imperial and racial violence underlying the "'innocent eye'" domestic sentiment granted white women photographers (*Tender Violence: Domestic Visions in an Age of U.S. Imperialism* (Chapel Hill: University of North Carolina Press, 2000, 6).
44. Shirley Samuels, introduction to *The Culture of Sentiment: Race, Gender, and Sentimentality in Nineteenth-Century America*, ed. Shirley Samuels (New York: Oxford University Press, 1992), 5.
45. Romero challenges a monolithic understanding of feminine conformity and masculine resistance, a binary constructed as much by domesticity's antebellum critics as its practitioners: "If one cannot stand entirely 'outside' of ideology, then one cannot stand entirely 'inside' of it either" (*Home Fronts*, 1–6). Noting that these structural forces cannot be reduced to individual morality, Amy Kaplan positions domesticity in relation to the national work of empire building: "When we contrast the domestic sphere with the market or the political realm, men and women inhabit a divided social terrain, but when we oppose the domestic to the foreign, man and women become national allies against the alien, and the determining division is not gender but racial demarcations of otherness" ("Manifest Domesticity," *American Literature* 70, no. 3 [September 1998]: 582). In her study of the relationship between domestic fiction and nineteenth century consumer culture, Lori Merish links debates over the liberating and constraining forces of sentimental domesticity to the ways that subjectivity and agency are constitutive within modern power structures (*Sentimental Materialism: Gender, Commodity Culture, and Nineteenth-Century American Literature* (Durham, NC: Duke University Press, 2000), 18).
46. Dillon, "Sentimental Aesthetics," 496–523; Joanne Dobson, "Reclaiming Sentimental Literature," *American Literature* 69, no. 2 (June 1997): 263–288; Richards, *Gender and the Poetics of Reception*, 24.
47. F. O. Matthiessen, *American Renaissance: Art and Expression in the Age of Emerson and Whitman* (New York: Oxford University Press, 1941), vii.
48. Matthiessen, *American Renaissance*, x–xi.
49. See Nina Baym, "Melodramas of Beset Manhood: How Theories of American Fiction Exclude Women Authors," *American Quarterly* 33, no. 2 (Summer 1981): 123–139. Baym traces the emergence of romance as the tradition claimed by critics seeking to establish a distinctive American literary tradition defined by its alienation from social conditions which are always described as feminine.

50. For Michael Gilmore, the romantic author's ambivalence towards the limitations and the possibilities of consumer culture is aesthetically generative: "disappointment impelled the romantics towards textual strategies of difficulty and concealment, causing them to reconstruct in their relations to their audience the alienation they criticized in society" (*American Romanticism and the Marketplace* [Chicago: University of Chicago Press, 1985], 13). For the Emersonian tradition as one of ineffectual "aesthetic dissent," as opposed to the political function of texts written within the antislavery and women's rights movements, see John Carlos Rowe, *At Emerson's Tomb: The Politics of Classic American Literature* (New York: Columbia University Press, 1997), 12–13.
51. Castiglia, "Aesthetics Beyond the Actual," 118; Hyde, *Civic Longing*, 15–17 and 119.
52. I concur with Paul Gilmore's claim that this move "has failed to connect individual cases to a broader, international literary mode, thereby neglecting the significant work categories as mode and genre enable" ("John Neal, American Romance, and International Romanticism," *American Literature* 84, no. 3 [September 2012]: 490).
53. Maurice S. Lee, "Introduction: A Survey of Survey Courses," *J19: The Journal of Nineteenth-Century Americanists* 4, no. 1 (Spring 2016): 125–130.
54. Jackson, "American Romanticism, Again," 321.
55. On romance as a theory of fiction rather than a stable genre, see Hyde, *Civic Longing*, 126. On realism "not as a genre but an aesthetic mode," see Murison, *Faith in Exposure*, 16. For Hyde, the romance is characterized by "its departure from the descriptive regime of the indicative," while Murison argues that realism is characterized by "the expression of privacy and the appraisal of other people's private lives." As Hyde's and Murison's studies show, these elements of romance and realism can appear across genres and have traditionally given rise to different critical approaches.
56. Michael Warner, *Letters of the Republic: Publication and the Public Sphere in Eighteenth-Century America* (Cambridge, MA: Harvard University Press, 1990), 173–174; Anne E. Boyd, *Writing for Immortality: Women and the Emergence of High Literary Culture in America* (Baltimore: The Johns Hopkins University Press, 2004), 120, Kindle.
57. Kyla Schuller and Jules Gill-Peterson, "Introduction: Race, the State, and the Malleable Body," *Social Text* 38.2 (June 2020): 6.
58. Although print capitalist accounts of the early national period have traditionally emphasized a divide between the abstracted disinterest of the public sphere and the embodied desires of the private sphere, more recently this divide (and the gendered assumptions it takes for granted) have been challenged. One common understanding that has emerged from public sphere theory is that "privacy is publicly constructed" (Michael Warner, *Publics and Counterpublics* [Brooklyn: Zone Books, 2002], 62). For Lauren Berlant, liberalism's fetishization of privacy as a signifier of freedom has resulted in a misrecognition of private sentiment for political action (*The Female Complaint: The Unfinished Business of Sentimentality in American Culture* [Durham, NC: Duke University Press, 2008]. Castiglia has argued that the melancholy that characterizes early national literature is a form of imaginative resistance to the "federalization of affect," the method by which early national citizens were encouraged to see state interests as corresponding to their individual interior states (*Interior States: Institutional Consciousness and the Inner Life of Democracy in the Antebellum United States* [Durham, NC: Duke University Press, 2008], 18–19). Countering the paranoid account of internalized discipline, Stacey Margolis finds that nineteenth century conceptions of privacy treat publicity "less as a space of exposure, surveillance, or discipline than as a condition of intelligibility for individual action" (*The Public Life of Privacy in Nineteenth-Century American Literature* [Durham, NC: Duke University Press, 2005], 14). As Dillon argues, it is precisely because privacy is not only constructed by the liberal public sphere but is also "crucial to the structure and meaning of liberalism" that "the rich and textured terrain of private life" continues to have political potential (*Gender of Freedom*, 3, 9).

CHAPTER 1 — CHARLES BROCKDEN BROWN'S DOMESTIC SCENES

1. Charles Brockden Brown, "The Difference between History and Romance," *The Monthly Magazine and the American Review* 2, no. 4 (April 1800): 251, Charles Brockden Brown Electronic Archive and Scholarly Edition. Hereafter referred to parenthetically.
2. On the conjectural mode and political critique, see Stephen Shapiro, *The Culture and Commerce of the American Novel: Reading the Atlantic World-System* (Philadelphia: Pennsylvania State University Press, 2007), 227. Linking Brown's theory of the romance to his narrative method, Shapiro describes Brown's sensational Gothic plots as punctuated by moments of conjectural contemplation. For Shapiro, Brown's Gothic plots are a pragmatic means of attracting readers who are then provided with opportunities to think critically about how to act virtuously when placed in situations of extreme environmental duress. See also Thomas Koenigs, *Founded in Fiction: The Uses of Fiction in the Early United States* (Princeton: Princeton University Press, 2021), 69–83. Taking *Wieland* as his representative example, Koenigs argues that Brown's fiction trains readers less in finding a stable interpretation than in the very nature of "possibilistic reasoning," "suppositional thought," and "speculative thinking" required of citizens in the early United States (79, 82).
3. Charles Brockden Brown, *Edgar Huntly; Or, Memoirs of a Sleep-Walker*, ed. Norman S. Grabo (New York: Penguin, 1988), 87. Hereafter referred to parenthetically.
4. As Cahill has argued, Brown's fiction reflects a concern that the strict "principle of necessary causality" espoused by Godwin hews closely to "a dangerously deterministic view of history in which individuals, in spite of their efforts, play no part other than that which is assigned to them" (*Liberty of the Imagination*, 186). I depart from Cahill's claim that Brown's resolutions demonstrate the triumph of an "ordering imagination," as characters are ultimately able to organize their own traumatic history into readable narrative. For example, Huntly is unable or unwilling to complete his narrative and relinquishes narrative control to Sarsefield.
5. Hyde, *Civic Longing*, 126.
6. Hyde, *Civic Longing*, 5, 119. Castiglia argues that New Historicism is "the logical outgrowth . . . of late nineteenth-century realism, which itself was a response to the counteractuality of romanticism" ("Aesthetics Beyond the Actual," 118). On the early national romance genre more generally, see Woertendyke, who argues that the self-consciously "future-oriented form" of the romance "offered imaginative solutions to pressing problems haunting the nation" (*Hemispheric Regionalism*, 3–4). Woertendyke works to "render the fantastic sensibilities of romance, and the cultural work it performs, visible," disrupting a critical tradition that, by conflating the romance and the novel, privileges the consolidating, nationalist aims of the realist novel (6, 10). For Sizemore, the imaginative and "as-yet-unresolved" future-passing temporal mode of the historical romance suggests a way forward for literary historicism that allows us "to engage literature as the site of not only multiple and competing tracks of history but also open and as-yet-unrealized futures" (*American Enchantment*, 170).
7. Hyde, *Civic Longing*, 15.
8. Hyde, *Civic Longing*, 122.
9. Berlant, *Female Complaint*, 4. Here and throughout, my reading aligns with Erica Burleigh's, who argues that Brown's final two novels "tweak" the "narrative expectations" of the sentimental marriage plot ("Incommensurate Equivalences: Genre, Representation, and Equity in *Clara Howard* and *Jane Talbot*," *Early American Studies* [Fall 2011]: 754).
10. On this move to "un-novel" Brown, see the group of essays included in the "Symposium on Scholarly Editing and the New Charles Brockden Brown Studies," *Early American Literature* 57, no. 2 (2022): 531–569. See especially Elizabeth Hewitt, Stephen Shapiro, and Karen A. Weyler, "Introduction," 531–535, and Philip Barnard and Stephen Shapiro, "Un-Noveling Brown: Liberalism and Its Literary Discontents," 549–554.
11. Many critics have noticed Huntly's lack of interest in the marriage plot that at first appears to provide the justification for his tale. For Huntly's "liberal cosmopolitanism," see Dillon, *Gender of Freedom*, 161–183. For the "carnality" of Huntly's refusal of the patriarchal

marriage plot, see Dana Luciano, "'Perverse Nature': Edgar Huntly and the Novel's Reproductive Disorders," *American Literature* 70, no. 1 (March 1998): 1–27. For Brown's "nascent ideal of male-male sexuality," see Stephen Shapiro, "'Man to Man I Needed Not to Dread His Encounter': Edgar Huntly's End of Erotic Pessimism," in *Revising Charles Brockden Brown: Culture, Politics, and Sexuality in the Early Republic*, ed. Philip Barnard, Mark L. Kamrath, and Stephen Shapiro (Knoxville: University of Tennessee Press, 2004), 216.

12. For an overview of this critical narrative see Burnham, "Epistolarity, Anticipation, and Revolution in *Clara Howard*," in *Revising Charles Brockden Brown: Culture, Politics, and Sexuality in the Early Republic*, ed. Philip Barnard, Mark L. Kamrath, and Stephen Shapiro, (Knoxville: University of Tennessee Press, 2004), 260–263, and Bruce Burgett, *Sentimental Bodies: Sex, Gender, and Citizenship in the Early Republic* (Princeton: Princeton University Press, 1998). Burgett puts it well: "Brown becomes the antetype of nineteenth- and twentieth-century male authors whose (masculine) art resists (feminine) sentimentality, even as it eventually falls prey to the demands of the mass market and the unenlightened taste of a female reading public" (114). On the unique endurance of the epistolary form in early national fiction, see Karen A. Weyler, *Intricate Relations: Sexual and Economic Desire in American Fiction, 1789–1814* (Iowa City: University of Iowa Press, 2004), 29–33.
13. Sydney Krause is one of the first to make this argument, arguing that *Clara Howard* and *Jane Talbot* "confirm and consummate the tendency of the early novels," particularly through a "testing out" of Godwin's political philosophy ("*Clara Howard* and *Jane Talbot*: Godwin on Trial," in *Critical Essays on Charles Brockden Brown*, ed. Bernard Rosenthal [New York: G. K. Hall, 1981], 186). On the final two novels as debating the conflicting ideals of disinterested republicanism and liberal individualism in the early national period, see Burgett, *Sentimental Bodies*, 112–133; Burnham, "Epistolarity, Anticipation, and Revolution"; Burleigh, "Incommensurate Equivalences." On Brown's turn to literary magazines, see Jared Gardner: "Instead of a two-year novel-writing career followed by abandonment and betrayal of the novel . . . we see instead a consistent and radical attempt to revise and reimagine the function of literature and the role of the editor in the new republic" (*The Rise and Fall of American Periodical Culture* [Urbana: University of Illinois Press, 2012] 6, Kindle).
14. As Burnham notes, "despite critical assumptions about Brown's sudden shift to domestic concerns" in his final two novels, "marriage and the role of money in romantic and marital matters are of course central to nearly all of his novels" ("Epistolarity, Anticipation, and Revolution," 264).
15. Charles Brockden Brown, *Jane Talbot* (Philadelphia: John Conrad, 1801), 57, Kindle. Hereafter cited parenthetically.
16. On domestic fiction as marking a new emphasis on gender difference, see Armstrong, *Desire and Domestic Fiction*, 4–5. On the early national context specifically, see Dillon, *Gender of Freedom*, 127.
17. Burgett, *Sentimental Bodies*, 131.
18. Rust, "Into the House of an Entire Stranger," 285.
19. Leonard Tennenhouse, "Libertine America," *differences: A Journal of Feminist Cultural Studies* 11, no. 3 (Fall 1999): 16.
20. Also arguing that *Jane Talbot* and *Clara Howard* are not sentimental, Burleigh claims the two novels critique "the limitations of the contractual logic underlying the sentimental novel" ("Incommensurate Equivalences, 752–753).
21. See Armstrong on domestic fiction as ideological tool: "[domestic fiction] helped to formulate the ordered space we now recognize as the household, made that space totally functional, and used it as the context for representing normal behavior" (*Desire and Domestic Fiction*, 24). For the aesthetic potential of the sentimental home and its relation to the pastoralization of domestic labor, see Dillon, "Sentimental Aesthetics."

22. According to historian Amy Dru Stanley, domestic labor during the early national period was theoretically considered to be "unwaged service that a woman owed her husband as his dependent by law and custom" (Stanley, *From Bondage to Contract*, 80).
23. Jeanne Boydston, *Home and Work: Housework, Wages, and the Ideology of Labor in the Early Republic* (New York: Oxford University Press, 1990), 44. Boydston demonstrates that civic republicanism worked "not simply to conceive of women as economic dependents, but to deny that they contributed to the household economy at all." Rendering women's household labor invisible bolstered a Republican masculinity characterized by an "economic independence [that] was evidenced by the presence of economic *dependents*."
24. Merish, *Sentimental Materialism*, 15.
25. Merish, *Sentimental Materialism*, 40.
26. Merish, *Sentimental Materialism*, 3.
27. On "the federalization of affect" during the early national period, see Castiglia: "citizenship was becoming an interior state in which individuals were being encouraged to recognize the interests and disciplines of the state as originating not in coercive legalisms or competitive capitalism, but in their 'deep' selves" (*Interior States*, 18).
28. See Margolis on how we might think of nineteenth-century literature as working "to disarticulate privacy and individuality by emphasizing what seems external, even peripheral, to the self" (*The Public Life of Privacy*, 3).
29. Barnes, *States of Sympathy*, 72.
30. The novel thus registers the relationship between consensual citizenship and affectionate marriage, and what Barnes describes as an uneasy correspondence between seduction and the sentimental reading practices of the early American novel. As Dillon argues, however, early national fiction is just as populated with texts that protest this appropriative redirecting of individual desire by "thematizing a dissonance between marital structure and affect" (*Gender of Freedom*, 136).
31. See Burleigh for how the endings of both *Jane Talbot* and *Clara Howard*, by tentatively implying but not ensuring marriage, highlight Brown's skepticism about the generic conventions that sentimentalize the coercive and unequal nature of contracts ("Incommensurate Equivalences," 750–753 and 777–780).
32. Hyde, *Civic Longing*, 25.
33. Hyde, *Civic Longing*, 33.
34. Gardner, *Rise and Fall*, 3.
35. Gardner, *Rise and Fall*, 73.
36. Elizabeth Harries, *The Unfinished Manner: Essays on the Fragment in the Later Eighteenth Century* (Charlottesville: University of Virginia Press, 1994), 6.
37. Harries, *Unfinished Manner*, 8.
38. Harries, *Unfinished Manner*, 9.
39. Matthew Garrett, *Episodic Poetics: Politics and Literary Form after the Constitution* (Oxford: Oxford University Press, 2014), 10.
40. For Garrett, "representational government is the most direct form of the abstract problem of the part and the whole within politics" during the early national period (*Episodic Poetics*, 16). For Gardner, comparisons between the early national magazine and the novel are analogous to textual and originalist theories of the constitution: "If the unalterable constitutions called for by some was the book, forever sacrosanct in closed covers, growing increasingly obsolete (and tyrannical) on library shelves, the magazine was to be a living document, forever responding to the needs of the moment" (*Rise and Fall*, 77).
41. Daniel Diez Couch, *American Fragments: The Political Aesthetic of Unfinished Forms in the Early Republic* (Philadelphia: University of Pennsylvania Press, 2022), 9–10.
42. Couch, *American Fragments*, 6.
43. "The Household. A Fragment." *The Monthly Magazine and the American Review* 3, no. 2 (August 1800): 86, 85, Charles Brockden Brown Electronic Archive and Scholarly Edition. Hereafter referred to parenthetically.

44. Tennenhouse, *Libertine America*, 15.
45. Stern, *Plight of Feeling*, 28.
46. On the common theme of incest in early American fiction as registering anxiety about a newly fluid social order, see Anne Dalke, "Original Vice: The Political Implications of Incest in the Early American Novel," *Early American Literature* 23 (1988): 188–201; as registering the confusion that arises from a moral philosophy that requires sameness for sympathetic identification and that naturalizes authority through family metaphors, see Stern, *Plight of Feeling*, 29, and Barnes, *States of Sympathy*, 19.
47. Dillon, *Gender of Freedom*, 157–158.
48. Couch, *American Fragments*, 176–180.
49. Charles Brockden Brown, *Ormond; or, The Secret Witness* (Kessinger Publishing, 2004), 149. Hereafter referred to parenthetically.
50. Shapiro, *Culture and Commerce*, 218.
51. See Sedgwick, "Character in the Veil," 256: "the veil that conceals and inhibits sexuality comes by the same gesture to represent it." See also Goddu on the figure of the veiled lady and the domestic woman in nineteenth-century American literary culture (*Gothic America*, 97–98). Ann M. Little's research on convent narratives demonstrates that although "supposed impenetrability" was a consistent element of the antebellum fascination with convents, historical accounts of convents suggest that despite this obsession with "the closed nature of the convent," "the evidence they present of their interactions with the Ursulines suggest that the convent was in fact quite open to them" ("Cloistered Bodies: Convents in the Anglo-American Imagination in the British Conquest of Canada," *Eighteenth-Century Studies* 39, no. 2 [Winter 2006)]: 188).
52. Much work has been done on the operations of sympathy, particularly as theorized by Adam Smith, in the early American novel. On a reading of how sympathy in the early American novel "subordinates difference to sameness," and thus teaches "that difference is to be negated rather than understood," see Barnes, *States of Sympathy*, 17–18. On spectacle as a failure of sympathy, see Stern, *Plight of Feeling*, 19. See Gardner for how an understanding of early American magazine culture can shift how we read early American fiction more generally: "If the new nation required a new literature, then one important contribution the novel might offer as it sought out national legitimation was a space that spoke the spectacularly contradictory voices of that nation" (*Rise and Fall*, 14). Gardner insightfully argues that "Brown's turn from gothic spectacles to the 'romance of real life' is part and parcel with a larger critique of the tendencies in narrative history and fiction to diminish the possibilities of the present" (22–23).
53. Couch, *American Fragments*, 178.
54. Charles Brockden Brown, "Portrait of an Emigrant. Extracted from a Letter," *The Monthly Magazine and the American Review* 1, no. 3 (June 1799): 162–3, Charles Brockden Brown Electronic Archive and Scholarly Edition. Hereafter referred to parenthetically.
55. Sizemore, *American Enchantment*, 138.
56. Woertendyke, *Hemispheric Regionalism*, 2–4.
57. I concur here with Gardner: "By reading the world around her not through the plots scripted by her factional age but through active and close investigation, she is able to read more 'justly' than those whose reading has been schooled by a newspaper—or by novels such as *Edgar Huntly*" (*Rise and Fall*, 1). Woertendyke notes that Haiti is a crucial space for the speculative futurity of the U.S. Gothic romance: "Haiti provides a geographic, political, and ultimately imagined space onto which early American fears are projected" (*Hemispheric Regionalism*, 38).
58. Kaplan, *Manifest Domesticity*, 582.
59. Kaplan, *Manifest Domesticity*, 591.
60. Elizabeth Maddock Dillon, "The Secret History of the Early American Novel: Leonora Sansay and Revolution in Saint Domingue," *NOVEL* (Fall 2006/Spring 2007): 99.
61. Dillon, "Secret History," 86.

62. Dillon, "Secret History," 94.
63. As Barnard and Shapiro note, the fact that Madame de Lisle is employed by Lailson's circus suggests she may have been involved in a performance of George Coleman's antislavery play *The American Heroine*, a production Brown and his circle might have seen and would at least have been familiar with (Barnard and Shapiro, *Arthur Mervyn, with Related Texts*, 351).
64. See Couch, *American Fragments*, 167–168: "these formal elements provided a means of emphasizing the compositional, in-process nature of writing that could confer the status of 'author.'"

CHAPTER 2 — *SALMAGUNDI*'S ELBOW-CHAIR DOMESTICITY

1. Richard H. Dana, "The Sketch Book of Geoffrey Crayon, Gent.," *The North American Review and Miscellaneous Journal* 9, no. 25 (Sept. 1819): 322, American Periodical Series Online. Hereafter referred to parenthetically.
2. Washington Irving et al., *Salmagundi; or The Whim-whams and Opinions of Launcelot Langstaff, Esq. & Others*, in *Letters of Jonathan Oldstyle, Gent.; Salmagundi; or the Whim-whams and Opinions of Launcelot Langstaff, Esq. & Others*, ed. Bruce I. Granger and Martha Hartzog (Boston: Twayne Publishers, 1977), 70. Hereafter referred to parenthetically. Despite circulating irregularly for only one year, *Salmagundi* was immediately popular in New York and eventually nationwide. See Amos Herold, *James Kirke Paulding: Versatile American* (New York: AMS Press, 1966), 31–32: "Many of the separate numbers passed through several editions . . . 800 copies at a shilling apiece were sold in a day—a record for that time."
3. Like the bachelors who publish his letters, Mustapha is a cultural outsider. Although the humor of Mustapha's social commentary, like that of Goldsmith's Chinese philosopher Lien Chi Altangi, is often based on the fact that it is voiced by an inferior and misinformed foreigner, his language seeps into the other essays of *Salmagundi*, suggesting that his assessment of American politics and print culture is not so inaccurate. See William L. Hedges, *Washington Irving: An American Study, 1802–1832* (Baltimore: The Johns Hopkins Press, 1965), 54–55.
4. Claudia Stokes, "Bachelor Sketches: Invisible Women in Irving's Domestic Writings," *Early American Literature* 57, no. 2 (2022): 193–219. See also Walter Sondey, who considers Irving as using the domestic and the sentimental to offer readers opportunities to participate in a conservative national identity that has lost sway in the public realm ("From Nation of Virtue to Virtual Nation: Washington Irving and American Nationalism," in *Narratives of Nostalgia, Gender, and Nationalism*," ed. Jean Pickering and Suzanne Kehde [Houndmills, UK: Macmillan Press, 1997], 52–73).
5. Stokes, "Bachelor Sketches," 211.
6. Stokes, "Bachelor Sketches," 204.
7. On the transition from "preindustrial to modern industrial work patterns," and the implication of this transition on gendered work, see Cott, *Bonds of Womanhood*, 57–62. Cott documents the notion of home as "retreat" beginning in the first decade of the nineteenth century.
8. For an overview of this history of Irving criticism, see Jeffrey Insko, "Diedrich Knickerbocker, Regular Bred Historian," *Early American Literature* 43, no. 2 (2008): 606–607, Project Muse.
9. Claudia Stokes, *Old Style: Unoriginality and Its Uses in Nineteenth-Century U.S. Literature* (Philadelphia: University of Pennsylvania Press, 2022), 2–3.
10. See Michael T. Gilmore, "The Literature of the Revolutionary and Early National Periods," in *The Cambridge History of American Literature*, ed. Sacvan Bercovitch (Cambridge: Cambridge University Press, 1994), 1: 662–663; William L. Hedges, *Washington Irving: An American Study, 1802–1832* (Baltimore: The Johns Hopkins Press, 1965), 45; Martin Roth, *Comedy and America: The Lost World of Washington Irving* (Port Washington, NY: Kennikat Press, 1976), 36.

11. William Hazlitt, *The Spirit of the Age; or, Contemporary Portraits*, in *The Complete Works of William Hazlitt*, ed. P. P. Howe (London: Frank Cass and Co., 1967), 11: 183.
12. I refer to the Habermasian print capitalist narrative of the "the public sphere of a rational-critical debate" (Jürgen Habermas, *The Structural Transformation of the Public Sphere: An Inquiry into a Category of Bourgeois Society*, 7th ed., trans. Thomas Burger [Cambridge, MA: MIT Press, 1995], 51). Scholars of eighteenth-century periodicals agree that an Enlightenment belief in universal reason animates Addison's and Steele's attempts to appeal to a broad public readership. For the representative function of Mr. Spectator, see Paul Trolander and Zeynep Tenger, "Addison and the Personality of the Critic," in *The Spectator: Emerging Discourses*, ed. Donald J. Newman (Newark: University of Delaware Press, 2005), 190; Greg Polly, "A Leviathan of Letters," in *The Spectator: Emerging Discourses*, ed. Donald J. Newman (Newark: University of Delaware Press, 2005), 118; Terry Eagleton, *The Function of Criticism* (London: Verso, 1984), 22. For *Salmagundi* and the 1807 New York City public sphere specifically, see Hedges, *Washington Irving*, 33, and Richard Squibbs, *Urban Enlightenment and the Eighteenth-Century Periodical Essay: Transatlantic Retrospects* (London: Palgrave, 2014): 167.
13. Lucy Newlyn, *Reading, Writing, and Romanticism: The Anxiety of Reception* (Oxford: Oxford University Press, 2000), 14.
14. As Michael Gilmore notes, "most interpretations of the romantic writers see them as oppositional in their attitude toward the values and social consequences of the market revolution" (*American Romanticism*, 5).
15. Gardner, *Rise and Fall*, 51.
16. Gardner, *Rise and Fall*, 161.
17. Warner, *Letters of the Republic*, 173–174.
18. Boyd, *Writing for Immortality*, 120.
19. For an overview and critique of the separate spheres model, see Cathy Davidson, "Preface: No More Separate Spheres!" *American Literature* 70, no. 3 (September 1998): 443–463, JSTOR. The bachelors are situated at the transition from class-based aristocracy to gender-based liberalism that Armstrong argues marks the parallel rise of domestic fiction and the self-regulating liberal subject (*Desire and Domestic Fiction*, 4). On the transition from class difference to sexual difference in the early American context specifically, see Dillon, *Gender of Freedom*, 44–48.
20. Using Hawthorne as a case study of a "major author" who performatively rejected his years of success as a periodical author when he turned to novels, McGill argues that "the fiction of obscurity itself is one of the means by which Hawthorne, who is thoroughly, and in many ways successfully embedded in the literary marketplace, *renegotiates* a relation to the reading public" (*American Literature*, 221–226).
21. Roth points to an apparent scarcity of women in the burlesque humor that links *Salmagundi* to the "Romantic genius," claiming "Irving's fiction, like that of most of the major American writers who followed him, is devoted to an essentially male world" (*Comedy and America*, 42, 84).
22. Although I share Stokes's concern that a critical tendency to conflate sentimental and domestic literature keeps us from seeing the full range and complexity of domestic literature in the nineteenth century, here I depart from her characterization of Irving as an author of domestic fiction who is not a sentimentalist ("Bachelor Sketches," 215). As I go on to argue, throughout *Salmagundi* the editors use good humor and sympathy to reform their readers.
23. American Romanticism is traditionally defined against the reformist energies of domesticity (Romero, *Home Fronts*, 1; Gilmore, "Literature," 557), and *Salmagundi* in particular has been claimed as proto-Romantic because of its antiutilitarian investment in pleasure, whim, and eccentricity rather than reform and didacticism (Gilmore, "Literature," 662–663; Roth, *Comedy and America*, 34–36).
24. Newlyn, *Reading, Writing, and Romanticism*, 42–43.

25. In his study of literary performance in the American Renaissance, Stephen Railton challenges the critical impulse to "assume that the popular failure of writers like Melville and Thoreau measures only the failure of their culture" (*Authorship and Audience: Literary Performance in the American Renaissance* [Princeton, NJ: Princeton University Press, 1991], 201). But Railton also continues a critical narrative that contrasts Melville and Thoreau's "unwillingness to concede to the expectations of the American public" with Harriet Beecher Stowe's ability to "cross the gap between great and popular fiction," even as that ability is dependent on her blindness toward the "feminine pieties" that corrupt her readers (86). Following Romero, I'm more interested in how the very alienation that dogged Melville and his Renaissance cohort can itself be understood as a "creative effort" (Romero, *Home Fronts*, 105).
26. Leslie Fiedler, *Love and Death in the American Novel* (1960; repr., Funks Grove, IL: Dalkey Archive Press, 2003), 25–26.
27. Michael Warner, "Irving's Posterity," *ELH* 67, no. 3 (Fall 2000): 791, Project Muse; Bryce Traister, "The Wandering Bachelor: Irving, Masculinity, and Authorship," *American Literature* 74, no. 1 (Mar. 2002): 112, Project Muse.
28. Scholars have argued that the bachelor's antagonism toward domesticity is less a sign of misogyny than part of a much larger critique of capitalism. See Gregg Camfield, *Necessary Madness: The Humor of Domesticity in Nineteenth-Century American Literature* (New York: Oxford University Press, 1997), 42–45; C. Michael Hurst "Reinventing Patriarchy: Washington Irving and the Autoerotics of the American Imaginary," *Early American Literature* 47, no. 3 (2012), 649–78, Project Muse; Vincent Bertolini, "Fireside Chastity: The Erotics of Sentimental Bachelorhood in the 1850s," *American Literature* 68, no. 4 (December 1996): 707–737, JSTOR. For Hurst, Irving's bachelor storyteller "eschews the materialistic emphasis of capitalism altogether in favor of nonmaterial, noncompetitive products of the imagination. Part of this refusal includes the avoidance of marriage, because married life is inextricably tangled with the capitalist desire that corrupted it in the first place" (668). Bertolini argues that Melville uses bachelor fiction to "imagine tentative forms of practical resistance to heteroerotic and procreative norms" (722).
29. Katherine Snyder, *Bachelors, Manhood, and the Novel, 1850–1925* (Cambridge: Cambridge University Press, 1999), 7.
30. The Cockloft bachelors' claim of independence and "general benevolence" links them to the republican ideals of civic disinterest that still circulated in the early national period. See Christopher Looby, "Republican Bachelorhood: Sex and Citizenship in the Early United States," *Historical Reflections* 33, no. 1 (Spring 2007): 92–3, JSTOR. John Bryant argues that early national debates about humor were informed by anxieties about factionalism; for Bryant, Irving helps shift the bachelor narrator from signifying misanthropy to achieving "a comic indifference that is paradoxically communal" (*Melville and Repose: The Rhetoric of Humor in the American Renaissance* [New York: Oxford University Press, 1993], 55).
31. See Snyder on how competing notions of manhood during the nineteenth century pitted masculinity against domesticity, particularly "sporting male culture" and "primitive masculinity" (*Bachelors, Manhood, and the Novel*, 25–28). See also Sarah Wilson's reading of Melville's subversion of the ways that a newly developing gender segregation within the domestic space "limits masculine identification with the spaces and labors of domesticity" ("Melville and the Architecture of Antebellum Masculinity," *American Literature* 76, no. 1 [March 2004]: 60, Project Muse).
32. Dillon, "Sentimental Aesthetics," 509–511.
33. Newlyn, *Reading, Writing, and Romanticism*, 265.
34. On originality and moral influence, see Newlyn, *Reading, Writing, and Romanticism*, 266–268. In her discussion of Hawthorne's career change from periodical contributor to novelist, McGill argues that "the antebellum 'poetics of repose'" achieves originality through a fragile negotiation of "fanciful speculation that is tempered with but not

overwhelmed by didacticism" (*American Literature*, 233). Perhaps signaling an earlier moment in the transition McGill is tracing, *Salmagundi*'s project follows a similar method but with a different emphasis: rather than tempering fancy with didacticism, the bachelor-editors transact with their readers by tempering an overtly didactic message with whim and humor.

35. Gilmore, "Literature," 663.
36. For the political referents of *Salmagundi*, including this sketch, see Mary Weatherspoon Bowden, "Cocklofts and Slang-whangers: The Historical Sources of Washington Irving's 'Salmagundi,'" *New York History* 61, no. 2 (April 1980): 133–160.
37. Richards, *Gender and the Poetics of Reception*, 4.
38. *Salmagundi*'s characterization of women as humorless and unimaginative is an example of the "defensive" nature of the rhetoric that Richards traces as a response to the robust collaboration across genders in nineteenth-century literary culture; as Camfield documents, the many men and women who wrote domestic humor shared similar concerns about the restrictions domesticity posed to individual freedom (*Necessary Madness*, 21, 26). See also Newlyn on how women poets resisted high Romanticism's defensive strategy of constructing women "as temporary rather than permanent, sympathetically receptive rather than creative" (*Reading, Writing, and Romanticism*, 252). See also Wilson on Melville: "the ostensibly feminized character of the literary marketplace in Melville's time may have suggested that literary production, taking place as it often has with domestic space, had been ceded to women in the separation of the spheres . . . Success for Melville thus relied on a figurative male reclaiming of a domesticated space" ("Melville," 78).
39. In 1788 New York banned the slave trade. In 1799 a gradual manumission act was passed, which freed all enslaved people born after July 4, 1799—men at age twenty-eight, women at age twenty-five. Enslaved people born before July 4, 1799 were renamed indentured servants for life.
40. Note the similarity between Caesar in this pastoral fantasy and the housewife in sentimental discourse. See Dillon's reading of Frances Sargent Osgood's poetry, where household labor is characterized as "the production of song, rather than, say, the production of dinner and the caretaking of children" ("Sentimental Aesthetics," 510).
41. On Irving's nostalgia for forms of anticapitalist aristocratic patriarchy, see Warner, "Irving's Posterity," and Hurst, "Reinventing Patriarchy."
42. As Shawn Lisa Maurer argues, eighteenth-century periodicals like the *Spectator* "worked to consolidate men's interests by creating and then effacing an artfully conceived female Other" (*Proposing Men: Dialectics of Gender and Class in the Eighteenth-Century English Periodical* [Stanford: Stanford University Press, 1998], 119). See also Snyder paraphrasing Eve Kosofsky Sedgwick: the fraught logic and shifting terms of bourgeois manhood meant bachelors were perceived simultaneously as "both a separate species of man and a representative modern man" (*Bachelors, Manhood, and the Novel*, 4).
43. See Squibbs, who, using *Salmagundi* as an example, links the early national periodical's investment in whim's potential to "renounc[e] the distractions of fashion and novelty in favor of the more durable pleasures of enriching character through reading, reflection, and sociable exchange" to Emerson's "Self-Reliance," "one of the key texts of American romanticism" ("Civic Humorism," 389–390).
44. This "thwarted suitor" performance is a frequent convention in bachelor literature that is more complicated than a defensive assertion of normative masculinity; as Snyder argues, by making "the inaccuracy of their self-portrayal as contenders so conspicuously evident to readers," the bachelor narrator openly broadcasts his rejection of normative masculinity and thus gains the "the privileged position of spectator-in-the-text" (*Bachelors, Manhood, and the Novel*, 67–68). This strategy also allows the chaste editors to displace anxieties about transgressive bachelor sexuality onto spinsters. By midcentury, the bachelor figure was a lightning rod for anxieties about the potentially detrimental effects of urbanization, industrialization, and Western expansion on the home and on normative masculinity (Bertolini, "Fireside Chastity," 708).

45. The periodical's success may have been its downfall; Paulding and the Irving brothers decided to end the project after their publisher, David Longworth, acquired a copyright and started raking in profits that the authors would never see (Herold, *James Kirke Paulding*, 32).
46. See *The Structural Transformation of the Public Sphere*, where Habermas connects eighteenth-century novels and early periodicals via the reflexivity the bourgeois reading public demanded: in early periodicals, "the public held up a mirror to itself" as it "read and debated about itself" (*Structural Transformation*, 43). For the collaborative function of early American magazines, see Gardner, *Rise and Fall.*
47. It is unclear when, exactly, Paulding and the Irving brothers came clean. Herold finds "the authorship was so well concealed that . . . even as late as March, 1832, the editor of the *New York Mirror* after careful enquiry felt the need of publishing an authentic statement, assigning all the poetry and all but two of the prose articles to William Irving and James K. Paulding" (Herold, *James Kirke Paulding*, 33–34). According to Dana's 1819 review, "it was not long before the authors of *Salmagundi* were as well known as their writings. Probably the secrecy was a mere matter of sport, and that after it had served its turn, they cared little whether they were known or not. It is now well understood who the gentlemen were, and that Washington Irving was the principal contributor to the work" ("The Sketch Book," 322). See also Bryant, who traces readers' "expectancy of concealment" to a much larger tradition of genial humor writing that challenges "any special aesthetic relevance" credited to Hawthorne and Melville's beleaguered relationship to the literary marketplace (*Melville and Repose*, 23–24).
48. On anonymity in republican print culture as a method of civic representation rather than "authorship" or "fictionality," see Warner, *Letters of the Republic*, 84.
49. In Armstrong's Foucauldian account of domestic fiction, a gendered divide between public and private is precisely what accords domestic fiction the apolitical status that implicates it in "a new form of state power" (*Desire and Domestic Fiction*, 15–24).

CHAPTER 3 — THE VOICE OF NATURE

1. Catharine Maria Sedgwick, *Hope Leslie; or, Early Times in the Massachusetts*, reprint ed. (New York: Penguin, 1998), 4. Hereafter referred to parenthetically.
2. Griswold, preface to *Female Poets*, 8.
3. Rufus Wilmot Griswold, preface to *The Female Poets of America*, 2nd ed. (Philadelphia: Henry C. Baird, 1852), 8.
4. Kaplan, "Manifest Domesticity," 588.
5. Throughout this chapter I use the term "Indian" to refer to the fictional characters and stereotypes of antebellum literary culture. I use the terms "American Indian" and "indigenous" to refer to the historical referents of this fiction. The term "native" is especially slippery in this context. As Griswold's preface demonstrates, its connotations of *indigenous* and *innate* are difficult to separate, particularly since early Romanticists worked to appropriate indigenous status for white Americans by inventing national character traits that could be imagined as derived from the American landscape and its original inhabitants. In this chapter I use the term "native" to capture this desire for an indigeneity that both legitimizes settlement and signals exceptionalism.
6. On this stubborn genealogy of American Romanticism, see Jackson, "American Romanticism, Again," 320.
7. See Jackson, who notes that one lingering symptom of the American Renaissance tradition is a privileging of "metrical innovation" ("Bryant; or, American Romanticism," in *The Traffic in Poems*, ed. Meredith L. McGill [New Brunswick, NJ: Rutgers University Press, 2008], 187). See also Kinereth Meyer's claim that "the aesthetic touches the political" in representations of American land and landscape ("Landscape and Counter-Landscape in the Poetry of William Cullen Bryant," *Nineteenth-Century Literature* 48, no. 2 [1993]: 199).

8. As an example of the critical consensus I am addressing here, consider Buell's characterization of Bryant's new-world pastoralism as postcolonial, still "affected by the European gravitational field," whereas Whitman's "anxious patriotic hubris" has an imperialist trajectory. I argue below that despite Bryant's "bondage to old-world language and form," his theory of national literature is closely related to the imperialistic narratives of progress Buell identifies in Whitman and Thoreau's "fully Americanized art" ("American Literary Emergence as a Postcolonial Phenomenon," in *American Literature, American Culture*, ed. Gordon Hutner, 605–609 [New York: Oxford University Press, 1999]).
9. Sizemore, *American Enchantment*, 138.
10. Jeffrey Insko, *History, Abolition, and the Ever-Present Now in Antebellum American Writing* (Oxford: Oxford University Press, 2018), 56–57.
11. Koenigs, *Founded in Fiction*, 143.
12. Virginia Jackson, "'Our Poets': William Cullen Bryant and the White Romantic Lyric," *New Literary History* 49, no. 4 (Autumn 2018), 526–527.
13. Jackson, "'Our Poets,'" 540. On the ballad tradition in particular, see Meredith Martin, "'Imperfectly Civilized': Ballads, Nations, and Histories of Form," *ELH* 82, no. 2 (Summer 2015): 345–363, Project Muse; Michael Cohen, "Whittier, Ballad Reading, and the Culture of Nineteenth-Century Poetry," *Arizona Quarterly: A Journal of American Literature, Culture, and Theory* 64, no. 3 (Autumn 2008): 1–29, Project Muse.
14. On refusal to engage with history, see Ann Douglas, *The Feminization of American Culture* (New York: Knopf, 1977), 184–185, and Laurence Buell, *New England Literary Culture from Revolution through Renaissance* (Cambridge: Cambridge University Press, 1986), 242. On subversive critique, see Sandra A. Zagarell, "Expanding 'America': Lydia Sigourney's *Sketch of Connecticut*, Catharine Sedgwick's *Hope Leslie*," *Tulsa Studies in Women's Literature* 6, no. 2 (1987): 225, and Christopher Castiglia, "In Praise of Extra-Vagant Women: *Hope Leslie* and the Captivity Romance," *Legacy* 6, no. 2 (1989): 3. On limited ability to negotiate racial difference, see Dana Nelson, "Sympathy as Strategy in Sedgwick's *Hope Leslie*" in *The Culture of Sentiment: Race, Gender, and Sentimentality in Nineteenth-Century America*, ed. Shirley Samuels (New York: Oxford University Press, 1992), 192; Judith Fetterley, "'My Sister! My Sister!': The Rhetoric of Catharine Sedgwick's *Hope Leslie*," *American Literature* 70, no. 3 (1998): 492–493, 511; Douglas Ford, "Inscribing the 'Impartial Observer' in Sedgwick's *Hope Leslie*," *Legacy* 14, no. 2 (1997): 81–82.
15. Romero, *Home Fronts*, 19; Kaplan, "Manifest Domesticity," 581–583.
16. Tremaine McDowell, introduction to *William Cullen Bryant: Representative Selections*, ed. Tremaine McDowell (New York: American Book Co., 1935), lxi; Buell, "American Literary Emergence," 605–609; Jackson, "Bryant; or, American Romanticism," 188; Meyer, "Landscape and Counter-Landscape," 196–197.
17. Jackson, "'Our Poets,'" 526.
18. Jackson, "'Our Poets,'" 540, 526.
19. William Cullen Bryant, "Lectures on Poetry," in *Prose Writings of William Cullen Bryant*, ed. Parke Godwin (New York: Russell & Russell, 1964), 1:16–17. Hereafter cited parenthetically.
20. William Cullen Bryant, "*Redwood*," review of *Redwood*, by Catharine Maria Sedgwick, *North American Review* 20, no. 47 (1825): 270–271, *The Nineteenth Century in Print*. Hereafter cited parenthetically.
21. For the Vanishing American convention in antebellum verse culture, see Kate Flint, "Is the Native an American? National Identity and the British Reception of *Hiawatha*," in *The Traffic in Poems: Nineteenth-Century Poetry and Transatlantic Exchange*, ed. Meredith L. McGill (New Brunswick, NJ: Rutgers University Press, 2008), 64–65.
22. Kaplan, "Manifest Domesticity," 582.
23. Meyer, "Landscape and Counter-Landscape," 196; Richards, *Gender and the Poetics of Reception*, 17.
24. Dillon, "Sentimental Aesthetics" 509–510.

25. In this sense I depart from Stacy Alaimo, who argues that the novel opposes the domestic space to the natural landscape. Although I agree that "Sedgwick justifies Hope's rebellious, impetuous, and even illegal actions by appealing to something beyond the law, rooted in the heart and in nature—a 'natural' ethic that the Indians share," I find that the nineteenth-century ideology of domesticity presented the home as a similar extralegal space of natural morality (*Undomesticated Ground: Recasting Nature as Feminist Space* [Ithaca: Cornell University Press, 2000], 30). Sedgwick replaces the home with the frontier but maintains its symbolic function.
26. Meyer, "Landscape and Counter-Landscape," 198.
27. Priscilla Wald, "Terms of Assimilation: Legislating Subjectivity in the Emerging Nation," *boundary 2* 19, no. 3 (1992): 86.
28. Dillon, *Gender of Freedom*, 21; Kaplan, "Manifest Domesticity," 582; Richards, *Gender and the Poetics of Reception*, 38.
29. Martin, "'Imperfectly Civilized,'" 348.
30. Insko, *History, Abolition, and the Ever-Present Now*, 63.
31. Colin Jager, *The Book of God: Secularization and Design in the Romantic Era* (Philadelphia: University of Pennsylvania Press, 2006), 142.
32. Anna E. Beaudry, "Provocation: Magawisca's Light: A Recuperative Approach to Catharine Maria Sedgwick's Hope Leslie," *Early American Literature* 57, no. 2 (2022): 368–369, Project Muse.
33. George C. Callcott, *History in the United States 1800–1860* (Baltimore: Johns Hopkins University Press, 1970), 177.
34. Insko, *History, Abolition, and the Ever-Present Now*, 62–63.
35. Buell, *New England*, 241.
36. Insko, *History, Abolition, and the Ever-Present Now*, 67.
37. Lucy Maddox, *Removals: Nineteenth-Century American Literature and the Politics of Indian Affairs* (New York: Oxford University Press, 1991), 94.
38. Maddox, *Removals*, 111–112.
39. Romero, *Home Fronts*, 35.
40. Romero, *Home Fronts*, 35.
41. Douglas, *Feminization*, 181–185; Maddox, *Removals*, 107–110; Barnes, *States of Sympathy*, 78–79.
42. More recent criticism has tried to move beyond what Judith Fetterley calls "the Alternating phases of celebration and critique" by arguing that the novel's conventional resolution shouldn't shut down analysis of its progressive possibilities ("'My Sister! My Sister!'" 492). Amanda Emerson argues that Magawisca's disappearance signals the limit of what nineteenth-century society can imagine ("History, Memory, and the Echoes of Equivalence in Catharine Maria Sedgwick's *Hope Leslie*," *Legacy* 24, no. 1 [2007]: 32). Quentin Miller argues that despite "Hope's racism," her overall development as a character constitutes "narrative progress" ("'A Tyrannically Democratic Force': The Symbolic and Cultural Function of Clothing in Catharine Maria Sedgwick's *Hope Leslie*," *Legacy* 19, no. 2 [2002]: 133, 122). Even these more nuanced arguments, however, continue to contrast the novel's conservative resolution to its larger narrative of progress, rather than considering that the resolution might signal Sedgwick's skepticism of these narratives of progress.
43. Part of Tawil's purpose is to challenge the critical history I have just described, where the recovery of women's fiction "seems to have reproduced the central terms of the antithesis between domestic and frontier fiction" (*The Making of Racial Sentiment: Slavery and the Birth of the Frontier Romance* [Cambridge: Cambridge University Press, 2006], 93–96). Although I share Tawil's interest in the ways that sympathy and racism operate together in both men's and women's frontier fiction, this understanding of the frontier romance as "anticipatory" also predetermines a reading of *Hope Leslie* as supporting conventions and values that were not as firmly established for Sedgwick as they would be for Stowe midcentury.
44. Castiglia, "In Praise of Extra-Vagant Women," 4–5.

45. "Hope Leslie," review of *Hope Leslie*, by Catharine Maria Sedgwick, *North American Review* 26, no. 59 (Apr. 1828): 410. Making of America.
46. Review of *Hope Leslie, North American Review*, 411.
47. "Hope Leslie; or, Early Times in the Massachusetts," review of *Hope Leslie*, by Catharine Maria Sedgwick, *Western Monthly Review* 1, no. 5 (1827): 290. Internet Archive.
48. Review of *Hope Leslie, Western Monthly Review*, 290.
49. Consider, for example, Lydia Maria Child's assessment of Sedgwick's' "kind and playful humour" in her review of Sedgwick's fiction in Sarah Hale's *Ladies' Magazine* ("Miss Sedgwick's Novels," *Ladies' Magazine* 2, no. 5 (1829): 234, Google Books.
50. Romero, *Home Fronts*, 7.
51. On the marriage plot in the domestic frontier romance, see Tawil, *Making of Racial Sentiment*, 93.
52. Zagarell, "Expanding 'America,'" 237–238; Castiglia, "In Praise of Extra-Vagant Women," 4; Fetterley, "'My Sister! My Sister!'" 505.
53. Meyer, "Landscape and Counter-Landscape," 195; Maria Karafilis, "Catharine Maria Sedgwick's *Hope Leslie*: The Crisis between Ethical Political Action and US Literary Nationalism in the New Republic," *American Transcendental Quarterly* 12, no. 4 (1998): 338–339.
54. Zagarell, "Expanding 'America,'" 238–239; Maddox, *Removals*, 103; Philip Gould, "Catharine Sedgwick's 'Recital' of the Pequot War," *American Literature* 66, no. 4 (1994): 649–650.
55. Philip Deloria argues that when colonists played Indian to protest British rule (the Boston Tea Party is the most obvious example), they "solidified their common understanding of themselves as Americans, their freedom an ancient thing linked intrinsically to the continent, its custom, and its nature" (*Playing Indian* [New Haven: Yale University Press, 1998], 32). Postrevolution, these performances "signified an American identity based upon republican order rather than revolutionary potential" (56).
56. Insko, *History, Abolition, and the Ever-Present Now*, 57.
57. Deloria explains that early-nineteenth-century national iconography replaced the Indian Princess with Columbia, who "signified the dignity and gentility of civilization" rather than "primitivism, sexuality, and miscegenation" (*Playing Indian*, 53).
58. Bethany Schneider, "New England Tales: Catharine Sedgwick, Catherine Brown, and the Dislocations of Indian Land," in *A Companion to American Fiction, 1780–1865*, ed. Shirley Samuels (Malden, MA: Blackwell, 2004), 354.
59. Schneider, "New England Tales," 355.
60. Karafilis argues that Magawisca serves as Hope's "host" and notes that the "darker side" to their friendship is Hope's "pernicious appropriation" of Magawisca's indigeneity ("Catharine Maria Sedgwick's *Hope Leslie*," 339). I agree, but it seems important to examine the borrowed nature of this indigeneity—Hope is a substitute but never becomes the original. Magawisca's disappearance from the Puritan community is crucial, not only because Hope's successful hybridity renders "the presence of Magawisca at the close of the novel less 'necessary'" (341) but also because, as I will argue below, maintaining the purity of the original is a crucial component of the novel's project of naturalizing nationalist ideology. See also Wald, "Terms of Assimilation," 92.
61. Nineteenth-century reviews of *Hope Leslie* also remark on Everell and Magawisca's relationship, and Lydia Maria Child's frontier romance *Hobomok*, a novel that also experiments with interracial marriage, would have been on Sedgwick's readers' minds.
62. Callcott, *History in the United States*, 173, 156.
63. See also Bradfield, who notes that that in the early national period "transgression began to be conceived of as a disciplinary activity" (*Dreaming Revolution: Transgression in the Development of American Romance* [Iowa City: University of Iowa Press, 1993], xi).
64. Barnes, *States of Sympathy*, 9.
65. Barnes, *States of Sympathy*, 80.
66. Insko, *History, Abolition, and the Ever-Present Now*, 72. Insko also notices this separation between the narrator and Hope and argues that although it is clear that "the otherwise 'pro-

gressive' Hope views her sister as transgressing against 'natural' racial boundaries," what is less clear is "that this view is shared by Sedgwick." I find this to be an overly generous reading, as it is the narrator, and not Hope, who tells us that Faith's face, "pale and spiritless, was only redeemed from absolute vacancy by an expression of gentleness and modesty" (Sedgwick, *Hope Leslie*, 240).

67. For some critics, Magawisca's refusal signifies that she is racially unsuited for the proper sentiment required for membership in Hope and Everell's enlightened and distinctly feminized community. See Maddox, *Removals*, 107–110. To me, the point of this final scene is that Everell and Hope cannot see that their friendship is what has endangered Magawisca all along.
68. Schweitzer argues that recognizing the choice Magawisca makes at the end of the novel allows its characters to recognize the "limits of their comprehension—and thus control—of the other." This recognition "clears the way for the future possibility of ethical friendship across difference" (*Perfecting Friendship: Politics and Affiliation in Early American Literature* [Chapel Hill: University of North Carolina Press, 2006], 205). I agree that Magawisca's choice opens up a space for equality with difference, but I'm not so sure Hope and Everell are in favor of keeping this space open. Hope, for example, belies sympathy's trajectory toward sameness when she wishes that she might retain Magawisca in order to teach her Christianity.
69. Rogers Smith, *Civic Ideals*, 158, 167.
70. Wald, "Terms of Assimilation," 77–78.
71. Warner argues that women in the early nineteenth century argued for equal rights "through the normative language of the liberal tradition" and "appealed to the ideal of a disinterested, abstract, universal public—just the kind of public in which particularized views and the gendered body would always seem matter out of place" (*Publics and Counterpublics*, 41).
72. Lauren Berlant, *The Anatomy of National Fantasy: Hawthorne, Utopia, and Everyday Life* (Chicago: University of Chicago Press, 1991), 4.
73. Again, see Warner: in the same way that the early nineteenth century's rhetoric of nationalism allowed for "imaginary participation" that could be extended to women "as symbolic members of the nation," the sentimental novel allowed women "to attribute public value to reader identification" (*Letters of the Republic*, 173–174). See also Barnes: "sentimental politics reveals itself to be a politics of affinity rather than of democracy" (*States of Sympathy*, 98).

CHAPTER 4 — EPICENE GENIUS IN THEODORE WINTHROP'S *CECIL DREEME*

1. Theodore Winthrop, *Cecil Dreeme*, 244.
2. Richards, *Gender and the Poetics of Reception*, 38–39.
3. On separate spheres as a simple but powerful organizing form, see Caroline Levine, *Forms: Whole, Rhythm, Hierarchy, Network* (Princeton, NJ: Princeton University Press, 2015), 93–97. For Levine, forms such as separate spheres that organize gender spatially collide with other forms of organization, including temporality and hierarchy, to produce uncertain effects. One example is how the domestic sphere becomes differently valued when men are relegated to it. Levine's argument follows from gender theorists like Jack Halberstam and Judith Butler who have demonstrated that the rigidity of gender binarism is correlative rather than oppositional to the fluidity of gender presentation: "In a way, gender's very flexibility and seeming fluidity is precisely what allows dimorphic gender to hold sway. Because so few people actually match any given community standards for male or female, in other words, gender can be imprecise and therefore multiply relayed through a solidly binary system. At the same time, because the definitional boundaries of male and female are so elastic, there are very few people in any given public space who are completely unreadable in terms of their gender" (Jack Halberstam, *Female Masculinity* [Durham, NC: Duke University Press, 1998], 20).

4. In his introduction to the novel, Peter Coviello draws connections between *Cecil Dreeme* and Walt Whitman, Edgar Allan Poe, George Lippard, Herman Melville, Nathaniel Hawthorne, and Henry James (Peter Coviello, introduction to *Cecil Dreeme*, by Theodore Winthrop, ed. Peter Coviello [New York: Washington Mews Books, 2016], xv–xvi). For an extended comparison of Winthrop and Hawthorne, see Christopher Castiglia, "Hawthorne/Winthrop," in *American Literature in Transition, 1820–1860*, ed. Justine Murison, vol. 2 (Cambridge, England: Cambridge University Press, 2022), 372–387. For a comparison of Winthrop and Whitman, see Michael Millner, "The Fear Passing the Love of Women: Sodomy and Male Sentimental Citizenship in the Antebellum City," *Arizona Quarterly: A Journal of American Literature, Culture, and Theory* 58, no. 2 (Summer 2002): 19–52, Project Muse.
5. If we were to transpose this novel's polar logic onto recent debates about critical method, we might see it as capturing the ways that the paranoid and the reparative are less choices to be fully occupied by critics than reactive positions subjects constantly move between. See Heather Love, "Truth and Consequences" and Eva Cherniavsky, "Cultural Studies Revisited." One larger takeaway is that debates about surface reading can themselves be historicized by an attention to how authors in the eighteenth and nineteenth centuries debated the relationship between surface and depth, exterior and interior, publicity and privacy.
6. See Coviello, introduction to *Cecil Dreeme*, xiii, and Michael Millner, "Fear Passing," 31–32. In his editor's introduction to the novel, Christopher Looby proposes a reading more aligned with the one I make here: while the Densdeth plot fits with Sedgwick's description of the "paranoid gothic," the Dreeme plot registers differently, "within the literary tradition of exalted same-sex romantic friendship" (Christopher Looby, introduction to *Cecil Dreeme*, by Theodore Winthrop, ed. Christopher Looby [Philadelphia: University of Pennsylvania Press, 2016], xviii). Looby makes the intriguing proposition that the novel is structured "stereoscopically," and that the "mismatched counterparts" of the two plots registers a historical transition between same-sex friendship as uncontroversial and stigmatized (xxi).
7. Sedgwick, "Character in the Veil," 256.
8. Sedgwick, *Between Men: English Literature and Male Homosocial Desire* (New York: Columbia University Press, 1985), 88–89.
9. On the cultural work of the Gothic novel in the early United States, particularly in relation to Enlightenment individualism, see Cathy Davidson, *Revolution and the Word*, 306–355; Teresa A. Goddu, *Gothic America*; Siân Silyn Roberts, *Gothic Subjects: The Transformation of Individualism in American Fiction, 1790–1861* (Philadelphia: University of Pennsylvania Press, 2014).
10. Saltz, "Rather Both than Neither," 73.
11. See Sean Trainor, "Fair Bosom/Black Beard: Facial Hair, Gender Determination, and the Strange Career of Madame Clofullia, 'Bearded Lady,'" *Early American Studies* 12, no. 3 (Fall 2014): 553, Project Muse.
12. On shifting our readings of *Cecil Dreeme* to transgender studies, see Travis Foster, "White Supremacist Submission," *TSQ: Transgender Studies Quarterly* 10, nos. 3–4 (November 2023): 430–431. Foster supplements this reading of *Cecil Dreeme* with attention to nineteenth-century sources that commented on Theodore Winthrop's gender variance and themes of gender variance within Winthrop's larger body of work.
13. David J. Getsy, "Capacity," *TSQ: Transgender Studies Quarterly* 1, nos. 1–2 (May 2014): 47–49.
14. LaFleur, "Sex and 'Unsex,'" 469–499.
15. Looby, introduction to *Cecil Dreeme*, x–xii. Coviello, introduction to *Cecil Dreeme*, xix–xx.
16. Danielle M. Seid, "Reveal." *TSQ: Transgender Studies Quarterly* 1, nos. 1–2 (May 2014): 177, https://doi.org/10.1215/23289252-2399947.
17. From this opening chapter, where the hotel's servant, whose speech is written in dialect, is labeled "A Patrick," the novel immediately performs the constructing and policing of bor-

ders between foreign and national that Amy Kaplan has determined to be central to the ideology of domesticity ("Manifest Domesticity," 581–606). As Foster has argued, the novel goes on to exemplify Jasbir Puar's concept of homonationalism. Densdeth is consistently described as a racial other and his interior ugliness is projected onto his "Afreet" servant. These racialized descriptions use whiteness to sanction Byng's virtuous attraction to Dreeme. See Foster, "The Queer Young American Comes of Age," *Commonplace: the journal of early American life* 17, no. 2 (Winter 2017), https://commonplace.online/article/the-queer-young-american-comes-of-age/. On the novel's deliberate strategy of depicting Densdeth as "ambiguously brown and decidedly Black," see Foster, "White Supremacist Submission," 436–437.

18. Sedgwick, *Between Men*, 91; Sedgwick, *Epistemology of the Closet* (Berkeley: University of California Press, 1990), 186–187.
19. On queer counterpublics, see Michael Warner, *The Trouble with Normal: Sex, Politics, and the Ethics of Queer Life* (Cambridge, MA: Harvard University Press, 1999), 177–180. On counterpublics more generally, see Warner, *Publics and Counterpublics*. As Castiglia notes, given that the white male residents of Chrysalis College protect one another but also regulate belonging and behavior, the community might be better described as a "subculture" rather than a "counterpublic" ("Hawthorne/Winthrop," 383).
20. Eve Kosofsky Sedgwick, *Epistemology of the Closet*, 186; Dillon, *Gender of Freedom*, 184–185.
21. Coviello, introduction to *Cecil Dreeme*, xiii–xiv. While Coviello argues that Densdeth is imbued with "sexual menace" but not specifically taxonomized as "homosexual," Millner argues that Densdeth is very specifically coded as the nineteenth-century type of the sodomite ("Fear Passing," 27).
22. On the female Gothic and the home as a space of terror, see Kate Ferguson Ellis, *The Contested Castle: Gothic Novels and the Subversion of Domestic Ideology* (Urbana: University of Illinois Press, 1989).
23. Christopher Lukasik, *Discerning Characters: The Culture of Appearance in Early America* (Philadelphia: University of Pennsylvania Press, 2011), 32.
24. The reading that follows is counter to Millner's, who describes a "voyeuristic Byng" in this first encounter ("Fear Passing," 25).
25. Lukasik, *Discerning Characters*, 32. On the "circuitous observational route" of physiognomy, see also Sarah Blackwood, *The Portrait's Subject: Inventing Inner Life in the Nineteenth-Century United States* (Chapel Hill: University of North Carolina Press, 2019), 25.
26. On Dreeme's gender transitivity as "the ultimate deflection," see Millner, "Fear Passing," 29.
27. Lukasik, *Discerning Characters*, 32.
28. On Byng's desire to be dominated and ruined by Densdeth, see Coviello, introduction to *Cecil Dreeme*, xiii–xiv, and Foster, "White Supremacist Submission."
29. This reading is informed by Bethany Schneider, "The Consummate Hermaphrodite," in *Philosophies of Sex: Critical Essays on* The Hermaphrodite, ed. Renee Bergland and Gary Williams (Columbus: The Ohio State University Press, 2012), 138–156. In this essay, Schneider counters the assumption that Julia Ward Howe invests the narrative's ambiguously sexed central character with a lack of sexual desire as a way of questioning gender without "without the complication of sexuality" (139).
30. On how the use of *trans* as a verb "signifies a process or practice without claiming to understand what it meant to that person or asserting any kind of fixed identity on them," see Jen Manion, *Female Husbands: A Trans History* (Cambridge: Cambridge University Press, 2020), 11.
31. On how gender inversion does not account for the archive surrounding Theodore Winthrop's life and writing, see Foster, "White Supremacist Submission," 431.
32. Although reverting to these stereotypical gender roles seems to be a conservative vision of queer domesticity that conforms to heteronormativity, as Manion writes of female husbands in the nineteenth century, "their ability to blend in—for a time—is precisely what sparked passionate rage and retaliation against them" (*Female Husbands*, 171).

33. Intriguingly, the novel disrupts the convention that claims male bonding as a democratic space that transcends differences of race, class, and gender: Byng's different relationships with Dreeme and Densdeth are defined by these very differences. On the nineteenth-century trope of male bonding "establishing the masculine as internally cohesive, as itself without difference," see Robyn Wiegman, "Melville's Geography of Gender," *American Literary History* 1, no. 4 (Winter 1989): 736.
34. Griswold, preface to *The Female Poets of America*, 7.
35. Richards, *Gender and the Poetics of Reception*, 38–39.
36. Blackwood, *Portrait's Subject*, 16.
37. Blackwood, *Portrait's Subject*, 17.
38. The novel thus performs the function of the marital Gothic Dillon describes: the Gothic highlights that the affectionate marriage celebrated by domestic fiction as a marker of individualism is in fact the most conventional plot of all (*Gender of Freedom*, 139).
39. See Judith Butler, *Undoing Gender* (New York: Routledge, 2004), 3: "we are constituted, invariably and from the start, by what is before us and outside of us."
40. Sedgwick, *Between Men*, 160. As Coviello notes, the Emma Denman subplot is akin to Henry James's novel *The Beast in the Jungle* (introduction to *Cecil Dreeme*, xvi), the very text Sedgwick uses to develop a reading of this figure.
41. Foster, "Queer Young American." On the "exotically raced Densdeth," see Millner, "Fear Passing," 27. More recently, Foster has argued that *Cecil Dreeme* establishes the "racial unidirectionality of plasticity," as Densdeth's racial indeterminacy is simultaneously a transferable but fixed feature ("White Supremacist Submission," 429). In this reading, Emma's racialization serves as a "cautionary tale" for Byng, whose desire to submit to Densdeth will result in becoming racially marked himself. The plasticity of whiteness carries with it both the potential for self-invention and the threat of vulnerability to racialized influence. In this sense, the novel helps us see how contemporary transgender narratives of self-determination should be considered within "a long history of racially differentiated access to malleability" (442–444).
42. Shawn Michelle Smith, *American Archives: Gender, Race, and Class in Visual Culture* (Princeton, NJ: Princeton University Press, 1999), 6.

CHAPTER 5 — TRACKING HARRIET E. WILSON'S SPIRITUALIST VISIONS

1. On reading Wilson's text as a slave narrative despite Frado's position as an indentured servant, see Julia Stern, "Excavating Genre in *Our Nig*," *American Literature* 67, no. 3 (September 1995): 440–441, JSTOR, and Hazel V. Carby, *Reconstructing Womanhood: The Emergence of the Afro-American Woman Novelist* (New York: Oxford University Press, 1987), 43. On the importance of Frado's status as free indentured servant rather than slave, see Lois Leveen, "Dwelling in the House of Oppression: The Spatial, Racial, and Textual Dynamics of Harriet Wilson's *Our Nig*," *African American Review* 35, no. 4 (2001).
2. Carby, *Reconstructing Womanhood*, 43. Despite this solicitation of funds, Wilson's relationship to her readers is far from conciliatory. As Barbara White asks, "Why, if Wilson wrote the narrative to earn money, did she do everything possible, seemingly, to make it unpopular?" ("'Our Nig' and the She-Devil: New Information about Harriet Wilson and the 'Bellmont' Family," *American Literature* 65, no. 1 [March 1993]: 22, JSTOR).
3. Wilson's title page is chock-full of playful and parodic critiques of genre and the racist practices of the United States. See Claudia Tate, *Domestic Allegories of Political Desire: The Black Heroine's Text at the Turn of the Century* (New York: Oxford University Press, 1992), 39–43.
4. Olaudah Equiano, *The Interesting Narrative of Olaudah Equiano, or Gustavus Vassa, The African, Written by Himself*, reprint ed. (New York: Norton, 2001), 84. Hereafter referred to parenthetically.

5. Frederick Douglass, *Narrative of the Life of Frederick Douglass*, reprint ed. (New York: Penguin, 2016), 87. Hereafter referred to parenthetically.
6. Harriet Jacobs, *Incidents in the Life of a Slave Girl*, reprint ed. (Mineola, NY: Dover Thrift, 2001), 3.
7. On how Douglass negotiated the limitations of witnessing and came to position himself as advocate, see Jeannine Marie DeLombard, *Slavery on Trial: Law, Abolitionism, and Print Culture* (Chapel Hill: University of North Carolina Press, 2007), 101–123. On how Frederick Douglass negotiated expectations for access from sentimental readers, see Thomas Koenigs, "The 'Mysterious Depths' of Slave Interiority: Fiction and Intersubjective Knowledge in *The Heroic Slave*," *J19: The Journal of Nineteenth-Century Americanists* 8, no. 2 (Fall 2020): 193–217, Project Muse. For a comparison of how Jacobs and Wilson participate in the hybrid genre of the slave narrative, see P. Gabrielle Foreman, "The Spoken and the Silenced in *Incidents in the Life of a Slave Girl* and *Our Nig*," *Callaloo* 13, no. 2 (Spring 1990): 313–324. On the hybrid nature of the slave narrative genre more generally, see Valerie Smith, *Self-Discovery and Authority in Afro-American Narrative* (Cambridge, MA: Harvard University Press, 1987). On the novelistic elements of Equiano's *Interesting Narrative*, see Cathy N. Davidson, "Olaudah Equiano, Written by Himself," *NOVEL: A Forum on Fiction* 40, no. 1/2 (Fall 2006/Spring 2007): 18–51.
8. On the novel's use of Gothic conventions, see Stern, "Excavating Genre." On its combination of the autobiographical slave narrative and the sentimental novel, see Jill Jones, "The Disappearing 'I' in *Our Nig*," *Legacy: A Journal of Women Writers* 13, no. 1 (1996): 38–53.
9. On "the aesthetics of sentimentalism which denies the hands of literary labor," see Cindy Weinstein, *The Literature of Labor and the Labors of Literature: Allegory in Nineteenth-Century American Fiction* (Cambridge: Cambridge University Press, 1995), 36–40.
10. Henry Louis Gates Jr., introduction to *Our Nig; or, Sketches from the Life of a Free Black*, by Harriet E. Wilson, ed. Henry Louis Gates Jr., 3rd ed. (New York: Vintage Books, 2002), 24. Similarly, Beth Maclay Doriani argues that as "fiction and autobiography become one discourse," Wilson gains "control over her self-presentation"; Doriani sees Wilson's decision to write a novelized version of her autobiography as "a bold move toward self-definition" ("Black Womanhood in Nineteenth-Century America: Subversion and Self-Construction in Two Women's Autobiographies," *American Quarterly* 43, no. 2 [June 1991]: 214, 218, JSTOR). Noting that the generic demands of slave narratives "tended to reinforce [the authors'] status as commodities," Carla Peterson argues that Wilson's text "strives" "to fuse narrating and narrated *I* into a coherent self" ("Capitalism, Black [Under]development, and the Production of the African-American Novel in the 1850s," *American Literary History* 4, no. 4 [Winter 1992]: 562, 565, JSTOR). Laura Doyle argues that the seeming incoherence of the text's doubled narration ultimately "seeks to repair" "the unhinging of corporeal self-relation" ("Ontological Crisis and Double Narration in African American Fiction: Reconstructing *Our Nig*," in *Thinking the Limits of the Body*, ed. Jeffrey Jerome Cohen and Gail Weiss [Albany: State University of New York Press, 2003]: 86).
11. Gates, introduction to *Our Nig*, 34, 16.
12. As Elizabeth Breau, who reads the text as a satire of the slave narrative genre, counters, "the expectation that nineteenth-century authored first-person narratives contain only unaltered truth restricts our ability to see authors of such texts as creative artists" ("Identifying Satire: *Our Nig*," *Callaloo* 16, no. 2 [Spring 1993]: 458, JSTOR).
13. See Stern, "Excavating Genre," 440: "It is only by commodifying her life into the narrative that becomes *Our Nig* that Frado can hope to reclaim the fruits of her reproductive labor." See Leveen, "Dwelling," 578: "The story of her physical subjection is what she can sell in lieu of her physical labor. Her paradoxical position, like that of her fictionalized protagonist, evidences the limits placed on free blacks, even as her novel exposes and challenges the mechanisms of power that impose those limits."
14. Examining how the novel deploys Gothic tropes to critique sentimental domestic ideology, Stern argues that this critique must be "excavated" before it can be found "seething

beneath the narrative's surface"; "encrypted within the sentimental frame of *Our Nig* is an insistent gothic story that yearns to be heard" ("Excavating Genre," 439, 449). The novel certainly weaponizes Frado's alienation from the protections and constraints of domesticity's fraught cultural power by fostering alliances through public performance rather than private confession. As Stern concludes, "what must be remembered is Wilson's impulse to turn away from the private sphere and to struggle for her race, class, gender, and maternity in public—that is, through her own reading public." But I'm not so sure that Wilson's critique of sentimental motherhood needs to be decrypted, or that within the text itself the violence of the private sphere is something that Wilson works to "reveal" or "expose" ("Excavating Genre," 440, 441, 442, 446).

15. Dillon, *Gender of Freedom*, 203.
16. Brodhead, *Culture of Letters*, 14.
17. See Stern: "In *Our Nig*, the affective associations with which nineteenth-century American culture coded its domestic and civic space undergo a fascinating reversal. Wilson privileges the public sphere as an arena of safety and freedom, in contrast to the private, which is figured as a gothic realm of violence and danger" ("Excavating Genre," 448).
18. See Berlant, *Female Complaint*, 22–23, on this legacy of nineteenth-century sentimental women's culture: "at moments of crisis persons violate the zones of privacy that give them privilege and protection in order to fix something social that feels threatening. They become public on behalf of privacy and imagine that their rupture of individuality by collective action is temporary and will be reversed once the national world is safe, once again, for a return to personal life."
19. As Peterson puts it, authors of slave narratives "discovered that the autobiographical act, far from freeing them from commodification, tended to reinforce their status as commodities. In writing their lives, they often found that they had created alienated images of themselves" ("Capitalism," 562). Third-person fiction became a way for African American authors to practice personal reinvention and to gain control over public and private histories (563). Ultimately Peterson finds that the shifts between first and third person are signs of Wilson's "difficulties in maintaining narrative distance" and of her desire to "fuse narrating and narrated *I* into a coherent self" (565). Doriani finds the device "heightening Wilson's control over her self-presentation" ("Black Womanhood," 214); Doyle argues the device allows Wilson to achieve "self-relation" ("Ontological Crisis," 88). In a sustained consideration of Wilson's shifts between the first and third person, Jones concludes that the authority Wilson gains through the third-person omniscient narrator collapses with the return of the first person in the novel's "abrupt and unsatisfactory finish" ("Disappearing 'I,'" 39). Jones takes this failed resolution as signaling the insufficiency of established genres to account for Wilson's experiences. My argument here is similar to the reading Koenigs develops about Frederick Douglass's novel *The Heroic Slave*; Koenigs argues that Douglass wields the explicitly speculative nature of fiction to cultivate an "epistemological humility" in his white readers about what they know of Black interiority ("'Mysterious Depths,'" 213).
20. See Sánchez-Eppler on this convention of nineteenth-century sentimental culture: "The bound and silent figure of the slave metaphorically represents the woman's oppression and so grants the white woman an access to political discourse denied the slave" ("Bodily Bonds: The Intersecting Rhetorics of Feminism and Abolition," *Representations* 24 [Autumn 1988]: 31, JSTOR).
21. On how the rhetoric of wage labor differentiated between freedom and bondage by a man's ability to maintain "a home unscathed by the market," see Stanley, *From Bondage to Contract*, 138. On the symbolic role women play in liberal subject formation, see Dillon: "the pastoralization of labor in the sentimental household has the important effect of defining the home as the location where necessity and labor end and where voluntary individual activity, animated by love, begins" (*Gender of Freedom*, 202). See also McClintock's research on the performance of idleness necessary to maintain this illusion of a domestic scene devoid

of labor, particularly in middle-class homes like the Bellmonts' ("Imperial Leather," 651), and Lori Merish on how Wilson links "racial phobia and class ambition" in her portrayal of how Mrs. Bellmont's "performance of domestic authority is meant to mask the ambiguities of her own class position" (*Archives of Labor: Working-Class Women and Literary Culture in the Antebellum United States* [Durham, NC: Duke University Press, 2017], 171).

22. Berlant describes women's culture as juxtapolitical because it "thrives in *proximity* to the political, occasionally crossing over in political alliance, even more occasionally doing some politics, but most often not, acting as a critical chorus that sees the expression of emotional response and conceptual recalibration as achievement enough" (*Female Complaint*, x).
23. Harriet Beecher Stowe, *Uncle Tom's Cabin; or, Life Among the Lowly*, reprint ed. (New York: Norton, 1994), 67–68. Hereafter referred to parenthetically.
24. Saidiya Hartman, *Scenes of Subjection: Terror, Slavery, and Self-Making in Nineteenth-Century America* (New York: Oxford University Press, 1997), 5.
25. Berlant, *Female Complaint*, 22.
26. James plays the part of Little Eva to Frado's Topsy, as he tells Frado on his deathbed that if she "will be a good girl, and love and serve God, it will be but a short time before we are in a *heavenly* home together" (53). Unlike Topsy, however, who is set on the path on Eva's deathbed to becoming a docile subject for Aunt Ophelia's domestic reform, Frado understands all too well that no matter how "good" she is, her position will not change, in the material or in the promised afterlife, a distinction that is reinforced in the contrast between James's promise that "she might hope for better things in the future" and the beating she endures a few paragraphs later when Mrs. Bellmont rather than James "found her weeping." Following James's death, Frado, now inundated by Mrs. Bellmont's teachings that "she could not go where James was," "resolved to give over all thought of the future world" (55, 58). For readings of Wilson revising Little Eva and Topsy, see Peterson, "Capitalism," 573, and Randi Lynn Tanglen, "Religious Popular Culture and the Critique of Romantic Racialism in Harriet E. Wilson's *Our Nig*," in *Nineteenth-Century American Women Write Religion: Lived Theologies and Literature*, ed. Mary McCartin Wearn (Farnham, England: Ashgate, 2013), 86–87.
27. On femininity as genre and the ends of female complaint as adaptation rather than transformation, see Berlant, *Female Complaint*, 4–19.
28. Christopher Castiglia, *Interior States*, 8. Castiglia argues that Black Americans came to be associated with a civic interiority that constituted white abolitionist publicity. Positioning James as a sentimental witness to Frado's private suffering, the novel demonstrates the relationship Castiglia describes between publicly acting white abolitionists and the private suffering of the Black Americans they appropriated (130). See also Berlant on how women's culture has "mobilized fantasies of what black and working-class interiority based on suffering must feel like in order to find a language for their own more privileged suffering" (*Female Complaint*, 6). Stern reads this moment as showing that Frado has "internalized" Mrs. Bellmont's attempts to silence her, as her lamentations "are so deeply encrypted that they reach audibility only because they happen to be overheard by a white male capable of transmitting them to a larger audience" ("Excavating Genre," 448). This reading accepts James's transcription as an accurate reading of Frado's deeply private thoughts.
29. Moments when Frado seems to be aware of an audience have typically been read as characterizing her as a minstrel figure whose performances objectify her and serve only to entertain her white audience. Peterson compares her to Topsy: "a figure of minstrelsy through which the dominant culture constructs, and economically exploits, black stereotypes" ("Capitalism," 573). White argues that "throughout the narrative she plays the part of clown for her so-called friends in the household" ("'Our Nig' and the She-Devil," 34). Stern finds that when Jack flippantly tosses a silver half-dollar to Frado after she humiliates his mother at the dinner table, "Frado's triumph is transformed into exploitation" ("Excavating Genre," 456). One exception is H. Jordan Landry, who reads Frado as a trickster figure who "exer-

cises her bodily powers to set herself apart from whites in a way that mocks the conventional racial and gender hierarchy." For Landry, "Frado pleasures herself first and, only incidentally, even unintentionally, entertains a white audience" ("Bringing Down the House: The Trickster's Signifying on Victimization in Harriet E. Wilson's *Our Nig*," *Callaloo* 36, no. 2 [Spring 2013]: 452–453, Project Muse). The incidental entertainment of a white audience does not undercut, and indeed might amplify, the subversion of Frado's tricksterism. See also Jones, who argues that Frado's rebellious nature "creat[es] the appearance of autonomy narratively even when the plot cannot sustain it" ("Disappearing 'I,'" 45). Merish links Frado's rebellious character to her class position as a free-born child of a white woman and a free Black laborer, arguing that through her theatrical antics, Frado "performs racialized class resistance" (*Archives of Labor*, 173–174).

30. As Landry notes, Frado's playful "merriment" is particularly difficult to square with accounts of the novel that follow a "critical framework places the novel almost entirely within the province of victimization," a tactic that "repeats the earlier anti-slavery discourse on black slave women's victimization" ("Bringing Down the House," 442).
31. Berlant, *Female Complaint*, 6.
32. See Landry: "black women must shape their bodies independent of white culture's attempt to masculinize their body into mere physical laborers and outside of a reverse discourse that strives to feminize their body into frail, near-white, and passive victim" ("Bringing Down the House," 451).
33. Here I disagree with Jones, who sees this moment as contrasting Frado's "lack of options" to Jane's "power to make real choices" ("Disappearing 'I,'" 47).
34. A sign of her white mother's "abjection and her transgressive choice," Stern argues that "Frado is a visible sign of the vulnerability of white women" for Mrs. Bellmont ("Excavating Genre," 458). My reading closely aligns with Merish: "Frado's humorous attempts to carnivalize white women's domestic authority expose the fragility of that authority, especially the Bellmont women's (material and psychic) dependence on her to ratify it" (*Archives of Labor*, 176). Landry argues that because antislavery fiction often used "the image of black women for their own designs in anti-slavery narrative . . . to dissociate any degrading experiences from the author's own specific body type and displace it onto the black woman's body," "the black woman had no hope of sloughing off her own experiences onto another more marginalized body"; Wilson thus is able to wield her embodied representation to imagine new possibilities for black women's bodies and desire that go beyond abject suffering and victimization ("Bringing Down the House," 443–444).
35. See Armstrong, *Desire and Domestic Fiction*, 20–21.
36. Sánchez-Eppler, "Bodily Bonds," 49. As Lauren Berlant has argued, this uneven and selective emphasis on "the monumental time of emotional recognition" only ever defers and dilutes the possibility of transformative political action to "an imaginary realm of possible acting" (*Female Complaint*, 21). See also Castiglia, *Interior States*, 2, on how interiority came to be misperceived as the location of democratic action.
37. For examples of this discourse, see Sánchez-Eppler, "Bodily Bonds," 30.
38. Castiglia, *Interior States*, 130.
39. See Tawil, *Making of Racial Sentiment*, 152–190 on Harriet Beecher Stowe's emphasis in *Uncle Tom's Cabin* on racial interiors and the link between her racialism and her antislavery argument and Castiglia, *Interior States*, 129–130, on how the antislavery public sphere depended on the relegation of Black Americans to the private sphere. Wilson seems particularly interested in challenging the abolitionist reader's confidence in their access to a transparent and readable slave interiority, the belief that "that the inner lives of enslaved persons were manifest on their bodies" (Koenigs, "'Mysterious Depths,'" 197).
40. Lydia Maria Child, "The Quadroons," *The Liberty Bell* (Boston, 1842): 118–119. *Uncle Tom's Cabin & American Culture: A Multi-Media Archive*, http://utc.iath.virginia.edu.
41. See Michael Warner on the "principle of negativity" that came to define the print public sphere: "the rhetorical strategy of personal abstraction is both the utopian moment of the

public sphere and a major source of domination, for the ability to abstract oneself in public discussion has always been an unequally available resource" (*Publics and Counterpublics*, 165). As Dillon argues, this narrative of the public sphere "tends to describe privacy and embodiment as inert—as that which can be left behind in the act of abstraction—rather than as that which is produced in and through the public sphere, in and through the very process of abstraction" (*Gender of Freedom*, 38).

42. Peterson, "Capitalism," 573.
43. As Margolis argues, this understanding of race as intrinsic also operates to characterize it as permanent: "Both the tragic mulatta genre . . . and the passing fiction . . . take for granted that race is intrinsic, an attribute that must be hidden because it can never be changed" (*Public Life of Privacy*, 110). In an intriguing reading given the previous chapter's consideration of *Cecil Dreeme* as a prototrans novel, Margolis goes on to argue that Charles Chesnutt diverges from this tradition by portraying passing as self-determination rather than pretense.
44. For the ways that Wilson uses Frado's complex relationship with Christianity to challenge the period's romantic racialism, see Tanglen, "Religious Popular Culture."
45. As Goddu has argued, the veiled lady of spiritualist performances served as an apt metaphor for "how the private sphere was created in and by the public sphere" (*Gothic America*, 98). For a reading of how Wilson uses this Biblical allusion to the story of Joseph and the butler to prophesize a renewed future for Black Americans, see Tanglen, "Religious Popular Culture," 87.
46. As Richards has argued, the spiritualist movement captured the confusion between the spiritual and the material that plagues romantic notions of feminine genius, as the medium is granted access to the spiritual world because of essentialist assumptions about the "receptivity to outside influences" of "'feminine' sensibility" (*Gender and the Poetics of Reception*, 120). On how the feminine propensity for mediumship was grounded in biological arguments, see Elizabeth Lowry, "Embodying Essence: Corporeality, Dualism and Rhetorical Invention in the Autobiographies of Nineteenth-Century Female Spirit Mediums," *Word and Text: A Journal of Literary Studies and Linguistics* 3, no. 2 (December 2013), 44–56. Additionally, R. J. Ellis and Gates have found evidence that Native American and African American mediums were stereotyped as having greater access to the spiritual world ("'Grievances at the treatment she received': Harriet E. Wilson's Spiritualist Career in Boston, 1868–1900," *American Literary History* 24, no. 2 [Summer 2012]: 259). Erin Forbes and Russ Castronovo have argued that slave narratives in particular deployed spiritualist rhetoric to invest the spiritual with the material: "As an evidence-based practice, Spiritualism sought to verify material relations between the living and the dead" (Forbes, "Do Black Ghosts Matter?: Harriet Jacobs' Spiritualism," *ESQ: A Journal of Nineteenth-Century American Literature and Culture* 62, no. 3 [2016]: 445).
47. See Foreman, "Spoken and Silenced," 314; Jones, "Disappearing 'I,'" 43–51; Peterson, "Capitalism," 565–574.
48. These readings tend to fully conflate Wilson the author with a newly literate and empowered fictional creation. Gates, for example, argues that "In these final scenes of instruction, Harriet Wilson's text reflects upon its own creation, just as surely as Frado's awakened speaking voice signifies her consciousness of herself as a subject" ("Introduction," 52). This imposition of a linear structure that reads the novel for confirmation of Wilson's autobiography—which in turn is interpreted as a rise to literacy and economic self-reliance—does not account for the ongoing precarity Frado faces after leaving the Bellmont home, in part because of the ways that the rhetoric of self-sufficiency is used against her.
49. Russ Castronovo draws a connection between spiritualism and the antislavery literary public sphere: "slave narrative, like spiritualist narrative, requires the presence of an editor-medium to translate voice into text" (*Necro Citizenship: Death, Eroticism, and the Public Sphere in the Nineteenth-Century United States* [Durham, NC: Duke University Press, 2001], 177). This operation grants the white amanuensis who speaks for the formerly enslaved an abstract authority similar to what is required of citizens in a representative democracy. In

this sense, spiritualism trained citizens in a representative democracy. Castronovo argues that the unevenly realized abstraction that is required to enter the public sphere is "a ghostly operation that dematerializes uniquely embodied and specifically historical citizens in its production of the liberal subject" ("Souls That Matter: Social Death and the Pedagogy of Democratic Citizenship," in *Materializing Democracy: Toward a Revitalized Cultural Politics*, ed. Russ Castronovo and Dana D. Nelson [Durham, NC: Duke University Press, 2002], 124).

50. Castronovo, *Necro Citizenship*, 186. See Forbes on the structural similarity between the relationships of medium and spirit and pseudonymous author and autobiographical subject in Jacobs's *Incidents in the Life of a Slave Girl* ("Do Black Ghosts Matter?" 458). See also Suzanne Ashworth on the posthuman elements of spiritualism in Julia Ward Howe's *The Hermaphrodite*, a novel that carefully attends to both the transcendent possibilities of the spirit and "bodily remainders" ("Spiritualized Bodies and Posthuman Possibilities: Technologies of Intimacy in Julia Ward Howe's *The Hermaphrodite*," *ESQ: A Journal of the American Renaissance* 57, no. 4 [2011]: 338, Project Muse). Ashworth positions the novel in relation to a nineteenth-century spiritualist tradition where "mediumship turned a womanly constitution into a vehicle of agency and subjectivity" (300–301).
51. Stern, "Excavating Genre," 462: "Frado has become a transparent eyeball, possessed of a vision to obsessive that it extends itself indefinitely through both space and time . . . it becomes her goal to trouble the family's 'rest' throughout the hereafter, to deny them peace for all eternity." Peterson, "Capitalism," 574: "Frado develops no self-identity independent of the Bellmonts, and the last line of the narrative leaves us with a sense of her continuing obsession." Landry, "Bringing Down the House," 457: "Most ironic though is the idea that Frado oversees everything."
52. Richards, *Gender and the Poetics of Reception*, 120.
53. More immediately, as Leveen argues, "her presence as the laborer and sufferer within their parents' house clearly serves those children, not only in motivating their own exits from the family homestead but in directly enabling their escapes" ("Dwelling," 573). Although Jones notes that Frado's sense of self is developed negatively in relation to Mrs. Bellmont, both Mr. Bellmont's sense of himself as the head of a household free of coercion and Mrs. Bellmont's sense of herself as removed from the material aspects of domestic labor are reliant on Frado's position (Jones, "Disappearing 'I,'" 49).

CODA

1. For representative examples of a consistent emphasis in this advice on setting clear boundaries between domestic labor and real work, see Zara Abrams, "Psychologists' Advice for Newly Remote Workers," *American Psychological Association*, March 20, 2020, https://www.apa.org/news/apa/2020/newly-remote-workers; Joan Hope, "Working from home? Follow these tips for successful remote work," *Recruiting & Retaining Adult Learners* 22, no. 8 (2020): 9, https://www.ncbi.nlm.nih.gov/pmc/articles/PMC7264770/; Bryan Lufkin, "Coronavirus: How to Work from Home, the Right Way," *BBC*, March 12, 2020, https://www.bbc.com/worklife/article/20200312-coronavirus-covid-19-update-work-from-home-in-a-pandemic; Yuki Noguchi, "8 Tips to Make Working from Home Work for You," *NPR*, March 15, 2020, https://www.npr.org/2020/03/15/815549926/8-tips-to-make-working-from-home-work-for-you; Kate Whiting, "8 Tips to Work from Home and Manage Time More Effectively," *World Economic Forum*, October 14, 2020, https://www.weforum.org/agenda/2020/10/8-tips-work-from-home-time-management/.
2. Armstrong, *Desire and Domestic Fiction*, 75.
3. See Sara Matthiesen, "Academic Work Is Labor, Not Romance," *The Chronicle of Higher Education* 63, no. 2 (September 9, 2016): https://www.chronicle.com/article/academic-work-is-labor-not-romance/; Barry Eidlin, "A New Force in American Labor: Academe," *The Chronicle of Higher Education*, November 29, 2021, https://www.chronicle.com/article/a

-new-force-in-american-labor-academe; Maximillian Alvarez, "Stonewalled, Disrespected, and Dismissed," *The Chronicle of Higher Education*, March 17, 2023, https://www.chronicle.com/article/stonewalled-disrespected-and-dismissed; Maximillian Alvarez, "Laboring Academia," *The Baffler*, July 20, 2021, https://thebaffler.com/latest/laboring-academia; Michael Sainato, "'Many of us are struggling': why US universities are facing a wave of strikes," *Guardian*, April 21, 2023, https://www.theguardian.com/us-news/2023/apr/21/us-universities-wave-strikes.

4. See Sarah Mesle and Sara Petersen, "The Cult of Ideal Motherhood," *Guernica*, May 1, 2023, https://www.guernicamag.com/the-cult-of-ideal-motherhood/ and Sara Peterson "Victorian Era-Inspired Momfluencers Are Taking Over Instagram," *InStyle*, March 25, 2021, https://www.instyle.com/lifestyle/momfluencers-nostalgia-instagram. On a recent call for women to find happiness in marriage, see Rebecca Traister, "The Return of the Marriage Plot: Why Everyone Is Suddenly So Eager for Men and Women to Get Hitched," *The Cut*, September 22, 2023, https://www.thecut.com/article/why-is-everyone-so-eager-for-men-and-women-to-get-married.html. Nineteenth-century women novelists have also been reappropriated for this domestic nostalgia, their fiction dubiously misread as emotionally invested in a marriage plot divorced from economic considerations. See David Brooks, "To Be Happy Marriage Matters More than Career," *New York Times*, August 17, 2023, https://www.nytimes.com/2023/08/17/opinion/marriage-happiness-career.html.
5. Nicole Bateman and Martha Ross, "Why Has COVID-19 Been Especially Harmful for Working Women?" *The Brookings Institution*, October 2020, https://www.brookings.edu/articles/why-has-covid-19-been-especially-harmful-for-working-women/.
6. On the speculative nature of citizenship before the Fourteenth Amendment, see Hyde, *Civic Longing*, 18–39. Hyde establishes that the capaciousness of theories of citizenship in the early national period is precisely what originalist legal interpretations must repress in their determination to establish historical precedent.

BIBLIOGRAPHY

Abrams, Zara. "Psychologists' Advice for Newly Remote Workers." *American Psychological Association*, March 20, 2020. https://www.apa.org/news/apa/2020/newly-remote-workers.

Alaimo, Stacy. *Undomesticated Ground: Recasting Nature as Feminist Space*. Ithaca, NY: Cornell University Press, 2000.

Alteri, Charles. Afterword to *American Literature's Aesthetic Dimensions*, 393–404. Edited by Cindy Weinstein and Christopher Looby. New York: Columbia University Press, 2012.

Alvarez, Maximillian. "Laboring Academia." *The Baffler*, July 20, 2021. https://thebaffler.com/latest/laboring-academia.

———. "Stonewalled, Disrespected, and Dismissed." *The Chronicle of Higher Education*, March 17, 2023. https://www.chronicle.com/article/stonewalled-disrespected-and-dismissed.

Anker, Elizabeth S., and Rita Felski, eds. *Critique and Postcritique*. Durham, NC: Duke University Press, 2017.

Armstrong, Nancy. *Desire and Domestic Fiction: A Political History of the Novel*. New York: Oxford University Press, 1987.

Ashworth, Suzanne. "Spiritualized Bodies and Posthuman Possibilities: Technologies of Intimacy in Julia Ward Howe's *The Hermaphrodite*." *ESQ: A Journal of the American Renaissance* 57, no. 4 (2011): 314–354. Project Muse.

Barnard, Philip, and Stephen Shapiro, eds. *Arthur Mervyn; or, Memoirs of the Year 1793, with Related Texts*. Indianapolis: Hackett Publishing Company, 2008.

Barnard, Philip, and Stephen Shapiro. "Un-Noveling Brown: Liberalism and Its Literary Discontents." *Early American Literature* 57, no. 2 (2022): 549–554.

Barnard, Philip, Mark Kamrath, and Stephen Shapiro, eds. *Revising Charles Brockden Brown: Culture, Politics, and Sexuality in the Early Republic*. Knoxville: University of Tennessee Press, 2004.

Barnes, Elizabeth. *States of Sympathy: Seduction and Democracy in the American Novel*. New York: Columbia University Press, 1997.

Bateman, Nicole, and Martha Ross. "Why Has COVID-19 Been Especially Harmful for Working Women?" *The Brookings Institution*, October 2020. https://www.brookings.edu/articles/why-has-covid-19-been-especially-harmful-for-working-women/.

Baym, Nina. "Melodramas of Beset Manhood: How Theories of American Fiction Exclude Women Authors." *American Quarterly* 33, no. 2 (Summer 1981): 123–139. JSTOR.

Beaudry, Anna E. "Provocation: Magawisca's Light: A Recuperative Approach to Catharine Maria Sedgwick's *Hope Leslie*." *Early American Literature* 57, no. 2 (2022): 367–386. Project Muse.

Bentley, Nancy. "Warped Conjunctions: Jacques Rancière and African American Twoness." In *American Literature's Aesthetic Dimensions*, edited by Cindy Weinstein and Christopher Looby, 291–312. New York: Columbia University Press, 2012.

Bercovitch, Sacvan, ed. *The Cambridge History of American Literature*. Vol. 1, 1590–1820. Cambridge: Cambridge University Press, 1994.

Bergland, Renée, and Gary Williams, eds. *Philosophies of Sex Critical Essays on* The Hermaphrodite. Columbus: The Ohio State University Press, 2012.

Berlant, Lauren. *The Anatomy of National Fantasy: Hawthorne, Utopia, and Everyday Life*. Chicago: University of Chicago Press, 1991.

———. *The Female Complaint: The Unfinished Business of Sentimentality in American Culture.* Durham, NC: Duke University Press, 2008.

Bertolini, Vincent J. "Fireside Chastity: The Erotics of Sentimental Bachelorhood in the 1850s." *American Literature* 68, no. 4 (December 1996): 707–737. JSTOR.

Best, Stephen, and Sharon Marcus. "Surface Reading: An Introduction." *Representations* 108, no. 1 (Fall 2009): 1–21. JSTOR.

Blackwood, Sarah. *The Portrait's Subject: Inventing Inner Life in the Nineteenth-Century United States.* Chapel Hill: University of North Carolina Press, 2019.

Bowden, Mary Weatherspoon. "Cocklofts and Slang-whangers: The Historical Sources of Washington Irving's 'Salmagundi.'" *New York History* 61, no. 2 (April 1980): 133–160.

Boyd, Anne E. *Writing for Immortality: Women and the Emergence of High Literary Culture in America.* Baltimore: The Johns Hopkins University Press, 2004. Kindle.

Boydston, Jeanne. *Home and Work: Housework, Wages, and the Ideology of Labor in the Early Republic.* New York: Oxford University Press, 1990.

Bradfield, Scott. *Dreaming Revolution: Transgression in the Development of American Romance.* Iowa City: University of Iowa Press, 1993.

Breau, Elizabeth. "Identifying Satire: *Our Nig.*" *Callaloo* 16, no. 2 (Spring 1993): 455–465. JSTOR.

Brodhead, Richard H. *Cultures of Letters: Scenes of Reading and Writing in Nineteenth-Century America.* Chicago: University of Chicago Press, 1993.

Brooks, David. "To Be Happy Marriage Matters More than Career." *New York Times,* August 17, 2023. https://www.nytimes.com/2023/08/17/opinion/marriage-happiness-career.html.

Brown, Charles Brockden. *Arthur Mervyn; or, Memoirs of the Year 1793.* Philadelphia: H. Maxwell, 1799. Reprinted with an introduction and notes by Philip Barnard and Stephen Shapiro. Indianapolis: Hackett Publishing Company, 2008.

———. "The Difference between History and Romance." *The Monthly Magazine and the American Review* 2, no. 4 (April 1800): 251–253. Charles Brockden Brown Electronic Archive and Scholarly Edition.

———. *Edgar Huntly; Or, Memoirs of a Sleep-Walker.* Philadelphia: H. Maxwell, 1799. Reprinted with preface by Norman S. Grabo. New York: Penguin, 1988.

———. "The Household. A Fragment." *The Monthly Magazine and the American Review* 3, no. 2 (August 1800): 81–87. Charles Brockden Brown Electronic Archive and Scholarly Edition.

———. *Jane Talbot.* Philadelphia: John Conrad, 1801. Kindle.

———. "A Literary Wife." *The Literary Magazine and American Register* 3, no. 18 (March 1805): 195–196. Charles Brockden Brown Electronic Archive and Scholarly Edition.

———. *Ormond; or, The Secret Witness.* New York: G. Forman for H. Caritat, 1799. Reprinted by Kessinger Publishing, 2004.

———. "Portrait of an Emigrant. Extracted from a Letter." *The Monthly Magazine and the American Review* 1, no. 3 (June 1799): 161–164. Charles Brockden Brown Electronic Archive and Scholarly Edition.

Brown, Gillian. *The Consent of the Governed: The Lockean Legacy in Early American Culture.* Cambridge, MA: Harvard University Press, 2001.

———. *Domestic Individualism: Imagining Self in Nineteenth-Century America.* Berkeley: University of California Press, 1990.

Bryant, John. *Melville and Repose: The Rhetoric of Humor in the American Renaissance.* New York: Oxford University Press, 1993.

Bryant, William Cullen. "Lectures on Poetry." Vol. 1 of *Prose Writings of William Cullen Bryant,* edited by Parke Godwin, 3–44. New York: Russel & Russel, 1964.

———. "*Redwood.*" Rev. of *Redwood,* by Catharine Maria Sedgwick. *North American Review* 20, no. 47 (1825): 245–272. *The Nineteenth Century in Print.*

Buell, Lawrence. "American Literary Emergence as a Postcolonial Phenomenon." In *American Literature, American Culture,* edited by Gordon Hutner, 592–612. New York: Oxford University Press, 1999.

———. *New England Literary Culture from Revolution through Renaissance.* Cambridge: Cambridge University Press, 1986.

Burgett, Bruce. *Sentimental Bodies: Sex, Gender, and Citizenship in the Early Republic.* Princeton, NJ: Princeton University Press, 1998.

Burleigh, Erica. "Incommensurate Equivalences: Genre, Representation, and Equity in *Clara Howard* and *Jane Talbot.*" *Early American Studies* (Fall 2011): 748–780.

Burnham, Michelle. "Epistolarity, Anticipation, and Revolution in *Clara Howard.*" In *Revising Charles Brockden Brown: Culture, Politics, and Sexuality in the Early Republic,* edited by Philip Barnard, Mark L. Kamrath, and Stephen Shapiro, 260–280. Knoxville: University of Tennessee, 2004.

Butler, Judith. *Undoing Gender.* New York: Routledge, 2004.

Cahill, Edward. *Liberty of the Imagination: Aesthetic Theory, Literary Form, and Politics in the Early United States.* Philadelphia: University of Pennsylvania Press, 2012.

Callcott, George C. *History in the United States 1800–1860.* Baltimore: Johns Hopkins University Press, 1970.

Camfield, Gregg. *Necessary Madness: The Humor of Domesticity in Nineteenth-Century American Literature.* New York: Oxford University Press, 1997.

Carby, Hazel V. *Reconstructing Womanhood: The Emergence of the Afro-American Woman Novelist.* New York: Oxford University Press, 1987.

Castiglia, Christopher. "Aesthetics Beyond the Actual: *The Marble Faun* and Romantic Sociality." In *American Literature's Aesthetic Dimensions,* edited by Cindy Weinstein and Christopher Looby, 117–136. New York: Columbia University Press, 2012.

———. "Hawthorne/Winthrop." Vol. 2 of *American Literature in Transition, 1820–1860,* edited by Justine S. Murison, 372–387. Cambridge: Cambridge University Press, 2022.

———. "Hope for Critique?" In *Critique and Postcritique,* edited by Elizabeth S. Anker and Rita Felski, 211–229. Durham, NC: Duke University Press, 2017.

———. "In Praise of Extra-Vagant Women: *Hope Leslie* and the Captivity Romance." *Legacy* 6, no. 2 (1989): 3–16.

———. *Interior States: Institutional Consciousness and the Inner Life of Democracy in the Antebellum United States.* Durham, NC: Duke University Press, 2008.

Castronovo, Russ. *Necro Citizenship: Death, Eroticism, and the Public Sphere in the Nineteenth-Century United States.* Durham, NC: Duke University Press, 2001.

———. "Souls That Matter: Social Death and the Pedagogy of Democratic Citizenship." In *Materializing Democracy: Toward a Revitalized Cultural Politics,* edited by Russ Castronovo and Dana D. Nelson, 116–143. Durham, NC: Duke University Press, 2002.

Castronovo, Russ, and Dana D. Nelson, eds. *Materializing Democracy: Toward a Revitalized Cultural Politics.* Durham, NC: Duke University Press, 2002.

Cherniavsky, Eva. "Cultural Studies Revisited: Determinate Conditions and the Depressive Position." *American Literary History* 34, no. 1 (Spring 2022): 54–66. Project Muse.

Child, Lydia Maria. "Miss Sedgwick's Novels." *Ladies' Magazine* 2, no. 5 (1829): 234–238. Google Books.

———. "The Quadroons." *The Liberty Bell.* Boston, 1842. *Uncle Tom's Cabin & American Culture: A Multi-Media Archive.* http://utc.iath.virginia.edu.

Cohen, Jeffrey Jerome, and Gail Weiss, eds. *Thinking the Limits of the Body.* Albany: State University of New York Press, 2003.

Cohen, Michael. "Whittier, Ballad Reading, and the Culture of Nineteenth-Century Poetry." *Arizona Quarterly: A Journal of American Literature, Culture, and Theory* 64, no. 3 (Autumn 2008): 1–29, Project Muse.

Cott, Nancy F. *The Bonds of Womanhood: "Woman's Sphere" in New England, 1780–1835.* 2nd ed. New Haven, CT: Yale University Press, 1997.

Couch, Daniel Diez. *American Fragments: The Political Aesthetic of Unfinished Forms in the Early Republic.* Philadelphia: University of Pennsylvania Press, 2022.

Coviello, Peter. Introduction to *Cecil Dreeme*, by Theodore Winthrop, ix–xx. Reprinted with a preface by Peter Coviello. New York: Washington Mews Books, 2016.

Dalke, Anne. "Original Vice: The Political Implications of Incest in the Early American Novel." *Early American Literature* 23 (1988): 188–201.

Dana, Richard H. "The Sketch Book of Geoffrey Crayon, Gent." *The North American Review and Miscellaneous Journal* 9, no. 25 (Sept. 1819): 322–356. American Periodical Series Online.

Davidson, Cathy N. "Olaudah Equiano, Written by Himself." *NOVEL: A Forum on Fiction* 40, no. 1/2 (Fall 2006/Spring 2007): 18–51.

———. "Preface: No More Separate Spheres!" *American Literature* 70, no. 3 (September 1998): 443–463. JSTOR.

———. *Revolution and the Word: The Rise of the Novel in America*. 2nd ed. Oxford: Oxford University Press, 2004.

DeLombard, Jeannine Marie. *Slavery on Trial: Law, Abolitionism, and Print Culture*. Chapel Hill: University of North Carolina Press, 2007.

Deloria, Philip J. *Playing Indian*. New Haven, CT: Yale University Press, 1998.

Dillon, Elizabeth Maddock. *The Gender of Freedom: Fictions of Liberalism and the Literary Public Sphere*. Stanford: Stanford University Press, 2004.

———. "The Secret History of the Early American Novel: Leonora Sansay and Revolution in Saint Domingue." *NOVEL* (Fall 2006/Spring 2007): 77–103.

———. "Sentimental Aesthetics." *American Literature* 76, no. 3 (2004): 496–523. EBSCO.

Dobson, Joanne. "Reclaiming Sentimental Literature." *American Literature* 69, no. 2 (June 1997): 263–288. JSTOR.

Doriani, Beth Maclay. "Black Womanhood in Nineteenth-Century America: Subversion and Self-Construction in Two Women's Autobiographies." *American Quarterly* 43, no. 2 (June 1991): 199–222. JSTOR.

Douglas, Ann. *The Feminization of American Culture*. New York: Knopf, 1977.

Douglass, Frederick. *Narrative of the Life of Frederick Douglass*. Boston: Anti-Slavery Office, 1845. Reprinted in *The Portable Frederick Douglass*, edited by John Stauffer and Henry Louis Gates Jr., 3–100. New York: Penguin, 2016.

Doyle, Laura. "Ontological Crisis and Double Narration in African American Fiction: Reconstructing *Our Nig*." In *Thinking the Limits of the Body*, edited by Jeffrey Jerome Cohen and Gail Weiss, 85–100. Albany: State University of New York Press, 2003.

Eagleton, Terry. *The Function of Criticism*. London: Verso, 1984.

Eidlin, Barry. "A New Force in American Labor: Academe." *The Chronicle of Higher Education*, November 29, 2021. https://www.chronicle.com/article/a-new-force-in-american-labor-academe.

Ellis, Kate Ferguson. *The Contested Castle: Gothic Novels and the Subversion of Domestic Ideology*. Urbana: University of Illinois Press, 1989.

Ellis, R. J., and Henry Louis Gates Jr. "'Grievances at the treatment she received': Harriet E. Wilson's Spiritualist Career in Boston, 1868–1900." *American Literary History* 24, no. 2 (Summer 2012): 234–264.

Emerson, Amanda. "History, Memory, and the Echoes of Equivalence in Catharine Maria Sedgwick's *Hope Leslie*." *Legacy* 24, no. 1 (2007): 24–49.

Equiano, Olaudah. *The Interesting Narrative of Olaudah Equiano, or Gustavus Vassa, The African, Written by Himself*. London, 1794. Reprinted with preface and notes by Werner Sollers. New York and London: Norton, 2001.

Fetterley, Judith. "'My Sister! My Sister!': The Rhetoric of Catharine Sedgwick's *Hope Leslie*." *American Literature* 70, no. 3 (1998): 491–516.

Fiedler, Leslie. *Love and Death in the American Novel*. 1960. Reprinted with an introduction by Charles B. Harris. Funks Grove, IL: Dalkey Archive Press, 2003.

Fleissner, Jennifer L. "Romancing the Real: Bruno Latour, Ian McEwan, and Postcritical Monism." In *Critique and Postcritique*, edited by Elizabeth S. Anker and Rita Felski, 99–126. Durham, NC: Duke University Press, 2017.

Flint, Kate. "Is the Native an American?: National Identity and the British Reception of *Hiawatha*." In *The Traffic in Poems: Nineteenth-Century Poetry and Transatlantic Exchange*, edited by Meredith L. McGill, 63–80. New Brunswick, NJ: Rutgers University Press, 2008.

Forbes, Erin. "Do Black Ghosts Matter?: Harriet Jacobs' Spiritualism." *ESQ: A Journal of Nineteenth-Century American Literature and Culture* 62, no. 3 (2016): 443–479.

Ford, Douglas. "Inscribing the 'Impartial Observer' in Sedgwick's *Hope Leslie*." *Legacy* 14, no. 2 (1997): 81–92.

Foreman, Gabrielle P. "The Spoken and the Silenced in *Incidents in the Life of a Slave Girl* and *Our Nig*." *Callaloo* 13, no. 2 (Spring 1990): 313–324.

Foster, Travis M. "The Queer Young American Comes of Age." *Commonplace: the journal of early American life* 17, no. 2 (Winter 2017). https://commonplace.online/article/the-queer-young-american-comes-of-age/.

———. "White Supremacist Submission." *TSQ: Transgender Studies Quarterly* 10, nos. 3–4 (November 2023): 426–448.

Gardner, Jared. *The Rise and Fall of American Periodical Culture*. Urbana: University of Illinois Press, 2012. Kindle.

Garrett, Matthew. *Episodic Poetics: Politics and Literary Form after the Constitution*. Oxford: Oxford University Press, 2014.

Gates, Henry Louis Jr. Introduction to *Our Nig; or, Sketches from the Life of a Free Black*, by Harriet E. Wilson, xxv–lxi. Edited by Henry Louis Gates Jr. 3rd ed. New York: Vintage Books, 2002.

Getsy, David J. "Capacity." *TSQ: Transgender Studies Quarterly* 1, nos. 1–2 (May 2014): 47–49.

Gilmore, Michael T. *American Romanticism and the Marketplace*. Chicago: University of Chicago Press, 1985.

———. "The Literature of the Revolutionary and Early National Periods." In *The Cambridge History of American Literature*. Vol. 1, 1590–1820, edited by Sacvan Bercovitch, 539–694. Cambridge: Cambridge University Press, 1994.

Gilmore, Paul. "John Neal, American Romance, and International Romanticism." *American Literature* 84, no. 3 (September 2012): 477–504.

Goddu, Theresa A. *Gothic America: Narrative, History, and Nation*. New York: Columbia University Press, 1997.

Gould, Philip. "Catharine Sedgwick's 'Recital' of the Pequot War." *American Literature* 66, no. 4 (1994): 641–662.

Griswold, Rufus Wilmot. Preface to *The Female Poets of America*, 7–10. Edited by Rufus Wilmot Griswold. Philadelphia: Carey and Hart, 1848.

———. Preface to *The Female Poets of America*, 2nd ed, 7–10. Edited by Rufus Wilmot Griswold. Philadelphia: Henry C. Baird, 1852.

Habermas, Jürgen. *The Structural Transformation of the Public Sphere: An Inquiry into a Category of Bourgeois Society*. 7th ed. Translated by Thomas Burger with the assistance of Frederick Lawrence. Cambridge, MA: MIT Press, 1995.

Halberstam, Jack. *Female Masculinity*. Durham, NC: Duke University Press, 1998.

Harries, Elizabeth. *The Unfinished Manner: Essays on the Fragment in the Later Eighteenth Century*. Charlottesville: University of Virginia Press, 1994.

Hartman, Saidiya V. *Scenes of Subjection: Terror, Slavery, and Self-Making in Nineteenth-Century America*. New York: Oxford University Press, 1997.

Hazlitt, William. *The Spirit of the Age; or, Contemporary Portraits*. In Vol. XI of *The Complete Works of William Hazlitt*, edited by P. P. Howe. London: Frank Cass and Co., 1967.

Hedges, William L. *Washington Irving: An American Study, 1802–1832*. Baltimore: The Johns Hopkins Press, 1965.

Herold, Amos. *James Kirke Paulding: Versatile American*. New York: AMS Press, 1966.

Hewitt, Elizabeth, Stephen Shapiro, and Karen A. Weyler. "Introduction to Symposium on Scholarly Editing and the New Charles Brockden Brown Studies." *Early American Literature* 57.2 (2022): 531–535. Project Muse.

Hope, Joan. "Working from home? Follow these tips for successful remote work." *Recruiting & Retaining Adult Learners* 22, no. 8 (2020): 9. https://www.ncbi.nlm.nih.gov/pmc/articles/PMC7264770/.

"Hope Leslie." Review of *Hope Leslie*, by Catharine Maria Sedgwick. *North American Review* 26, no. 59 (Apr. 1828): 403–421. Making of America.

"Hope Leslie; or, Early Times in the Massachusetts." Review of *Hope Leslie*, by Catharine Maria Sedgwick. *Western Monthly Review* 1, no. 5 (1827): 289–295. Internet Archive.

Hurst, Michael C. "Reinventing Patriarchy: Washington Irving and the Autoerotics of the American Imaginary." *Early American Literature* 47, no. 3 (2012): 649–678. Project Muse.

Hutner, Gordon, ed. *American Literature, American Culture*. New York: Oxford University Press, 1999.

Hyde, Carrie. *Civic Longing: The Speculative Origins of U.S. Citizenship*. Cambridge, MA: Harvard University Press, 2018.

Insko, Jeffrey. "Diedrich Knickerbocker, Regular Bred Historian." *Early American Literature* 43, no. 2 (2008): 605–641. Project Muse.

———. *History, Abolition, and the Ever-Present Now in Antebellum American Writing*. Oxford: Oxford University Press, 2018.

Irving, Washington, William Irving, and James Kirke Paulding. *Salmagundi; or The Whim-whams and Opinions of Launcelot Langstaff, Esq. & Others*. In *Letters of Jonathan Oldstyle, Gent.; Salmagundi; or the Whim-whams and Opinions of Launcelot Langstaff, Esq. & Others*, edited by Bruce I. Granger and Martha Hartzog. Vol. 6 of *The Complete Works of Washington Irving*, edited by Henry A. Pochman et al. Boston: Twayne Publishers, 1977.

Jackson, Virginia. "American Romanticism, Again." *Studies in Romanticism* 55 (Fall 2016): 319–346.

———. "Bryant; or, American Romanticism." In *The Traffic in Poems: Nineteenth-Century Poetry and Transatlantic Exchange*, edited by Meredith L. McGill, 185–204. New Brunswick, NJ: Rutgers University Press, 2008.

———. "'Our Poets': William Cullen Bryant and the White Romantic Lyric." *New Literary History* 49, no. 4 (Autumn 2018): 521–551.

Jacobs, Harriet. *Incidents in the Life of a Slave Girl*. Mineola, NY: Dover Thrift, 2001. First published 1861 (Boston).

Jager, Colin. *The Book of God: Secularization and Design in the Romantic Era*. Philadelphia: University of Pennsylvania Press, 2006.

Jones, Jill. "The Disappearing 'I' in *Our Nig*." *Legacy: A Journal of Women Writers* 13, no. 1 (1996): 38–53.

Kamrath, Mark L., Philip Barnard, Rudy McDaniel, William Dorner, Kevin Jardaneh, Patricia Carlton, and Josejuan Rodriguez. "The Charles Brockden Brown Electronic Archive: Mapping Archival Access and Metadata." *Archive Journal* 4 (April 2014). http://www.archivejournal.net/essays/the-charles-brockden-brown-electronic-archive-mapping-archival-access-and-metadata/.

Kaplan, Amy. "Manifest Domesticity." *American Literature* 70, no. 3 (September 1998): 581–606. JSTOR.

Karafilis, Maria. "Catharine Maria Sedgwick's *Hope Leslie*: The Crisis between Ethical Political Action and US Literary Nationalism in the New Republic." *American Transcendental Quarterly* 12, no. 4 (1998): 327–344.

Kehde, Suzanne, and Jean Pickering, eds. *Narratives of Nostalgia, Gender and Nationalism*. Houndmills, UK: Macmillan Press, 1997.

Koenigs, Thomas. *Founded in Fiction: The Uses of Fiction in the Early United States*. Princeton, NJ: Princeton University Press, 2021.

———. "The 'Mysterious Depths' of Slave Interiority: Fiction and Intersubjective Knowledge in *The Heroic Slave*." *J19: The Journal of Nineteenth-Century Americanists* 8, no. 2 (Fall 2020): 193–217. Project Muse.

Krause, Sydney. "*Clara Howard* and *Jane Talbot*: Godwin on Trial." In *Critical Essays on Charles Brockden Brown*, edited by Bernard Rosenthal, 184–211. New York: G. K. Hall, 1981.

LaFleur, Greta. "Sex and 'Unsex'": Histories of Gender Trouble in Eighteenth-Century North America." *Early American Studies: An Interdisciplinary Journal* 12, no. 2 (Fall 2014): 469–499. Project Muse.

Landry, H. Jordan. "Bringing Down the House: The Trickster's Signifying on Victimization in Harriet E. Wilson's *Our Nig*." *Callaloo* 36, no. 2 (Spring 2013): 440–457. Project Muse.

Lee, Maurice S. "Introduction: A Survey of Survey Courses." *J19: The Journal of Nineteenth-Century Americanists* 4, no. 1 (Spring 2016): 125–130.

Leveen, Lois. "Dwelling in the House of Oppression: The Spatial, Racial, and Textual Dynamics of Harriet Wilson's *Our Nig*." *African American Review* 35, no. 4 (2001): 561–580.

Levine, Caroline. *Forms: Whole, Rhythm, Hierarchy, Network*. Princeton, NJ: Princeton University Press, 2015.

Lewis, Reina, and Sara Mills, eds. *Feminist Postcolonial Theory: A Reader*. New York and London: Routledge, 2003.

Little, Ann M. "Cloistered Bodies: Convents in the Anglo-American Imagination in the British Conquest of Canada." *Eighteenth-Century Studies* 39, no. 2 (Winter 2006): 187–200.

Looby, Christopher. Introduction to *Cecil Dreeme*, by Theodore Winthrop, viii–xxii. Reprinted with a preface by Christopher Looby. Philadelphia: University of Pennsylvania Press, 2016.

———. "Republican Bachelorhood: Sex and Citizenship in the Early United States." *Historical Reflections* 33, no. 1 (Spring 2007): 89–100. JSTOR.

Love, Heather. "Close but Not Deep: Literary Ethics and the Descriptive Turn." *New Literary History* 41, no. 2 (Spring 2010): 371–391. Project Muse.

———. "Truth and Consequences: On Paranoid Reading and Reparative Reading." *Criticism* 52, no. 2 (Spring 2010): 235–241.

Lowry, Elizabeth. "Embodying Essence: Corporeality, Dualism and Rhetorical Invention in the Autobiographies of Nineteenth-Century Female Spirit Mediums." *Word and Text: A Journal of Literary Studies and Linguistics* 3, no. 2 (December 2013): 44–56.

Luciano, Dana. "'Perverse Nature': Edgar Huntly and the Novel's Reproductive Disorders." *American Literature* 70, no. 1 (March 1998): 1–27.

Lufkin, Bryan. "Coronavirus: How to Work from Home, the Right Way." *BBC*, March 12, 2020. https://www.bbc.com/worklife/article/20200312-coronavirus-covid-19-update-work-from-home-in-a-pandemic.

Lukasik, Christopher J. *Discerning Characters: The Culture of Appearance in Early America*. Philadelphia: University of Pennsylvania Press, 2011.

Maddox, Lucy. *Removals: Nineteenth-Century American Literature and the Politics of Indian Affairs*. New York: Oxford University Press, 1991.

Manion, Jen. *Female Husbands: A Trans History*. Cambridge: Cambridge University Press, 2020.

Margolis, Stacey. *The Public Life of Privacy in Nineteenth-Century American Literature*. Durham, NC: Duke University Press, 2005.

Martin, Meredith. "'Imperfectly Civilized': Ballads, Nations, and Histories of Form." *ELH* 82, no. 2 (Summer 2015): 345–363. Project Muse.

Matthiesen, Sara. "Academic Work Is Labor, Not Romance." *The Chronicle of Higher Education* 63, no. 2 (September 9, 2016). https://www.chronicle.com/article/academic-work-is-labor-not-romance/.

Matthiessen, F. O. *American Renaissance: Art and Expression in the Age of Emerson and Whitman*. New York: Oxford University Press, 1941.

Maurer, Shawn Lisa. *Proposing Men: Dialectics of Gender and Class in the Eighteenth-Century English Periodical*. Stanford: Stanford University Press, 1998.

McClintock, Anne. "Imperial Leather: Race, Cross-Dressing and the Cult of Domesticity." In *Feminist Postcolonial Theory: A Reader*, edited by Reina Lewis and Sara Mills, 635–666. New York and London: Routledge, 2003.

McDowell, Tremaine. Introduction to *William Cullen Bryant: Representative Selections*, xiii–lxviii. Edited by Tremaine McDowell. New York: American Book Co., 1935.

McGill, Meredith L. *American Literature and the Culture of Reprinting, 1834–1853*. Philadelphia: University of Pennsylvania Press, 2003.

McGill, Meredith, ed. *The Traffic in Poems: Nineteenth-Century Poetry and Transatlantic Exchange*. New Brunswick, NJ: Rutgers University Press, 2008.

Merish, Lori. *Archives of Labor: Working-Class Women and Literary Culture in the Antebellum United States*. Durham, NC: Duke University Press, 2017.

———. *Sentimental Materialism: Gender, Commodity Culture, and Nineteenth-Century American Literature*. Durham, NC: Duke University Press, 2000.

Mesle, Sarah, and Sara Petersen. "The Cult of Ideal Motherhood." *Guernica*, May 1, 2023. https://www.guernicamag.com/the-cult-of-ideal-motherhood/.

Meyer, Kinereth. "Landscape and Counter-Landscape in the Poetry of William Cullen Bryant." *Nineteenth-Century Literature* 48, no. 2 (1993): 194–211.

Miller, Quentin. "'A Tyrannically Democratic Force': The Symbolic and Cultural Function of Clothing in Catharine Maria Sedgwick's *Hope Leslie*." *Legacy* 19, no. 2 (2002): 121–136.

Millner, Michael. "The Fear Passing the Love of Women: Sodomy and Male Sentimental Citizenship in the Antebellum City." *Arizona Quarterly: A Journal of American Literature, Culture, and Theory* 58, no. 2 (Summer 2002): 19–52. Project Muse.

Murison, Justine S., ed. *American Literature in Transition, 1820–1860*. Vol. 2 of *American Literature in Transition*. Cambridge: Cambridge University Press, 2022.

Murison, Justine S. *Faith in Exposure: Privacy and Secularism in the Nineteenth-Century United States*. Philadelphia: University of Pennsylvania Press, 2023.

Nelson, Dana. "Sympathy as Strategy in Sedgwick's *Hope Leslie*." In *The Culture of Sentiment: Race, Gender, and Sentimentality in Nineteenth-Century America*, edited by Shirley Samuels, 191–202. New York: Oxford University Press, 1992.

Newlyn, Lucy. *Reading, Writing, and Romanticism: The Anxiety of Reception*. Oxford: Oxford University Press, 2000.

Newman, Donald J., ed. *The Spectator: Emerging Discourses*. Newark: University of Delaware Press, 2005.

Noguchi, Yuki. "8 Tips to Make Working from Home Work for You." *NPR*, March 15, 2020. https://www.npr.org/2020/03/15/815549926/8-tips-to-make-working-from-home-work-for-you.

Peterson, Carla L. "Capitalism, Black (Under)development, and the Production of the African-American Novel in the 1850s." *American Literary History* 4, no. 4 (Winter 1992): 559–583. JSTOR.

Petersen, Sara. "Victorian Era-Inspired Momfluencers Are Taking Over Instagram." *InStyle*, March 25, 2021. https://www.instyle.com/lifestyle/momfluencers-nostalgia-instagram.

Pethers, Matthew, and Len von Morzé. "Early American Magazine Writing in and out of the Charles Brockden Brown Canon." *Early American Literature* 57.2 (2022): 554–560. Project Muse.

Polly, Greg. "A Leviathan of Letters." In *The Spectator: Emerging Discourses*, edited by Donald J. Newman, 105–128. Newark: University of Delaware Press, 2005.

Railton, Stephen. *Authorship and Audience: Literary Performance in the American Renaissance*. Princeton, NJ: Princeton University Press, 1991.

Richards, Eliza. *Gender and the Poetics of Reception in Poe's Circle*. Cambridge: Cambridge University Press, 2004.

Roberts, Siân Silyn. *Gothic Subjects: The Transformation of Individualism in American Fiction, 1790–1861*. Philadelphia: University of Pennsylvania Press, 2014.

Romero, Lora. *Home Fronts: Domesticity and Its Critics in the Antebellum United States*. Durham, NC: Duke University Press, 1997.

Rosenthal, Bernard, ed. *Critical Essays on Charles Brockden Brown*. New York: G.K. Hall, 1981.

Roth, Martin. *Comedy and America: The Lost World of Washington Irving*. Port Washington, NY: Kennikat Press, 1976.

Rowe, John Carlos. *At Emerson's Tomb: The Politics of Classic American Literature*. New York: Columbia University Press, 1997.

Rust, Marion. "'Into the House of an Entire Stranger': Why Sentimental Doesn't Equal Domestic in Early American Fiction." *Early American Literature* 37, no. 2 (2002): 281–309.

Sainato, Michael. "'Many of us are struggling': why US universities are facing a wave of strikes." *Guardian*, April 21, 2023. https://www.theguardian.com/us-news/2023/apr/21/us-universities-wave-strikes.

Saltz, Laura. "'Rather Both than Neither': The Polarity of Gender in Howe's *Hermaphrodite*." In *Philosophies of Sex: Critical Essays on* The Hermaphrodite, edited by Renée Bergland and Gary Williams, 72–92. Columbus: The Ohio State University Press, 2012.

Samuels, Shirley, ed. *A Companion to American Fiction, 1780–1865*. Malden, MA: Blackwell, 2004.

Samuels, Shirley. Introduction to *The Culture of Sentiment: Race, Gender, and Sentimentality in Nineteenth-Century America*, 3–8. Edited by Shirley Samuels. New York: Oxford University Press, 1992.

Sánchez-Eppler, Karen. "Bodily Bonds: The Intersecting Rhetorics of Feminism and Abolition." *Representations* 24 (Autumn 1988): 28–59. JSTOR.

Schneider, Bethany. "The Consummate Hermaphrodite." In *Philosophies of Sex: Critical Essays on* The Hermaphrodite, edited by Renée Bergland and Gary Williams, 138–156. Columbus: The Ohio State University Press, 2012.

———. "New England Tales: Catharine Sedgwick, Catherine Brown, and the Dislocations of Indian Land." In *A Companion to American Fiction, 1780–1865*, edited by Shirley Samuels, 353–365. Malden, MA: Blackwell, 2004.

Schuller, Kyla, and Jules Gill-Peterson. "Introduction: Race, the State, and the Malleable Body." *Social Text* 38.2 (June 2020): 1–17.

Schweitzer, Ivy. *Perfecting Friendship: Politics and Affiliation in Early American Literature*. Chapel Hill: University of North Carolina Press, 2006.

Sedgwick, Catharine Maria. *Hope Leslie; or, Early Times in the Massachusetts*. New York: White, Gallaher, and White, 1827. Reprinted with preface and notes by Carolyn L. Karcher. New York: Penguin, 1998. Page references are to the 1998 edition.

Sedgwick, Eve Kosofsky. *Between Men: English Literature and Male Homosocial Desire*. New York: Columbia University Press, 1985.

———. "The Character in the Veil: Imagery of the Surface in the Gothic Novel." *PMLA* 96, no. 2 (March 1981): 256. JSTOR.

———. *Epistemology of the Closet*. Berkeley: University of California Press, 1990.

———. "Paranoid Reading and Reparative Reading, or, You're So Paranoid, You Probably Think This Essay Is About You." In *Touching Feeling: Affect, Pedagogy, Performativity*, 123–151. Durham, NC: Duke University Press, 2003.

Seid, Danielle M. "Reveal." *TSQ: Transgender Studies Quarterly* 1, no. 1–2, 176–177. https://doi.org/10.1215/23289252-2399947.

Shapiro, Stephen. *The Culture and Commerce of the American Novel: Reading the Atlantic World-System*. Philadelphia: Pennsylvania State University Press, 2007.

———. "'Man to Man I Needed Not to Dread His Encounter': Edgar Huntly's End of Erotic Pessimism." In *Revising Charles Brockden Brown: Culture, Politics, and Sexuality in the Early Republic*, edited by Philip Barnard, Mark L. Kamrath, and Stephen Shapiro, 216–251. Knoxville: University of Tennessee Press, 2004.

Sizemore, Michelle. *American Enchantment: Rituals of the People in the Post-Revolutionary World*. Oxford: Oxford University Press, 2018.

Slauter, Eric. *The State as a Work of Art: The Cultural Origins of the Constitution*. Chicago: University of Chicago Press, 2009.

Smith, Caleb. "From the Critique of Power to the Poetics of Justice." *J19: The Journal of Nineteenth-Century Americanists* 1, no. 1 (2013): 160–166. ProQuest Central.

Smith, Rogers M. *Civic Ideals: Conflicting Visions of Citizenship in U.S. History.* New Haven, CT: Yale University Press, 1997.

Smith, Shawn Michelle. *American Archives: Gender, Race, and Class in Visual Culture.* Princeton, NJ: Princeton University Press, 1999.

Smith, Valerie. *Self-Discovery and Authority in Afro-American Narrative.* Cambridge, MA: Harvard University Press, 1987.

Snyder, Katherine V. *Bachelors, Manhood, and the Novel, 1850–1925.* Cambridge: Cambridge University Press, 1999.

Sondey, Walter. "From Nation of Virtue to Virtual Nation: Washington Irving and American Nationalism." In *Narratives of Nostalgia, Gender and Nationalism,* edited by Jean Pickering and Suzanne Kehde, 52–73. Houndmills, UK: Macmillan Press, 1997.

Squibbs, Richard. "Civic Humorism and the Eighteenth-Century Periodical Essay." *ELH* 75, no. 2 (Summer 2008): 389–413. Project Muse.

———. *Urban Enlightenment and the Eighteenth-Century Periodical Essay: Transatlantic Retrospects.* London: Palgrave, 2014.

Stanley, Amy Dru. *From Bondage to Contract: Wage Labor, Marriage, and the Market in the Age of Slave Emancipation.* Cambridge: Cambridge University Press, 1998.

Stern, Julia. "Excavating Genre in *Our Nig.*" *American Literature* 67, no. 3 (September 1995): 439–466. JSTOR.

———. *The Plight of Feeling: Sympathy and Dissent in the Early American Novel.* Chicago: University of Chicago Press, 1997.

Stokes, Claudia. "Bachelor Sketches: Invisible Women in Irving's Domestic Writings." *Early American Literature* 57, no. 2 (2022): 193–219.

———. *Old Style: Unoriginality and Its Uses in Nineteenth-Century U.S. Literature.* Philadelphia: University of Pennsylvania Press, 2022.

Stowe, Harriet Beecher. *Uncle Tom's Cabin; or, Life Among the Lowly.* Boston: John P. Jewett & Company: 1852. Reprinted with preface and notes by Elizabeth Ammons. New York and London: Norton, 1994.

Tanglen, Randi Lynn. "Religious Popular Culture and the Critique of Romantic Racialism in Harriet E. Wilson's *Our Nig.*" In *Nineteenth-Century American Women Write Religion: Lived Theologies and Literature,* edited by Mary McCartin Wearn, 77–88. Farnham, England: Ashgate, 2013.

Tate, Claudia. *Domestic Allegories of Political Desire: The Black Heroine's Text at the Turn of the Century.* New York: Oxford University Press, 1992.

Tawil, Ezra. *The Making of Racial Sentiment: Slavery and the Birth of the Frontier Romance.* Cambridge: Cambridge University Press, 2006.

Tennenhouse, Leonard. "Libertine America." *differences: A Journal of Feminist Cultural Studies* 11, no. 3 (Fall 1999): 1–28.

Tompkins, Jane. *Sensational Designs: The Cultural Work of American Fiction 1790–1860.* New York: Oxford University Press, 1985.

Trainor, Sean. "Fair Bosom/Black Beard: Facial Hair, Gender Determination, and the Strange Career of Madame Clofullia, 'Bearded Lady.'" *Early American Studies* 12, no. 3 (Fall 2014): 548–575. Project Muse.

Traister, Bryce. "The Wandering Bachelor: Irving, Masculinity, and Authorship." *American Literature* 74, no. 1 (Mar. 2002): 111–137. Project Muse.

Traister, Rebecca. "The Return of the Marriage Plot: Why Everyone Is Suddenly So Eager for Men and Women to Get Hitched." *The Cut,* September 22, 2023. https://www.thecut.com/article/why-is-everyone-so-eager-for-men-and-women-to-get-married.html.

Trolander, Paul, and Zeynep Tenger. "Addison and the Personality of the Critic." In *The Spectator: Emerging Discourses,* edited by Donald J. Newman, 175–199. Newark: University of Delaware Press, 2005.

Wald, Priscilla. "Terms of Assimilation: Legislating Subjectivity in the Emerging Nation." *boundary 2* 19, no. 3 (1992): 77–104.

Warner, Michael. "Irving's Posterity." *ELH* 67, no. 3 (Fall 2000): 773–799. Project Muse.

———. *Letters of the Republic: Publication and the Public Sphere in Eighteenth-Century America*. Cambridge, MA: Harvard University Press, 1990.

———. *Publics and Counterpublics*. Brooklyn: Zone Books, 2002.

———. *The Trouble with Normal: Sex, Politics, and the Ethics of Queer Life*. Cambridge, MA: Harvard University Press, 1999.

Wearn, Mary McCartin, ed. *Nineteenth-Century American Women Write Religion: Lived Theologies and Literature*. Farnham, England: Ashgate, 2013.

Weinstein, Cindy. *The Literature of Labor and the Labors of Literature: Allegory in Nineteenth-Century American Fiction*. Cambridge: Cambridge University Press, 1995.

Weinstein, Cindy and Christopher Looby. Introduction to *American Literature's Aesthetic Dimensions*, 1–36. Edited by Cindy Weinstein and Christopher Looby. New York: Columbia University Press, 2012.

Wexler, Laura. *Tender Violence: Domestic Visions in an Age of U.S. Imperialism*. Chapel Hill: University of North Carolina Press, 2000.

Weyler, Karen A. *Intricate Relations: Sexual and Economic Desire in American Fiction, 1789–1814*. Iowa City: University of Iowa Press, 2004.

———. "Reader-Centered Periodicals and the Literary Commons." *Early American Literature* 57.2 (2022): 543–548. Project Muse.

White, Barbara. "'Our Nig' and the She-Devil: New Information about Harriet Wilson and the 'Bellmont' Family." *American Literature* 65, no. 1 (March 1993): 19–52. JSTOR.

Whiting, Kate. "8 Tips to Work from Home and Manage Time More Effectively." *World Economic Forum*, October 14, 2020. https://www.weforum.org/agenda/2020/10/8-tips-work-from-home-time-management/.

Wiegman, Robyn. "Melville's Geography of Gender." *American Literary History* 1, no. 4 (Winter 1989): 735–763. JSTOR.

Wilson, Harriet E. *Our Nig; or, Sketches from the Life of a Free Black*. Boston: George C. Rand & Avery, 1859. Reprinted with preface and notes by P. Gabrielle Foreman. New York: Penguin, 2005.

Wilson, Sarah. "Melville and the Architecture of Antebellum Masculinity." *American Literature* 76, no. 1 (March 2004): 59–87. Project Muse.

Winthrop, Theodore. *Cecil Dreeme*. Boston: Ticknor and Fields, 1861. Reprinted with preface by Peter Coviello. New York: Washington Mews Books, 2016.

Woertendyke, Gretchen J. *Hemispheric Regionalism: Romance and the Geography of Genre*. Oxford: Oxford University Press, 2016.

Zagarell, Sandra A. "Expanding 'America': Lydia Sigourney's *Sketch of Connecticut*, Catharine Sedgwick's *Hope Leslie*." *Tulsa Studies in Women's Literature* 6, no. 2 (1987): 225–245.

INDEX

Addison, Joseph, 140n12
aesthetic turn, the, 6–11, 20
Alaimo, Stacy, 145n25
American Indians, 62, 63, 66, 69, 74, 75, 143n5, 146n57, 146n55
Armstrong, Nancy, 122, 130n20, 136n21, 140n19, 143n49
Ashworth, Suzanne, 156n50

ballad, the, 59, 63
Barnard, Philip, 132n33, 139n63
Barnes, Elizabeth, 7, 28, 72–73, 137n30, 138n52
Baym, Nina, 12–13, 133n49
Berlant, Lauren, 74, 110, 114, 134n58, 153n22, 154n36; on the female complainant, 112; on "generic performance," 20; on women's culture, 152n18, 153n28
Best, Stephen, 132n34
Blackwood, Sarah, 92, 93, 149n25
Boyd, Anne E., 43
Boydston, Jeanne, 137n23
Bradfield, Scott, 146n63
Breau, Elizabeth, 151n12
Brodhead, Richard, 108, 133n43
Brown, Charles Brockden, 17, 39, 41, 58, 80, 101, 124; "The Difference Between History and Romance," 8, 18–19; and domestic fiction, 6, 9, 14–15, 20–29, 30–33, 34–38, 131n22, 136n14; and domestic labor, 1–2, 9, 14, 21–22, 23–26, 27, 30–31, 33, 34, 35, 38; *Edgar Huntly*, 19, 21, 135n4; "The Household: a Fragment," 29, 30–34; *Jane Talbot*, 21–22, 23–29, 31, 65, 76, 135n9, 136n13, 137n31; "A Literary Wife," 1–2, 5, 8, 92, 123; *Ormond or, the Secret Witness*, 33; periodical fiction of, 20, 21, 22, 29–38, 136n13; "Portrait of an Emigrant. Extracted from a Letter," 29, 34–38, 49, 138n57; and race, 35, 37, 139n63; and romance, 9–10, 13–14, 18–21, 135n2, 135n4; and Romanticism, 19–21, 23, 30, 38; *Wieland*, 135n2
Brown, Gillian, 129n3, 131n28
Bryant, John, 141n30, 143n47
Bryant, William Cullen, 57, 58, 60–62, 63, 64, 68, 69, 71–72; *Lectures on Poetry*, 60–61
Buell, Lawrence, 65, 144n8
Burgett, Bruce, 22–23, 136n12
Burleigh, Erica, 135n9, 137n31
Burnham, Michelle, 136n14
Butler, Judith, 147n3, 150n39

Cahill, Edward, 131n28, 135n4
Callcott, George, 64, 71
Carby, Hazel V., 103, 105
Castiglia, Christopher, 10, 113, 116, 132n31, 134n58, 135n6, 137n27, 153n28; on *Cecil Dreeme*, 149n19; on *Hope Leslie*, 67
Castronovo, Russ, 119, 155n46, 155n49
Chesnutt, Charles, 155n43
Child, Lydia Maria: *Hobomok*, 146n61; "The Quadroons," 117
consensual citizenship, 2–3, 8–9, 10, 17, 20, 74, 107, 157n6; and individualism, 137n27; inequality of, 26, 57, 131n23, 155n49; and the right to disaffiliate 7–8, 28–29, 131n25, 131n28. *See also* marriage; marriage plot, the
Cooper, James Fenimore: *The Last of the Mohicans*, 66
Cott, Nancy F., 3, 4, 139n7
Couch, Daniel Diez, 30, 33, 34–35, 139n64
COVID-19, 122, 123
Coviello, Peter, 148n4, 149n21, 150n40
creole, 34–35, 37–38
critical methodology, 6, 8–12, 20, 86, 132n31, 132nn33–34, 148n5

Dana, Richard H., Sr., 39, 40, 49, 51–52, 53, 143n47
Davidson, Cathy N., 130n21

Deloria, Philip, 146n55, 146n57
Dillon, Elizabeth Maddock, 37, 47, 107, 130nn20–21, 137n30, 150n38; on separate spheres, 62–63, 129n9, 134n58, 142n40, 155n41; on subject formation, 32–33, 85, 152n21
domestic fiction: and fragments, 29–34; gendered assumptions regarding, 2, 6–7, 11–12, 23, 40–41, 64, 67; and the incest plot, 32; and interiority, 10; and physiognomy, 87; politics of, 6–7, 8–9, 12, 21–22, 27, 29, 30, 37, 79, 130n20, 133n43, 136n21, 140n19, 143n49; and realism, 6–7, 13–14, 20; and the romance, 20, 76; and Romanticism, 2, 11–12, 13–14, 18, 21, 44; and the slave narrative, 102, 107–108; and sympathy, 73. *See also* sentimentality. *See also under* Catharine Maria Sedgwick; Charles Brockden Brown; Harriet E. Wilson; Theodore Winthrop; Washington Irving
domesticity: and the bachelor, 3, 15, 39, 40, 41, 44–55, 140n19, 141n28, 142n42, 142n44; and citizenship, 124; and cosmopolitanism, 14, 34, 38; and eroticism, 28; and the Gothic, 34, 96, 150n38; and homosociality, 14, 38, 46–51, 83–85; ideology of, 4, 16–17, 24, 26, 41, 133n45, 149n17; and immigrant households, 30, 34–38; and individualism, 129n3; and market economy, 3–4, 32; and masculinity, 141n31; material conditions of, 1–2, 4, 5, 21, 23–26, 34, 39, 40, 41, 50–51, 62–63; and matriarchal households, 30–34; and morality, 26, 46–51, 145n25; and political potential, 7, 36–38; and queerness, 16–17; and race, 3–4, 12, 17, 37, 62, 63, 66, 69, 71, 74, 75, 99, 102, 109, 115, 124; and servants, 4, 44, 54; and slavery, 3–4; violence of, 17, 106–108, 109–110, 111–112, 114, 115. *See also* domestic fiction; domestic labor; domestic retreat; gender; sentimentality
domestic labor, 2, 3–4, 5–6, 122–124, 137nn22–23, 142n40. *See also* domesticity: material conditions of; labor. *See also under* Catharine Maria Sedgwick; Charles Brockden Brown; Harriet E. Wilson; Theodore Winthrop; Washington Irving
domestic retreat: and aesthetic potential, 2–3, 6, 11, 23, 46, 92; and autonomy, 5, 21, 22, 23, 24–26, 39, 92; emergence of, 1–3, 10, 14, 18, 20, 41, 139n7; and feminine virtue, 2, 4, 27, 32, 48, 57, 96; and heteronormativity, 33; as ideological fantasy, 1–3, 4, 5, 10, 14, 24, 102, 112; and intimacy, 89; and men, 4, 78, 91; and paranoid obsession, 86–87; and politics, 4, 14, 7, 15, 25–26, 76; and race, 3–4, 100, 102; and the reading public, 42–43, 44–51; and wilderness, 63. *See also* domestic fiction; domesticity; domestic labor; gender
Doriani, Beth Maclay, 151n10, 152n19
Douglass, Frederick, 108; *The Heroic Slave*, 152n19; *Narrative of the Life of Frederick Douglass*, 104–105
Doyle, Laura, 151n10, 152n19

Ellis, R.J., 155n46
Emerson, Amanda, 145n42
episode, the, 9, 14, 19, 20, 22, 29, 30
Equiano, Olaudah: *Interesting Narrative*, 103–105
extract, the, 34–38

Fetterley, Judith, 145n42
Fiedler, Leslie, 45
Follen, Eliza Lee Cabot, 57
Forbes, Erin, 155n46, 156n50
Foster, Travis, 99, 148n12, 149n17
fragments, 29–34, 139n64
Fuller, Margaret, 80

Gardner, Jared, 29, 30, 35, 43, 136n13, 137n40, 138n52, 138n57
Garrett, Matthew, 30, 137n40
Gates, Henry Louis, Jr., 102, 106, 155n46, 155n48
gender, 1–2; and authorship, 15, 56, 130n16; binary logic, 15, 22, 147n3; and contracts, 1, 3–4, 26, 28; denaturalization of, 10–11; deviant femininity, 40; essentialism, 55, 89; feminine genius, 4–5, 6, 38, 50, 56–57, 62, 76, 91–92, 101, 121, 155n46; indeterminacy, 90, 149n29; naturalization of women, 4–5, 56–57, 62, 63–64, 67–68; as performative, 5, 77–78; polarity of, 5, 80–81, 82, 86, 95, 96, 98; and race, 16–17, 81, 98–99, 102, 154n32. *See also* domestic fiction; domesticity; domestic labor; domestic

retreat; Romanticism; separate spheres ideology; Theodore Winthrop: transgender capacity; transgender studies
genius, 2, 16, 54–55, 91, 94. *See also* gender: feminine genius
Getsy, David J., 81
Gill-Peterson, Jules, 17
Gilmore, Michael, 11, 134n50, 140n14
Gilmore, Paul, 13, 134n52
Goddu, Theresa, 133n41, 138n51, 155n45
Godwin, William, 19, 135n4
Gothic, the: and domesticity, 34, 96, 150n38; and the fallen woman, 81; and identity, 10, 79, 85–86, 87; and paranoia, 82–83, 86, 89; and reading practices, 77; and the slave narrative, 105; and the veil, 138n51. *See also under* Theodore Winthrop
Griswold, Rufus Wilmot, 63; *The Female Poets of America*, 4–5, 56–57, 62, 75, 91

Habermas, Jürgen, 140n12, 143n46
Halberstam, Jack, 147n3
Halleck, Fitz-Greene, 57
Harries, Elizabeth, 29–30
Hartman, Saidiya, 112
Hawthorne, Nathaniel, 9, 20, 40; *House of the Seven Gables*, 93
Herold, Amos, 139n2, 143n47
Howe, Julia Ward, 80; *The Hermaphrodite*, 156n50
Hurst, C. Michael, 141n28
Hyde, Carrie, 7, 20, 28–29, 131n25, 132n31, 134n55, 157n6

Indian Removal Act, the, 66, 74
Insko, Jeffrey, 58, 63, 64, 65, 69, 73, 146n66
Irving, Washington, 38; critical reception, 42–44, 45, 56; and domestic fiction, 6, 15, 44–45, 51; and domesticity, 5, 6, 101, 124, 139n4; and domestic labor, 15, 39, 40, 41, 46, 50–51, 56, 142n40; "The Little Man in Black," 48–49; and moral reform, 15, 46–53; and the public sphere, 42, 53–54, 141n30; and race, 50; and Romanticism, 39–40, 42–46, 48, 52, 54, 140n21, 140n23; and the sketch, 38, 41, 42; "Sketches from Nature," 50–51; and whimsy, 5, 15, 40, 44, 46–51, 52, 142n43. *See also* domesticity: and the bachelor; *Salmagundi*
Irving, William. See *Salmagundi*

Jackson, Andrew, 66
Jackson, Virginia, 58, 60, 143n7
Jacobs, Harriet: *Incidents in the Life of a Slave Girl*, 104–105, 156n50
Jager, Colin, 63–64
James, Henry, 9, 20
Jones, Jill, 152n19, 154n29, 154n33, 156n53

Kaplan, Amy, 37, 57, 62, 133n45, 149n17
Karafilis, Maria, 146n60
Koenigs, Thomas, 58, 135n2, 152n19, 154n39
Krause, Sydney, 136n13

labor, 122–123; pastoralization of, 3–4, 17, 24, 51, 101, 120, 124, 152n21. *See also* domestic labor
Landry, H. Jordan, 153n29, 154n30, 154n32, 154n34, 156n51
Leveen, Lois, 151n13, 156n53
Levine, Caroline, 147n3
liberalism, 2, 4, 15–16, 43, 63, 74, 107, 117, 147n71; assimilative pressures of, 26, 29, 59
Literary Magazine and American Register, The, 1
Little, Ann M., 138n51
Looby, Christopher, 8, 148n6
Lukasik, Christopher, 87, 88
lyric, the, 59, 61, 63, 91, 120, 130n16

Maddox, Lucy, 66
Manion, Jen, 90, 149n30, 149n32
Marcus, Sharon, 132n34
Margolis, Stacey, 134n58, 137n28, 155n43
marriage, 1, 3–4, 25–26, 28, 29, 137n30. *See also* consensual citizenship; domestic labor; gender; marriage plot, the
marriage plot, the, 18, 20, 21–22, 25, 29, 31, 68, 98, 115–116; and the Gothic, 80; ideological work of, 4, 7, 8–10, 14, 87, 99, 124, 130n21; and the Vanishing American, 76. *See also* consensual citizenship; marriage
Martin, Meredith, 63
Matthiessen, F.O., 12
Maurer, Shawn Lisa, 142n42
McClintock, Anne, 4, 152n21
McGill, Meredith, 44, 133n41, 140n20, 141n34
Merish, Lori, 26, 133n45, 153n21, 154n29, 154n34
Mesle, Sarah, 123
Meyers, Kinereth, 143n7
Miller, Quentin, 145n42

Millner, Michael, 149n21, 149n24
Mitchell, Koritha, 123
Monthly Magazine and the American Review, 29
Murison, Justine, 132n34, 132n37, 134n55

National Labor Relations Board, the, 123
Newlyn, Lucy, 42–43, 47, 142n38
North American Review, 60, 67

Paulding, James Kirke. See *Salmagundi*
Peterson, Carla, 117, 151n10, 152n19, 153n29, 156n51
physiognomy, 87–89
Poe, Edgar Allan, 91
portraiture, 92–94
Pound, Ezra, 12
Puar, Jasbir, 149n17

Railton, Stephen, 141n25
Richards, Eliza, 5, 50, 91, 120, 130n16, 142n38, 155n46
romance, the: as conjectural mode, 7, 9–10, 13–14, 18–21, 26, 29, 35, 36, 58; and domestic fiction, 20, 76; and gender, 133n49; and nature, 72; political possibilities of, 13; and realism, 9, 13, 134n55, 135n6. *See also* Charles Brockden Brown
romanticism: and authorship, 5–6, 44, 47, 134n50, 140n14; as category, 12–14, 42–43, 57–58, 134n52, 140n23; and critical methodology, 6–7, 132n31, 135n6; and domestic fiction, 2, 6, 11–12, 13–14, 18, 21, 44; and the fragment, 30; gendered assumptions regarding, 2, 11–12, 15, 23, 40–41, 43–44, 45, 58, 101, 133n49, 142n38; and historiography, 6, 15–16, 56–57, 59–60, 62–63, 64–67, 76; and nationalism, 58–64; poetry, 13, 56, 58, 59, 60, 61, 63, 66, 69, 91, 120, 130n16, 143n7; and politics, 75, 105, 134n50, 140n14; and race, 143n5; and the reading public, 42–43, 45, 47; and realism, 132n31; romantic racialism, 10, 17, 116–117; and Catharine Maria Sedgwick, 56–57; and women's fiction, 57–64. *See also* genius; William Cullen Bryant. *See also under* Catharine Maria Sedgwick; Charles Brockden Brown; Harriet E. Wilson; Theodore Winthrop; William Irving
Romero, Lora, 11, 45, 66, 68, 133n45, 141n25
Roth, Martin, 140n21
Rowe, John Carlos, 134n50
Rust, Marion, 7, 23, 131n22

Salmagundi, 15, 38, 39–41, 42, 44–55, 56, 65, 76, 77, 120, 124, 139n3, 140nn22–23, 142n34, 142n38, 143n45, 143n47. *See also* domesticity: and the bachelor; Washington Irving
Saltz, Laura, 80
Samuels, Shirley, 12
Sánchez-Eppler, Karen, 116, 152n20
Sansay, Leonora: *Secret History*, 37
scene, the. *See* episode, the
Schneider, Bethany, 70–71, 149n29
Schuller, Kyla, 17
Schweitzer, Ivy, 147n68
Sedgwick, Catharine Maria: and consensual citizenship, 74; critical reception, 60, 66–68, 77, 146n61; and domestic fiction, 6, 15–16, 55, 57, 58, 59, 64, 67–68, 72–74; and domesticity, 15–16, 101, 123; and domestic labor, 63; and gender essentialism, 55; and historiography, 58, 64–67; *Hope Leslie*, 8, 15–16, 56–57, 59–60, 62, 63–75, 76, 102, 120, 145n25, 145n42, 146n60, 146n66, 147nn67–68; and the "Indian Woman," 15, 57, 60, 63, 64, 75, 143n5; and morality, 69–70, 73; and nationalism, 55, 58–59, 63, 64, 65, 69; and naturalism, 63, 72, 74–75; *A New England Tale*, 70–71; and race, 15, 57, 59–60, 62, 63–72, 74–75; and realism, 68; *Redwood*, 61, 68, 71; and Romanticism, 6, 15–16, 56–57, 58–60, 62–63, 65, 66–67, 70, 75, 76; and sympathy, 73
Sedgwick, Eve Kosofsky, 9–10, 79–80, 83, 86, 96, 132n33, 132n36, 138n51
seduction novel, the, 27, 32, 44–45, 78, 105
Seid, Danielle M., 82
sentimentality, 7, 34, 43, 58, 130n21, 152n20; and antislavery fiction, 10, 116–117; and domesticity, 5, 7, 12, 15, 23, 51, 131n22, 140n22; and the slave narrative, 102, 103–106. *See also under* Harriet E. Wilson
separate spheres ideology, 46, 59, 78, 100, 109, 111, 129n9, 134n58, 147n3. *See also* domesticity; domestic retreat; gender
sexology, 16, 82, 90
Shapiro, Stephen, 33, 132n33, 135n1, 139n63
Sizemore, Michelle, 36, 58, 64, 135n6
sketch, the, 38, 41, 42, 103, 139n64

Slauter, Eric, 131n28
slave narrative, the, 102, 103–106, 107–108, 112, 113–114, 152n19
Smith, Caleb, 132n39
Smith, Rogers, 131n23
Smith, Shawn Michelle, 99
Snyder, Katherine, 45–46, 141n31, 142n42, 142n44
Sondey, Walter, 139n4
Spectator, the, 42
speculative fiction, 9
Spiritualism, 119–121, 155nn45–46, 155n49
Squibbs, Richard, 142n43
Stanley, Amy Dru, 3, 137n22, 152n21
Steele, Richard, 140n12
Stern, Julia, 32, 151nn13–14, 152n17, 153nn28–29, 154n34, 156n51
Stokes, Claudia, 41, 42, 140n22
Stowe, Harriet Beecher: *Uncle Tom's Cabin*, 110–112, 116, 153n26

Tatler, the, 42
Tawil, Ezra, 67, 145n43
Tennenhouse, Leonard, 23, 32
Thoreau, Henry David, 144n8
Tompkins, Jane, 12–13
Traister, Bruce, 45
Transcendentalism, 6
transgender studies, 16–17, 81–82, 148n12, 149n30. *See also* Theodore Winthrop: transgender capacity

University of California system, the, 123

Wald, Priscilla, 74
Warner, Michael, 43, 45, 84, 134n58, 147n71, 147n73, 154n41
Weinstein, Cindy, 8, 105, 106
Western expansion, 56–57, 58, 59, 60
Western Monthly Review, 67–68
Wexler, Laura, 133n43
Wharton, Eliza: *The Coquette*, 79
White, Barbara, 102, 150n2, 153n29
Whitman, Walt, 144n8
Wiegman, Robyn, 150n33
Wilson, Harriet E., 102, 123, 124; on authenticity, 106, 112, 113–114, 154n39; and domestic fiction, 6, 17, 102–103, 107–108, 114–115, 121; and domestic labor, 5–6, 17, 100, 101–103, 105–106, 107, 109, 114, 115, 120–121, 123; and embodiment, 5–6, 10, 17, 105–106, 115, 117, 118–121; and exposure of abuse, 17, 102, 104, 110, 111, 113; *Our Nig*, 6, 10–11, 17, 99–100, 101–103, 104, 105–110, 111–121, 150nn2–3, 151n10, 151nn13–14, 152n17, 152n19, 153n26, 153nn28–29, 154n30, 154n34, 155n48, 156n51, 156n53; and race, 17, 100, 102, 105, 109, 116–119, 120, 121, 153nn28–29, 154n34, 155n43; and realism, 103; and Romanticism, 6, 10, 17, 102, 117, 121; and sentimentality, 17, 105, 107, 113–114, 118; and spiritualist movement, 17, 102, 118, 119–121; and third-person narration, 105, 108–109, 112–113, 119, 152n19
Wilson, Sarah, 141n31, 142n38
Winthrop, Theodore, 6, 79, 81, 82, 124; *Cecil Dreeme*, 10–11, 16–17, 76–99, 102, 148n4, 148n6, 148n17, 149n21, 150n33, 150n41; and domestic fiction, 6, 10, 16, 79, 80, 87, 98–99; and domestic labor, 84, 91–92; and gender polarity, 80–81, 82, 86, 95, 96, 98; and the Gothic, 10, 79–80, 82–83, 85–90, 95–96, 98; and homosociality, 83–85; and queerness, 16, 78, 79, 89, 97; and race, 16–17, 81, 98–99, 149n17, 150n41; and retrospective narration, 79, 95, 96, 97, 98, 102; and Romanticism, 16, 91; and transgender capacity, 16, 76, 77, 81–82, 89–91, 93–95, 101
Woertendyke, Gretchen J., 36, 135n6, 138n57
Wordsworth, William, 58, 60
work from home, 122–124

ABOUT THE AUTHOR

LAUREL V. HANKINS is an associate professor in the Department of English and Communication at the University of Massachusetts Dartmouth, where she teaches courses on literary theory and early and nineteenth-century American literature. Her essays and reviews can be found in *African American Review*, *Legacy: A Journal of American Women Writers*, *Nineteenth-Century Literature*, *Common-place: The Journal of Early American Life*, *The American Literary History Online Review*, *Early American Literature*, and *The Part and the Whole in Early American Literature, Print Culture, and Art* (Bucknell University Press).